This wax impression, bearing the abbreviated name of Jesus
encircled by the inscription
"The seal of the Superior of the Society of Jesus"
(SIGILLVM PREPOSITI SOCIETATIS IESV),
was made from the seal used
by St. Ignatius when he was the first general
of the order, 1541-1556.
The medieval spelling of *prepositi* is noteworthy.
This same seal was also used by St. Ignatius' earlier successors
and by General Congregations II-XI (1565-1661),
XIII (1687), and XV-XIX (1706-1758).
St. Ignatius' secretary, Juan de Polanco, used it
upon the official text of the *General Examen* on October 9, 1558,
and Lorenzo Maggio, Secretary of the Society, put it
upon the ameliorated text
of the *Constituciones de la Compañía de Jesús*
which was approved by General Congregation V (1593-1594).
In the series of volumes,
Monumenta Historica Societatis Iesu,
there are interesting facsimiles
in *Constitutiones Societatis Jesu,* Volume II, pages 123 and 727,
and *Fontes Narrativi,* Volume I, on the title page.
The photograph was taken
by the Reverend Algimantas Kezys, S.J.
The seal itself is now preserved in the Jesuit curia in Rome.

JOHN CARROLL FUTRELL, S.J.

MAKING AN
APOSTOLIC COMMUNITY
OF LOVE

*The Role of the Superior
according to St. Ignatius of Loyola*

"The well-being of the Company consists largely in
this, that it have good superiors" (*Cons*MHSJ, I, 303).

THE INSTITUTE OF JESUIT SOURCES
St. Louis, 1970

IMPRIMI POTEST: Very Reverend Gerald R. Sheahan, S.J.
Provincial of the Missouri Province
August 4, 1970

IMPRIMATUR: John J. Cardinal Carberry
Archbishop of St. Louis
August 18, 1970

©1970 The Institute of Jesuit Sources
St. Louis University, Fusz Memorial
3700 West Pine Blvd.
St. Louis, Missouri 63108

FOR ALL MY COMPANIONS
IN THE COMPANY OF JESUS

*Published through the aid of funds
donated by the late Mr. James L. Monaghan
of Milwaukee, Wisconsin,
1 8 6 7 - 1 9 6 3 ,
in memory of his brother,
Reverend Edward V. Monaghan, S.J.,
1 8 7 9 - 1 9 2 2 .*

CONTENTS

MAKING AN
APOSTOLIC COMMUNITY
OF LOVE

INTRODUCTION

THIS BOOK IS A CONDENSATION of a very long and complicated dissertation.[1] In the hope of presenting a study of the role of the superior according to St. Ignatius of Loyola which would be of reasonable brevity and easily accessible to superiors and to those whom they lead in their communities, I have deliberately kept documentation to a minimum. Hopefully, for those interested in scholarly research the original dissertation will be published in some form in the future. The purpose of this study is to discover as accurately as possible the personal conception which St. Ignatius had of the role of the superior in the Company of Jesus.[2]

One religious said to me, "Why do you discuss the role of the superior according to Ignatius? If his name were not in the title, I would read the book." One reason for such a study is that Vatican Council II called for a return to the original inspiration of the founders of religious orders.[3] Another is to show as simplistic and false the popular statement, "A man who lived four hundred years ago can have nothing to say to us today." As this study will show, Ignatius had a view of the role of the superior which is remarkably modern, which manifests great

For the ABBREVIATIONS USED THROUGHOUT THIS BOOK, see below, p. 215.

1 J. C. Futrell, S.J. *Making an Apostolic Community of Love: The Role of the Superior according to St. Ignatius Loyola.* A dissertation, still unpublished, presented to the Institut Catholique, Paris.

2 Throughout this study I have used the expression "Company of Jesus" rather than the usual English title, "Society of Jesus." The reason is that the word *Company* (despite certain unhappy "administrative" connotations) seems to me better to convey the notion of living companionship, than does the more abstract *Society.*

3 *The Documents of Vatican II,* ed. Walter M. Abbott (New York 1966), p. 468.

3

human wisdom, and from which we can learn much about the role of the superior today. He is still a teacher, although it is necessary to break through his language and cultural structures, which are the expression of the epoch in which he lived, in order to arrive at an understanding of his profound intention.

Ignatius has often been misunderstood, and some of the most classical Jesuit commentators have unwittingly misinterpreted him, especially concerning his ideas on authority and obedience. There is always some underlying truth in caricature and an anecdote told in France reflects this misinterpretation. "There are three steps in the historical degradation of the Catholic Church. The first was due to Constantine, who turned the Church into an institution. The second to St. Thomas Aquinas, who turned it into a system. And the third to St. Ignatius of Loyola, who turned it into a police force!" This study will show that the conception of authority and obedience therein indicated could not have been farther from the mind of St. Ignatius.

Although much has been written about the practice of Jesuit obedience, very few studies have been devoted to the role of the superior and none has attempted to grasp its essential nature through a complete study of the language of Ignatius expressing it.[4] Through an analysis of the entire vocabulary of Ignatius — words, phrases, and images he used to describe the role of the superior — it is possible to arrive at an understanding of his "mental structure," the way he approached reality, and the way he shaped experience. Understanding his mental structure, we are enabled to penetrate to his profound intention, which necessarily is expressed in his own language in terms of the cultural patterns which were his own.

The method followed in the original dissertation, then, was to construct a lexicon of all the words and the expressions used in

---

4 Many hortatory works appeared during the first century of the Company concerning the qualities of a good superior. See, in J. Gilmont, *Les écrits spirituels des premiers Jésuites* (Rome, 1960), the entries in the index under *gouvernement religieux,* and in I. Iparraguirre, *Répertoire de spiritualité ignatienne* (Rome, 1961), the entries under *supérieur.* A study which is useful, although restricted to one aspect of the role of the superior, is J. Lewis, *Le gouvernement spirituel selon Saint Ignace de Loyola* (Montreal, 1961). L. Mendizabal has written a brochure on *El Modo de mandar segùn San Ignacio* (Berriz, Viscaya, 1966).

the Ignatian texts to delineate the role of the superior. These terms were allowed to speak for themselves; that is to say, their significance was sought through an analysis of their employment in the contexts in which they occurred.[5] Once these words and expressions had been collected, it was found that it was possible to classify them into broad categories of meaning in the vocabulary of Ignatius. In order to have as complete an understanding as possible of the content of these terms — their total conceptual extension in the mind of Ignatius — they were studied in all contexts, even those not concerned with the role of the superior. Analysis of the language of Ignatius is complicated by the fact that we have very few manuscripts written by him. The editors of the primary sources, in the Monumenta Historica Societatis Jesu, have listed these texts and the other documents preparatory to the Constitutions most directly authored by Ignatius, even when written by Polanco or some other secretary.[6] In this study the analysis of the language of the Constitutions has been based upon text *a* (1547-1550), which is the most directly Ignatian in its redaction, since much of it is composed of texts written by Ignatius before Polanco became his secretary in March, 1547. Reference is made to text A (1550) and text B (1556), only when they make additions to the vocabulary of text *a*. Text B, the basis for the official Latin text of the *Constitutions,* is strongly influenced in its structure and organization of materials by the logical, scholastic mentality of Polanco.[7] The vocabulary analysis also involved study of various texts in the *Monumenta Praevia* which were rough drafts for certain parts

5 Reference is made occasionally to lexicons giving the general usage of words during the epoch of Ignatius. However, rather than relying on these definitions to understand the Ignatian employment of the terms, I have sought their meaning for Ignatius through the analysis of his own use of them.

6 *Constitutiones et Regulae Societatis Iesu,* 4 vols., I, *Monumenta Constitutionum praevia* (Rome, 1934), in the series Monumenta Historica Societatis Jesu, xciii (abbreviated hereafter as *Cons*MHSJ, I, xciii).

7 Text B bears very few corrections in the hand of Ignatius, and, indeed, Polanco testified in one instance that he did not know whether Ignatius had examined that part of the text (*Cons*MHSJ, II, 394, critical apparatus). For a detailed study of the quite different mental structures of Ignatius and of Polanco revealed in these texts of the *Constitutions,* see F. Roustang, *Saint Ignace Constitutions de la Compagnie de Jésus,* 2 vols. (Paris, 1966), II, 11-138.

of the Constitutions as well as of those expressions in the *Spiritual Exercises* and the *Spiritual Diary* which shed light upon the language of Ignatius concerning the role of the superior.[8]

To understand language one must understand the man who used it; the man himself — his own personal manner of structuring reality — is the living context of his language. One must also understand the historical and the cultural background which formed the man. Ignatius received his conceptions of the role of authority, whether parental, royal, or ecclesiastical, within a certain structure of reality, and he filtered them through his own personal experiences as a Basque *hidalgo* and a Castilian *caballero* and, especially, through his personal apostolic evolu-

---

8 The *Spiritual Exercises* is the manual giving Ignatius' program of meditations, contemplations and other spiritual activities aimed at freeing the person making them from "inordinate affections" so that he can make his "Election" — his choice of the state of life to which God calls him — in true spiritual liberty motivated by the unique desire to serve and praise God. The book also contains advice for the director of the Exercises and various "rules."

Especially important for this study of the role of the superior are the Rules for the Discernment of Spirits — for distinguishing the orientation of the different "motions" experienced in the soul of the exercitant during the Exercises — which helps him to recognize subtle self-love and to seek and find the will of God.

Unfortunately, the commentators have tended to treat almost exclusively the "discernment of spirits" which is described in the *Spiritual Exercises,* [313-336]. As a result, many readers overlook the fact that this discernment "of spirits" is only a part of a larger, much more complex, dynamic process of discernment or deliberation leading to both individual and communal decisions. These decisions pertain to action in response to a challenge posed to a man or to a community to live authentically the demands of the Jesuit vocation in an actual, concrete situation here and now. In other words, the discernment of spirits of *Exercises,* [313-316] is actually only a technique employed throughout the larger and prayerful process of Ignatian discernment of the will of God in order to arrive at a decision and to seek its confirmation. On all this, see below, ch. 7; also, especially pp. 47-52 of J. C. Futrell, "Ignatian Discernment," *Studies in the Spirituality of Jesuits* (St. Louis: the Assistancy Seminar of Jesuit Spirituality), II (April, 1970).

The *Spiritual Diary* is Ignatius' own account of his discernment of spirits and his final "Election" that professed houses of the Company, renouncing all fixed revenues, should have a regime of absolute poverty. Text in *Cons*MHSJ, I, 86-158; English translation by W. J. Young, S.J., *The Spiritual Journal of St. Ignatius of Loyola* (Woodstock, 1958).

tion which led to the foundation of the Company of Jesus.[9] Only through study of his personal evolution and the cultural context is it possible truly to grasp the mental structure of Ignatius and the profound intention which he expressed through his language. The various chapters of this study therefore, in general, present discussions of relevant historical, cultural and biographical data, analyze the vocabulary of Ignatius and interpret the profound intention which he wished to express through his language.[10]

The vocabulary analysis quickly revealed that the mental structure of Ignatius was so concrete and so rooted in real experience that the conceptual content of his words and expressions often overlapped and intermingled. He did not think in clear-cut theoretical categories or according to the methods of logical deduction. His ideas tended to be at the same time very simple and very dense and profound, and so a certain amount of verbal awkwardness marks their expression. This overlapping of areas of meaning is evident in Ignatius' frequent employment of certain terms (e.g., "service and praise and glory of God," "helping souls," "universal good of the Church and the Company," "union and love and obedience") as practically equivalent, and in his continual use of "triplets" or "doublets" which combined different words in a phrase where their meaning is quasi-identical. Indeed, it is characteristic of the Basque language to reduplicate words which are more or less synonomous in

---

9 Indeed, Guipúzcoa and Viscaya claimed that all of their inhabitants were *hidalgos* — "noblemen." Nobility was transmitted by blood to *los hijos de los bien nacidos*. The term *fijodalgo* from *filius alicui* (*hijo de alguién*) became *hidalgo* in Castile during the thirteenth century. The duty of the noble was to fight for his temporal lord or king, but not as a mere soldier. Rather, he went off to battle magnificently on horseback (*caballaris*) and so was called a *caballero*. See A. García-Gallo, *Manual de historia del derecho español,* 2nd ed., 2 vols. (Madrid, 1964), I, 576.

10 In the past there was a tendency to stress the role of divine grace in the formation of Ignatius to such an extent that he was presented as almost entirely liberated from normal cultural conditioning. This exaggerated approach caused studies of specific problems of Ignatian spirituality, such as authority and obedience, often to be a priori and insufficiently concerned with the precise historical and cultural meaning of the language of Ignatius. Actually, this language can be understood only in its cultural context. See Hugo Rahner, *The Spirituality of St. Ignatius Loyola* (Westminster, Md., 1953), ch. 1.

order to communicate the idea of the superlative.[11] Thus, these verbal "equations" are of great significance for understanding the mental structure of Ignatius and for interpreting the texts.

Because of the simplicity and the density of the mental structure of Ignatius, it will be found that the study of the various aspects of the role of the superior in the different chapters always returns to the same essential role. For this reason, the reader will be conscious of considerable repetition. A "spiral" approach rather than a "linear" approach to the study of the ideas of Ignatius was imposed upon me by the fact that for him everything revolved around the changeless axis of the "scope of our vocation" — *scopus vocationis nostrae*.[12] I use this expression repeatedly during this study because it was this which controlled all the efforts of Ignatius to frame the Constitutions and to delineate the role of the superior, and it is this which is the norm of all discernment in the Company.

The same density and unity of the mental structure of Ignatius is evident in his conception of the role of the superior, which accounts for his sometimes apparently ambiguous use of the term superior, which is used without qualification in many passages to refer either to the general or to subordinate superiors. Ignatius constantly envisioned the whole Company as one body made up of all the individual members throughout the whole world unified by their one head the superior general.[13] As the number of companions increased it became necessary to appoint subordinate superiors. The first mention of these occurs in the document "De collegiis et domibus fundandis" of 1541. Because of the necessity of multiplying superiors on provincial and local levels, Ignatius developed his principle of unity through hierarchical structure.[14] He conceived of all subordinate superiors

---

11 See M. Hernandez, "*Sentir* en el estilo literario de Ignacio de Loyola," *Manresa,* CXLIX (1966), 349-370; CXL (1967), 5-18. Hernandez gives the example of the frequent doublet *sentir y juzgar* which means *muy repensado:* deeply and repeatedly thought through.

12 *Cons*MHSJ, I, 2, in the Deliberation of the First Fathers, [1].

13 See below, ch. 3, pp. 71-73.

14 See below, ch. 3, pp. 79-83. The vicarious nature of the authority of all subordinate superiors in the Company is clearly expressed by Ignatius in his letter to the companions at Gandía, July 29, 1547 (*EppIgn,* I, 551-562). He tells them that they should elect one of their number as their superior to govern them in Ignatius' place (p. 552), since experience has shown him the impossibility of doing this

as vicars of the general — appointed or removed by him and given wide or limited powers at his discretion — in order to carry out on their own level the unifying role committed to the general by the whole Company. Lower superiors, therefore, vicariously share in the general's role as unifier of all the companions with one another and with their head.

Thus, like the general and through him, the provincials and local superiors are "emanations" of the whole Company who in the name of the Company give unifying direction to the life and action of the companions committed to their care. It is because of this vicarious sharing in the role of the one real superior of the Company, the general (himself a vicar of the vicar of Christ for the Company), that Ignatius remarks that all that is stated in the Ninth Part of the *Constitutions* about the general also applies *mutatis mutandis* to provincials and local superiors.[15]

In this book, then, the term superior, when not specifically qualified, is used in the Ignatian sense as referring to the role of the superior general which is shared vicariously with all the subordinate superiors, since this role is identical on the various levels of its exercise — general, provincial, or local.

The essential characteristic of the mental structure of Ignatius revealed through the analysis of his vocabulary is that it was completely dynamic. His language manifests an absolute docility to the teaching of living experience which provided him with the clearest indications of the will of God in the concrete circumstances here and now. Ignatius' words and images express an ever onward thrust of the spirit, always "on the way," never installed in a fixed or a priori position, constantly seeking the way to *bring the Company to be* for the accomplishment of its end here and now. Ignatius had realized within himself the total spiritual liberty which is the goal of the Spiritual Exercises, the interior freedom to desire only the ever greater service and praise of God through the vocation of the Company of Jesus. To attempt to fix the way of fulfilling this vocation in the static

himself from the distance of Rome, so that he must do this "por medio de otros" (p. 558). Ignatius reminds the companions that they should show the same obedience and respect to their rector as they would to himself and, above all, as they would to Jesus Christ "whom you obey in both and whose ministers they are" (p. 561).

15 See below, ch. 3, p. 74.

forms of any epoch — even that of Ignatius himself — is to fail completely to grasp the mental structure revealed in his language. A superior today who is to carry out his role as Ignatius conceived it must possess this same dynamic mental structure, this profound spiritual liberty.

The role of the superior described in the language of Ignatius takes all its meaning from the necessity to achieve the end of the Company: "the scope of our vocation." Therefore, it was necessary, first of all, to analyze the language expressing this end. Since the reason for the existence of the Company is to achieve this end, the role of the superior can be understood only through a study of what constitutes the *being* of the Company. It is for these reasons that the first two chapters concern the end and the being of the Company of Jesus. Thereafter, the various functions of the superior in carrying out his essential role in the concrete are studied. Since every aspect of the role of the superior involves making decisions, two chapters are devoted to a study of discernment: the process by which the superior seeks to discover the will of God in the concrete for the life and the action of the Company here and now. Finally, a chapter is given to the study of Ignatian obedience, since it is impossible to understand the meaning of authority fully without understanding the correlative, obedience of those who respond to it.

It will quickly be evident to the reader that the results of this study reflect my own language and mental structure. For instance, he will see that my own vocabulary is strongly influenced by the terminology of existentialist philosophy and that I have questioned the texts of Ignatius according to contemporary preoccupations. No one has expressed better than Michael de Certeau, S.J., how a scholar's own culture conditions his research:[16]

> The author carrying out this scrutiny takes up his position according to his own past, and is himself determined by it. In his very anxiety to be fair (which is typical of our age) and his own particular way of embodying it in a method (belonging to a specific environment), he is giving cultural expression to a spir-

---

16 "Culture and Spiritual Experience," *Concilium,* IX, no. 2 (1966), 3-16. Citation from p. 3. Cf. L. Febvre, *Au coeur religieux du XVIᵉ siècle* (Paris, 1957), pp. 7-8.

itual question even when he is making judgments on situations in the past and historical relationships between culture and the spiritual world.

The particular value of the method of vocabulary analysis followed in this study was that it forced me to pose questions which were new to me. The answers discovered through continuation of analysis frequently were astonishing to me. The advantage of this method over more traditional approaches is that it requires one to liberate his mind from preconceived theses or a priori "received positions" and "classical interpretations," for which he would then seek "proof texts." A complete vocabulary analysis can have an embarrassing and, sometimes, even explosive effect upon points of view that have been taken for granted.

Although this book is written primarily with Jesuits in mind, it is my hope that it may also be helpful to the many religious congregations which have found inspiration and guidance in the Constitutions written by the founder of the Company of Jesus as well as to others seeking clarification of the essential role of the religious superior. I have endeavored to discover the role of the superior according to St. Ignatius by arriving at an understanding of the profound intention he expressed in his own language. In spite of the necessary expression of the conclusions of this study in my own language, it seems justifiable, in the light of this analysis of the vocabulary of St. Ignatius, to present them as an accurate statement of his notion of the role of the superior as articulated in the vocabulary of our own times. All translations of texts are my own unless otherwise noted. It is my earnest hope and sincere prayer that with a clear understanding of the original inspiration of St. Ignatius, it will be possible, under the guidance of the Holy Spirit, to effect the adaptation to the "signs of the times" to which the Church in council has called us, through the united efforts of all those who are companions in the Company of Jesus today.

Finally, I have the pleasant duty of thanking those who have made this book possible. This includes many great Jesuits whose nameless influence has shown me by example the meaning and value of the "scope of our vocation." During the actual research invaluable help and encouragement were given by the director of my dissertation, Father Michael de Certeau, S.J.,

Introduction

and by Father Louis Cognet of the Oratory and Father Jean-Marie Le Blond, S.J. Whatever merit is to be found in the style and presentation of this book belongs to Sister Mary Janice Futrell, O.S.B., who patiently and firmly edited the writing, and to Father George E. Ganss, S.J., the general editor of the Institute of Jesuit Sources. I owe a special debt of gratitude to my superiors who made it possible for me to undertake the study of Ignatian spirituality, especially Father Frederick Kuijper, S.J., Father Theodore van der Putten, S.J., Father Harold O. Small, S.J., and Father Linus J. Thro, S.J. Above all, I must say "Thank you with love" to Father André Dethiou, S.J., my guide, my friend, my father in Christ.

Cushing, Oklahoma

Feast of Saint Ignatius, 1968

SERVICE OF CHRIST
THROUGH APOSTOLIC LOVE

THE ROLE OF THE SUPERIOR of a religious community — what
he is for — can be understood only through understanding the
end of this religious community — what it is for, its role in continuing salvation history within the Church. It is the ecclesial
end, the reason for the existence of the religious community,
which determines all its life and action, the vocation of its individual members, and the techniques and structures which it
adopts. This ecclesial end is specified by the original inspiration of the founder to serve the Church by living out the Christian life of the Gospel in a certain way which gradually is incarnated in the history of the community. The founder's original
inspiration — his particular vision of a way to serve Christ
living and acting in His Church — permanently determines the
vocation of the religious community as such and must remain
intact if the community is to be true to itself.

*The Superior
and the
"Scope of Our
Vocation"*

On the other hand, the group of techniques used by the community to achieve its end and to realize its vocation at any given
time in history must be adapted to the "signs of the times," even
though this requires radical changes in the techniques and
forms of expression employed by the founder himself to achieve
the end of the community within his own historical situation.[1]
Consequently, except for the essential vocation of the community — its ecclesial end —, everything is relative, everything
is a means to the end. True loyalty to the profound intention of

---

1 See the Decree on the Appropriate Renewal of the Religious Life
(*Perfectae Caritatis*), esp. nos. 1, 2, in *The Documents of Vatican II,*
ed. Walter M. Abbott (New York, 1966), p. 468.

the founder, therefore, requires the constant discernment of the means best suited to achieve the end of the community here and now, and the courage to adopt the new techniques and structures necessary to carry out the conclusions of this discernment. There can be no true discernment without a clear norm of judgment. The great danger during a time of dramatic cultural change is to retain or reject old structures and techniques and to refuse or adopt new ones without examining their true efficacy in the light of the norm: the essential vocation of the community.

To understand the role of the superior and to discern the best ways for him to exercise his function here and now, it is necessary first to understand the end of the religious community. Now the end of the Company of Jesus as it was conceived by Ignatius of Loyola can be expressed in its essence as *the service of Christ through the aid of souls in companionship.* All aspects of the reason for being of the Company of Jesus are implicit in this statement.

Following the gradual evolution of the personal vocation of Ignatus from his conversion at Loyola to the decision to found the Company of Jesus recorded in the Deliberation of the First Fathers in 1539, and his expression of the community vocation of the Company in the various documents culminating in the Constitutions, it becomes possible to express Ignatius' understanding of what he called the "scope of our vocation" in a succinct phrase composed of words which are constants in his vocabulary: *servicio de Cristo, ayudar las ánimas, compañeros,* and *Compañía.* The scope of our vocation is: *to serve Christ through the aid of souls in companionship.* In the early documents of the Society, the expression *scopus vocationis nostrae* refers to the specific end of the Society, its particular charism, that which, according to the Decree on Religious Life of Vatican Council II, must be authentically renewed.

Now, everything involved in the scope of our vocation is implicit in this phrase: (1) the personal love and commitment to Christ in faith of each individual Jesuit, nurtured in his prayer and realized in his holiness, which is the foundation of his individual vocation to the Company: to serve Christ; (2) the fact that in the Company this personal love of Christ is to be concretized in the active apostolic work of proclaiming the Kingdom of Christ to men in word and deed and life: through

14

the aid of souls;[2] (3) and the fact that in the Company this apostolic service of Christ is to be done in community in order to exercise the apostolate more effectively through the united force of a group of dedicated companions than it could be done individually: in companionship. This "in companionship" ideal also implicitly contains all that is involved in community life and work and the entire structure of authority and obedience.

It is evident that to serve Christ through the aid of souls in companionship is the essential end of all apostolic religious. That which specifies apostolic congregations among themselves is their particular approach to the apostolic service of Christ and the history of their community in carrying out this service. The particular approach of Ignatius is revealed through other constant expressions in his vocabulary: *más, mejor,* and other dynamic comparative terms explicitly urging Jesuits always to seek the ever greater service of Christ; *vicario de Cristo* and *discurrir* to insist that it is the work of Jesuit apostles to go anywhere in the world on missions for the Church under the direction of the vicar of Christ. The scope of the vocation of the Company of Jesus, then, is specified by the apostolic approach which is "the ever greater service of Christ who is working through His Church, by going anywhere in the world at the command of the vicar of Christ to aid souls in companionship". The specifying notes of the apostolic approach of the Company of Jesus, therefore, are three: (1) the constant dynamic thrust to ever greater service of Christ; (2) immediate service of the Church at the direction of the vicar of Christ; (3) mobility.

The history of an institution progressively characterizes this institution in its identity, just as the personal history of a man characterizes his identity. A man of forty carries with him the accumulated characteristics of his own personal evolution. Similarly, the Company of Jesus is characterized by four hundred years of living out the scope of its vocation. The key document for understanding the "scope of our vocation" is the Deliberation of the First Fathers, which describes the founding of the

---

2 The Spanish word *ánimas* at the time of Ignatius was much more concrete in referring to the whole body-person than is the English word *souls*. Perhaps a more accurate translation of the phrase "ayudar las ánimas" would be, therefore, "through helping people". Nevertheless, since this study is based upon direct vocabulary analysis, the phrase

15

Company for the achievement of its ecclesial end.[3] All the subsequent documents up to and including the Constitutions are really merely commentaries on the Deliberation of the First Fathers. Therefore, to understand the superior in the Constitutions or in the occasional letters on obedience, one must never allow the Deliberation to become lost in the background. It is the essential context in which all else must be placed if one is to have a true understanding of the role of the superior according to Ignatius.

The deliberation which resulted in the foundation of the Company of Jesus was brought about by the fact that the first companions were being dispersed on apostolic missions in fulfillment of their vow to go anywhere in the world where the Vicar of Christ on earth judged they might aid souls. This physical dispersal posed a question to the companions: should they remain united so that even physical separation could never really destroy their companionship, or should they simply go their separate ways as the inevitable result of their apostolic vocation? They concluded that since God had united them despite their great variety of race and origin, they should remain joined together. Furthermore, they should endeavor daily to strengthen and make more firm this God-given union, forming themselves into one body and caring for one another's needs with mutual understanding. The reason given for this decision was that thus united they could more effectively aid souls and, so, better fulfill the will of God according to the scope of their vocation.[4] The norm of their mutual discernment, therefore, was the common end about which they were already of one mind, and in function of which they were deciding the best means to achieve it. In view of this union for the sake of their apostolic end, and taking note that they had already vowed perpetual poverty and chastity in 1534, the companions then asked themselves in 1539 whether, as a means to fulfill the will of God in all things more sincerely and with greater praise and merit,

---

"through the aid of souls" will be retained throughout, with the caution that it is never to be understood in any neo-Platonic sense.

3 *Con*MHSJ, I, 1-7. The document was most probably written by Jean Codure or Pierre Favre. See ibid., I, xxxvii. For description of these deliberations, see *FN,* I, 129, 205, 269; II, 93, 202, 592-593. An English translation of the Deliberation is given below in Appendix I.

4 *Cons*MHSJ, I, 2.

they should add the vow of obedience to one of their own number. After further mutual discernment, the companions reached the decision that they should indeed pronounce the vow of obedience to one of their own as the most effective means to carry out their chief intention. This intention they divided into three parts: (1) to fulfill the will of God (understood always "according to the scope of our vocation" of aiding souls); (2) more effectively to preserve the Company for the achievement of its apostolic end; (3) to provide for all spiritual and temporal contingencies of the companions united in this apostolic Company.

In this statement of the necessity of obedience as a means to achieve the end of the Company, the role of the superior is already implicitly described. It consists of: (1) discerning the will of God for accomplishing the apostolic end of the Company; (2) preserving the being of the Company; (3) providing for the spiritual and the temporal needs of the members of the Company.

The implications of this role were developed by Ignatius in the Constitutions as he described the concrete way in which the superior must carry it out. The discernment of the will of God for the apostolate would involve the process of mutual discernment — the "circulation" of the whole body of the Company — which the companions had practiced from the beginning, but which now would terminate in the final decision of the superior speaking in the place of Christ. The preservation of the being of the Company would suppose that the superior, as the one head of the whole body, would be the living principle of the union of all its members in mutual love. His providence over the Company would involve ordering the lives and the actions of the companions for the greater spiritual perfection and material welfare of all.

This fundamental notion of the role of the superior was the fruit of years of experience of exercising an apostolic vocation in companionship. It issued from human life and was not derived from any traditional formula or imposed as an abstract principle. It would govern all the delineation of the role of the superior by Ignatius, whatever modes of expression he might eventually borrow from traditional religious rules. The structure of authority and obedience, the role of the superior, are means to achieve the ecclesial end of the Company, and the manner of their exercise must always be discerned here and now in the light of the "scope of our vocation": to serve Christ through the aid of souls in companionship. In order better to understand this end, it is well to examine it analytically, noting how it developed in the psychological evolution of the apostolic vocation of Ignatius of Loyola.

To Serve Christ   The conversion of Ignatius Loyola from the life of a vain and pleasure-loving knight to the service of Christ was the result in the natural order of his life and formation as a Basque *hidalgo* and a Castilian *caballero*. Born around 1491 in Guipúzcoa,[5] he had imbibed as a child the profound faith of his countrymen in God and the Church. From his prolonged contact with his nurse María de Garín, the wife of a blacksmith, the young Iñigo seasoned the faith of his seignorial parents with the simple devotion of the common people. At the age of thirteen or fourteen he went to serve the king in the household of Juan Velázquez de Cuéllar, overseer of the royal estates and collector of revenue for Ferdinand the Catholic. Here his mentality was permanently molded by Castilian notions of honor and of loyalty and service of his king. If during this period of adolescence at a worldly court, Iñigo succumbed to the temptations that surrounded him, nevertheless, he was still immersed in an atmosphere of profound and living faith.[6] If Ignatius recalled in his *Autobiography* the fruits of this period as "a great and vain desire to gain honor," it is also true that he lived in a milieu where the truth of the Christian faith was taken for granted as the ultimate meaning of life and that he developed positive qualities of knightly service. These qualities were deepened during his service of Antonio Manrique, Viceroy of Navarre, after the death of Velázquez in 1517, until that fateful May 20, 1521, at Pamplona, when a cannon ball changed his destiny.

Wounded in the service of his lord, frustrated in his efforts to find romances like *Amadís de Gaula* to while away the inter-

---

5 The chonology of the life of Ignatius, established by Pedro Leturia, is given with its proofs in *FN*, I, 26* - 62*.
6 Laynez says that Ignatius "had been attacked and conquered by sins of the flesh" (*FN*, I, 76). Gonçalves da Câmara reports that Ignatius told him he had had "the vicious habits of a youth" — *las travesuras de mancebo* (ibid., 358).

minable hours of convalescence, Iñigo rediscovered in Ludolph's *Life of Christ* and in the *Flos Sanctorum* the climate of faith that he had breathed as a child in the castle of Loyola and the cottage of María de Garín, and which had been the atmosphere created by the devotional practices in the house of Velázquez at Arévalo. His knightly imagination dreamed of emulating the heroic deeds of St. Francis and St. Dominic, of going barefoot to Jerusalem, of eating nothing but herbs and of performing all those hard actions the saints had done.[7] He thought of exercising his "hatred of himself" on returning from Jerusalem by becoming a Carthusian, if being a member of this order would not limit his freedom to perform the great penances he longed for.[8] When Ignatius finally left Loyola toward the end of February, 1522, to begin his pilgrimage to Jerusalem by way of Montserrat, the only evolution in his personal motivation was a change from preoccupation with satisfying for his sins to a desire to emulate the great penances of the saints simply to please God.[9] There was as yet no notion of an apostolic vocation. Ignatius was fired with the desire to serve Christ in a knightly and heroic fashion, but he had not yet discovered the concrete way in which God would call him to carry out his service. This ideal of divine service was the first step in his spiritual evolution, and his final commitment to an apostolic vocation exercised in companionship would be the result of his discovery through living experience that it was in this way that God wished Ignatius to serve Him. Father de Guibert has shown that the profoundest reaches of Ignatian mysticism were grounded in this desire to give himself totally to the service of the Divine Majesty.[10] It was inevitable that this ideal of service, identified with the praise and glory of God, would become the ruling spirit of the apostolic Company which Ignatius was to found.

It was during his months of prayer and penance — his "primitive Church" — at Manresa that Ignatius discovered that for him the service of Christ meant following his divine King

7 *FN,* I, 372.
8 Ibid., I, 376-378.
9 Ibid., I, 382.
10 J. de Guibert, *The Jesuits: Their Spiritual Doctrine and Practice,* trans. W. J. Young (Chicago, 1964), pp. 152-181.

into battle against Satan under the banner of the Cross to extend the Kingdom of Christ to all mankind. He remained at Manresa from March, 1522, until February of the following year. Here he experienced interior fluctuations of consolation and desolation and wondered to himself "what new manner of life he was now beginning." This was his own period of the Spiritual Exercises which led him to the "election" of his apostolic vocation. Through conversation with spiritual persons and the experience of the mutual gain received, he perceived the first glimmerings of apostolic motivation in the living revelation of human contact. Gradually, he worked out a rhythm of life which included, besides seven hours of prayer a day, the effort to help those souls who came to seek his spiritual aid.[11] He began to experience a series of great consolations, and this period of spiritual peace was helpful for reflection upon his manner of life. "After he began to be consoled by God and to see the fruit which occurred in the souls who conversed with him, he discontinued his previous extreme practices; and he began to cut his nails and his hair." [12]

Ignatius was passing through the human process of discovering his own identity — what his life was for — through the very experience of living and of discerning the will of God for him. This process reached its term in the great illumination at the river Cardoner, where he received the grace of clarity: a synthetic view of himself and of the meaning of reality which would integrate into an harmonious whole all his past experiences and which would provide him with the norm of discernment for all his future decisions. The *Autobiography* provides the most striking description of this illumination:

> The eyes of his understanding started to be opened. He had no vision; but he understood and knew many things, both spiritual and in the realm of letters. The illumination was so tremendous that it seemed to him that all things were made new. It is impossible to state the specific matters he then understood, although they were many. He can only say that he received such a great clarity in his understanding, that it seemed to him that if all the many helps he had received from God and all the many things he had known throughout the rest of his life up to his present

11 *FN,* I, 398.
12 Ibid., I, 402.

age of sixty-two were all put together, they would not amount to as much clarity as he had received this one time.[13]

This mystical elevation was the climax of all the work of nature and grace that had gone before in Ignatius. What the text insists upon is not the quantitative content of the experience but the overwhelming quality of light: a radiant clarity which opened up to him the pattern of his own history, illuminating his own life, an interior brilliance which enabled him to grasp a larger world and to find a larger self. This is why it seemed to him a greater light than all the other mystical graces of his life put together. Although he would have gifts of much more profound union with God later on, it was at the Cardoner that he discovered in the divine light the meaning of his own being in the world. All of the things he had actually known before were now bathed in a new light which enabled him to comprehend their meaning and interrelation in such a way that he seemed to have known them hardly at all until then. In the profoundest depths of his subjective consciousness, he felt an illuminating union with the source of the reality of all things. This is why it was impossible to analyze the details of this radiance; nevertheless, it was light, because it would illuminate all his life to come.[14]

Ignatius was still to pass through a long period of searching before he would discover the specific goal to which God was leading him: the foundation of the Company of Jesus. This would become fully clear only in the Deliberation of 1539. But

13 Ibid., I, 404; cf. 80, 160, 162.
14 The "inner light" has always been an important element in personal religious experience. Cf. Mircea Eliade, *Mephistopheles and the Androgyne: Studies in Religious Myth and Symbol* (New York, 1965), esp. pp. 57-59, where he discusses the Transfiguration of Christ, baptismal fire symbolism, the Jewish concept of the "light of glory" and of the glory that will appear as the Messiah shining like the sun, etc., and similar phenomena in other religions (pp. 59-77). Of particular interest in relation to the Illumination at the Cardoner are the ecstasy of Jacob Boehme, "an intellectual illumination so perfect that he seemed to have understood all mysteries" (65), and the long description of the experience of Dr. R. M. Bucke, who claimed that "he learnt more within the few seconds during which the illumination lasted than in previous months or years of study, and that he learnt much that no study could have taught him" (67).

after the Cardoner he was absolutely certain about the essence of his own vocation: the service of Christ through the aid of souls. This would be the principle that would guide him in all his future projects: going to Jerusalem as an apostle rather than as a penitent,[15] devoting himself to study at an advanced age,[16] seeking companions to serve Christ with him either in Jerusalem, or, if Divine Providence so disposed, through becoming immediate missionaries of the vicar of Christ; founding a new religious order of active apostles; and, finally, drawing up the Constitutions and delineating the role of the superior. For Ignatius, ever afterwards, his concrete service and praise and glorifying of God would be through the aid of souls, and this essentially apostolic vocation would become that of all the members of the Company of Jesus.

To Serve Christ through the Aid of Souls in Companionship

It was only after his return from Jerusalem to Barcelona in 1524 that Ignatius arrived at the conclusion that he should seek out companions to follow his apostolic ideal: "to become trumpets of Jesus Christ." [17] When embarking for Jerusalem in March, 1523, he had actually refused the offer of companions who might help him during the pilgrimage, because he wished to place all his hope in God alone.[18] But on his return he was convinced that the apostolate could be carried out more effectively by a group of companions bound together by mutual love and aiding one another corporally and spiritually.

This realization resulted from the teaching of living experience, beginning with Ignatius' first fruitful encounters with other spiritual persons in Manresa and continuing through his solitary efforts to aid souls there and in Barcelona and Jerusalem. Although there is no written testimony concerning the mental processes of Ignatius in arriving at that ideal, one can surmise that it was the concrete experience of the limitations imposed upon his apostolic efforts through undertaking them alone that brought him to realize that a group of companions, giving each other mutual aid and love and combining their personal forces in one united body, would be much

15 *FN,* I, 422; cf. 86; also *MonNad,* V, 276.
16 *FN,* I, 430; cf. 263; II, 202.
17 Ibid., I, 170.
18 Ibid., I, 408-410.

22

more effective as an instrument of Christ in the establishment of His Kingdom than a solitary apostle could ever be. As Ignatius gained companions in Barcelona and Salamanca, he became absolutely certain that he should find more men sharing the same ideal and that he should keep those he had already found. He planned to arrange matters in Paris to receive his Spanish companions there.[19] As is well known, these first companions did not remain with him, nor did the first three to whom he gave the Spiritual Exercises in Paris.[20] It would be at Paris, nevertheless, that the nucleus of companions would be formed which would evolve into the Company of Jesus.

Ignatius arrived at Paris on February 2, 1528, and remained there until the beginning of April, 1535, during which period he would finish his study of Latin at the College of Montaigu and take his Master of Arts degree at the College of Sainte Barbe. He began his studies at Sainte Barbe on October 1, 1529, and two of his fellow students were Francis Xavier and Pierre Favre. In October, 1532, he began a friendship with Simão Rodrigues. Laynez and Salmerón arrived in Paris around September, 1533, and they were soon comrades of Ignatius. He gave the month of Spiritual Exercises to Favre at the beginning of 1534, to Laynez and Salmerón during the spring of the same year, to Rodrigues and Bobadilla shortly afterwards, and, finally to Xavier the following September.[21]

These men were united through sharing the same personal identity. Each one discovered the meaning of his own life in their common vocation to serve Christ through the aid of souls in companionship. That this vocation would lead them to found a new, apostolic religious order was not yet clear to them and would not become fully so until the Deliberation, but gradually they were given the "grace of companionship" through living it. During discussions of their ideals and their hopes and dreams, they inevitably experienced the necessity imposed upon each of them individually to submit his own judgment to the control of their collective discernment of their apostolic mission. On August 15, 1534, at Montmartre, they pronounced vows of poverty and chastity and to go to Jerusalem or, if this

19 Ibid., I, 462.
20 Ibid., I, 100-102; 468.
21 Ibid., I, 32*-33*.

proved to be impossible, to place themselves at the disposal of the vicar of Christ to go anywhere in the world for the aid of souls. Although the decision to make this vow was unanimous, we have the word of Simão Rodrigues that it was arrived at only "longam post disputationem." [22] Having committed themselves to the same vocation, the companions felt bound together in a new intimacy of mutual love grounded in their identical life-ideal. Laynez remembered that from this time forward, although they did not live together, they would eat in the rooms of one another, besides having frequent visits and conversations which "inflamed their hearts with ardor." In retrospect, he saw this mutual familiarity and communication and unflagging attention to one another's needs, both spiritual and temporal, as the human bond of union which maintained their companionship for the aid of souls.[23] In 1539, after years of lived companionship with Laynez, Ignatius wrote a letter to Laynez' brother John in which he described the fruits of their manner of "conversando en perpetuo amor": that now "we are more inseparably united and joined together than ever, and on account of this I consider all of his interests as my own and his affairs as mine." [24]

The only head of this group of companions was Jesus Christ, although Ignatius had obvious personal and moral ascendancy. He was, however, an elder brother rather than a superior whose final decision the others must obey, and during this period of discovery of one another and of their common vocation their decisions were always, finally, unanimous. That even after the vow at Montmartre the relationship of the companions remained that of a family of brothers rather than that of a group structured by juridical authority is shown by the fact that when Ignatius left Paris for Azpeitia at the beginning of April, 1535, in the hope of regaining his health in his native air, he left Pierre Favre "como hermano mayor de todos," not to rule the others, but to watch over their needs with the affectionate care of an older brother.[25] The structure of authority and obedience and the role of the superior would appear only when it would

22 Ibid., III, 20.
23 Ibid., I, 102-104.
24 *EppIgn,* I, 153.
25 *FN,* I, 104.

become clear that they were necessary means to fulfill the scope of the vocation of the Company of Jesus.

On the other hand, while hopefully awaiting a ship to Jerusalem at Venice in 1536, the companions lived together, when possible, in small communities, and here they made their first experiments with obedience, taking weekly turns as the superior whom the others obeyed voluntarily, but as if bound by a vow of obedience. They were to continue this practice until Ignatius' election as general in April, 1541.[26] This obedience was conceived as a meritorious ascetical exercise, rather than as a juridical structuring of their common life. All of the companions were, of course, aware of the age-old tradition that obedience in imitation of Christ's submission to His Father's will was an act of high virtue. This motive would be an important help to individual companions in their practice of obedience in the future Company of Jesus, but it would not be the reason for the choice of obedience in fulfilling the scope of its vocation.[27]

Even though the companions were not yet thinking of founding a religious order, their little group had been increasing. Favre had attracted Claude Jay, a priest, to become one of them in 1535. By the time they left Paris to join Ignatius in Venice in 1536, two others were with them: Paschase Broët and Jean Codure. In Venice, Ignatius himself had accepted Diego Hozes as one of their number. After their ordination and while awaiting passage to Jerusalem, they sought to find other companions. The desire "to preserve and augment" their company which would lead to the foundation of a religious order was already strong within their hearts. In September, 1537, after the first Masses of all the priests except Ignatius, the companions not only discussed their way of serving God while waiting to go to Jerusalem, but also chose for themselves the name "the Company of Jesus." They arrived at this name after prayer and discussion because they had no head and no superior among them except Jesus Christ, whom alone they desired to serve.[28] Rather than having any military resonance, the name signified that they were companions of one another and of Jesus.[29]

---

26 Ibid., III, 86.
27 See below, pp. 34-38.
28 *FN*, I, 204; II, 504, 596-597.
29 J. Iturrioz, "Compañía de Jesùs. Sentido histórico y ascético de este nombre", *Manresa*, XXVII (1955), 43-53, has shown that the mili-

Since there was still no hope of going to Jerusalem by the end of October, 1537, Ignatius went to Rome with Favre and Laynez, there to wait out the year provided for in the vow of Montmartre. During this journey, in mid-November, Ignatius experienced the great vision of La Storta, where the heavenly Father placed him with His Son, saying, "I will be propitious to you at Rome"; and the Son said to him, "I will that you serve Us." [30] It is clear that at least on reflection Ignatius saw in this vision a confirmation of the name "Company of Jesus." [31] By hindsight, too, he would come to understand that the meaning of the vision was the vocation to found the religious order of the Company; but there is no evidence that Ignatius here received a "revelation" of the future Company. Indeed, we have his own testimony that he did not understand the meaning of the Father's words, but thought that they might signify that he would be crucified at Rome.[32] That the details of the "content" of the vision seemed of little consequence to Ignatius himself is proved by his remark to Gonçalves da

tary note given to this name later by Polanco (*FN,* II, 597; *Polchron,* I, 74) and Ribadeneyra (*De ratione instituti* [Rome, 1864], pp. 47-49), was for external reasons. In any case, it refers to the ascetical war against Satan in the soul, rather than to militarism. He notes the extremely common use of this name in Italy during the time of Ignatius for all sorts of pious groups (pp. 45-47), and concludes that the important word is not *Company* but *of Jesus.* But Th. Baumann, "Compagnie de Jésus. Origine et sens primitif de ce nom," *RAM,* XXXVII (1961), 47-60, rightly insists that Ignatius' use of the word *Company* was Spanish rather than Italian. It meant simply *companions* and was used for the group before they added the notion of "companions of Jesus" (49-57). B. Schneider, "Nuestro Principio y principal fundamento. Zum historischen Verständnis des papstgehorsamsgelübdes," *AHSJ,* XXV (1956), 488-513, also stresses the note of companionship in the word *Company.* The companions had a common program of work, not left to individual initiative: place, manner and time of the apostolate were determined by the community, and their whole manner of life was that of a unit.

30 For discussions solving the discrepancies in the various testimonies of this vision, see H. Rahner, "La vision de Saint Ignace à la chapelle de la Storta," *Christus,* no. 1 (1951), 48-65, and R. Rouquette, "Essai critique sur les sources relatant la vision de Saint Ignace de Loyola à la Storta," *RAM,* XXXIII (1957), 34-61, 150-170.

31 *FN,* I, 203-204; II, 377, 585, 595-597; *MonNad,* IV, 649. See also Th. Baumann, "Compagnie de Jésus: la confirmation de ce nom," *RAM,* XXXVIII (1962), 52-63.

32 Ibid., II, 133.

Câmara that he could obtain more accurate information from Laynez about the vision than from himself.[33] The essence of this vision must have been the interior experience of being placed with the Son by the Father and the mystical confirmation of the vocation of Ignatius to serve Them through the aid of souls in companionship.

On their subsequent arrival in Rome to place themselves at the disposal of the vicar of Christ for apostolic missions anywhere in the world in fulfillment of their vow at Montmartre, Ignatius and his companions already were certain of the scope of their vocation to serve Christ through the aid of souls in companionship. During the following months, highlighted by Ignatius' celebration of his first Mass on Christmas, 1538, the companions seriously contemplated their future. Finally, they came together from March until the middle of June, 1539, to engage in the mutual "discernment of spirits" which was to result in the foundation of the Company of Jesus described in the Deliberation. The companions saw that if their union of mutual love and mutual aid as a means to the greater service of Christ was to endure, they must stabilize their Company.[34] They must preserve it in being permanently and increase the number of its members. They must see to it that they would continue to be intimately bound together in one body, no matter how great might be the physical distances that would separate them in undertaking missions for the Church anywhere in the world. Their apostolic vocation required them to undertake labors in which, precisely, a group is less kept together ("minus conservetur societas"). For this reason they chose to vow obedience to one of their own ("alicui ex nobis"), since without this obedience the Company could not long remain in being, while nothing better preserves a community than obedience.[35]

Thus, the long years of discernment of the will of God for him led Ignatius to the idea of a new kind of religious order: a company of companions united in the common vocation to glorify God through serving Christ who had been sent by the Father on the mission to save all men. Made up of companions bound together by the bond of mutual love and united through

33 Ibid., I, 498.
34 Ibid., I, 28, 205; II, 205, 592.
35 *Cons*MHSJ, I, 2-3, 6-7.

obedience to one head, the Company was conceived as one corporate instrument of Christ's action through the Church to aid all souls to attain the end for which God created them. The individual member of the Company would realize his service of Christ in His Church through service of the Company whose corporate end is this divine service. The essential role of the superior to Ignatius, then, would be the unification of all these companions into an apostolic community of love for the service of Christ.

To Serve Christ in His Church Anywhere in the World

Although Ignatius of Loyola founded the first totally apostolic religious order, many have been founded since his time.[36] The essential end of any apostolic order may be expressed as the service of Christ through the aid of souls in companionship. As has already been noted, that which specifies any given order is its own history and the particular approach it takes to the apostolate. From the beginning, the Company of Jesus was characterized by specific apostolic procedures expressed in a special vow: the immediate service of the vicar of Christ and the mobility to go anywhere in the world where he might send them for the aid of souls.[37]

The Ignatian ideal of the ever greater service of Christ in His Church through the immediate service of His vicar on earth was not simply the result of theological reasoning, but it had been given to him at Guipúzcoa as part of his ancestral faith, nourished in the Basque hermitage of San Pedro at Loyola. As a *caballero* in Castile, Ignatius had deepened this loyalty to the Roman Pontiff. At Arévalo his parish church was dedicated to the Prince of the Apostles. In the royal household of Velázquez he must have heard of the perils of division within the Church, all of which implied a revolt against the primacy of the Roman Pontiff.[38] The faith of the childhood of Ignatius

36 Useful studies concerning the relationship of the Company of Jesus to older religious Orders are: J. L. de Urrutia, "Régimen de las órdenes religiosas a mediados del s. XVI y aportación de San Ignacio," *Miscelanea Comillas*, XXXVI (1961), 91-142; L. Moulin, *Le monde vivant des religieux* (Paris, 1964), pp. 27-39, and the tables, pp. 291-297.
37 *Cons*MHSJ, I, 67.
38 Around the year 1450, Torquemada had written eloquently about the need for Catholic champions to arm themselves to do battle in de-

at Loyola became that of a mature man in the Castile which from Isabel to Charles V had repeatedly chanted its faith in the hierarchical unity of the Church of Christ. One month before the wounding of Ignatius at Pamplona in 1521, the Castilian nobles, including the Loyolas, reacted against the first introduction of Lutheran propaganda into Spain in a manifesto strongly reaffirming their faith in "la Iglesia Romana neustra Madre." [39] Within his own cultural heritage, Ignatius found the basis for his ideal of the consecration of the Company of Jesus to the service of Christ through His vicar on earth.

The depth of Ignatius' faith that the will of God is communicated to Christians by the vicar of Christ on earth when his full authority is brought to bear is strikingly demonstrated by a painful act of obedience when the Franciscan Guardian ordered him to leave Jerusalem. Ignatius was absolutely determined to remain permanently in the city of Christ, following the actual footsteps of his King and exercising the apostolate there during the rest of his life.[40] However, the Guardian refused the necessary permission to Ignatius to remain because experience had shown the Franciscans that death or prison (with the Friars forced to pay the ransom!) was the normal outcome of such a project. This reasoning did not convince Ignatius, and his response to it contained a touch of Basque stubbornness. He was so set upon remaining in Jerusalem that nothing could persuade him to renounce the project; and even if the Guardian could not see the affair from Ignatius' point of view, no fear of consequences was going to change his mind.[41] Confronted with this defiance, the good Franciscan let Ignatius know that he was speaking with the authority of the Apostolic

fense of the Church against the attacks of those who would attempt to wound it mortally, rend its unity, and destroy its God-given organization, especially by attempting to paralyze the supreme authority which the Apostolic See had received from God. *Summa de ecclesia,* cited by A. Fliche and V. Martin, *Histoire de l'église,* XV (Paris, 1951), 17-18.

39 See P. Leturia, *Estudios Ignacianos,* ed. I. Iparraguirre, 2 vols. (Rome, 1957), I, 314. Leturia notes that there was considerable aversion in Spain from the time of Cisneros to the actual condition of the Roman curia and the politics of various popes. But faith in the dogma itself of the papal primacy was unshakable and made of Spain the *paladin del pontificado* during the Reformation.

40 *FN,* I, 422.

41 Ibid., I, 424.

See and that he would excommunicate the pilgrim if he did not obey. In spite of his personal determination to remain in Jerusalem, Ignatius immediately bowed to papal authority. Later on when recounting his effort to find God's will for his future activity ("pensando quid agendum"), he remarked that he was so doing because he had understood that it was the "will of God" that he should not remain in Jerusalem.[42] That this contradicted his own subjective discernment of the will of God was painful, but in the last analysis insignificant. Thus, for him an integral part of the order of reality was the conviction that an irrevocable decision of the vicar of Christ spoke for God.

Of importance in deepening Ignatius' ideal of loyalty to the pope was his encounter at the College of Sainte Barbe in Paris with the influence of Erasmus, an author for whose viewpoints he had already developed a strong dislike at Alcalá.[43] As did Lefèvre d'Estaples, Erasmus blended with his humanism and evangelism a strong dose of criticism of the pope. This was as much a scandal to the Castilian sense of fealty of Ignatius as it was a shock to his idea of proper submission to papal authority. In his *Supputationes* Erasmus wittily averred that if the pope were to approve the assertions of the arch-conservative and extravagant Noel Beda, he would appeal from the pope "nodding" to the pope "awake," since "black would not be white if the Roman Pontiff were to say so, which I know he will never do." In the thirteenth of the Rules for Thinking Rightly Within the Church, added to the Spiritual Exercises during his stay in Paris, Ignatius said precisely that we should hold it as certain that the white we see is black, if the hierarchical Church says so.[44] Strange as this statement appears to modern eyes and much as it needs nuancing, it is a rhetorical riposte to the terminology of Erasmus and a declaration of the profound faith of the Spanish Ignatius who had been certain in Jerusalem that papal authority expressed the will of God even when it contradicted his own firm election to remain there.

This consciousness of Ignatius and of his companions of the role of the pope as the vicar of Christ on earth led them to the "papal clause" in their vow at Montmartre, when they chose

42 Ibid., I, 30; see 90, 168.
43 Ibid., I, 454-456.
44 *SpEx,* [365].

to place themselves at the disposal of the Sovereign Pontiff to go anywhere in the world on apostolic missions, if Divine Providence made it impossible for them to go to Jerusalem or to remain there to aid souls. They looked to the pope as the vicar of Christ who would make the ultimate act of discernment of the vocation of the companions by deciding in what way they concretely should serve Christ apostolically. The emphasis in the vow was rather upon the pope as discerner of their apostolic missions rather than upon service of the pope. Pierre Favre explained this in a letter of November 23, 1538; "The cause of our agreement to submit ourselves to his judgment and will was that we felt sure that he had the greatest knowledge of what was expedient for universal Christianity." [45]

Ignatius was convinced that Christ would be best served in the world through service of the Church whose head is His vicar. This conception was the basis of the special vow in the Company of Jesus to go anywhere in the world to aid souls at the command of the vicar of Christ on earth. The one head of the Company is Christ; but Christ gives His commands on earth through His vicar, who is obeyed in His place. It was in this simple but dense and profound conception of Ignatius of the practical, existential way to serve God in the world that his notion of obedience to the superior in the place of Christ was rooted.[46] Since the end of the Company is the service of Christ through the aid of souls in companionship, to be realized in fulfillment of the vow to the vicar of Christ on earth, it is clear that for Ignatius the real superior of the Company is the pope. The role of the immediate superior of the Company, therefore, is, in a very true sense, to be the vicar of the Sovereign Pontiff and, thus, to represent Christ to his companions in the total realization of the "scope of our vocation."

In order to grasp fully the function of authority in the Company of Jesus, it is instructive to note the "limits" placed by Ignatius upon the discernment of the pope. Ignatius had no doubt that when he gave a direct command the pope expressed the will of God for a Christian, since he is the vicar of Christ on earth who must be obeyed in the place of Christ when he invokes his plenary authority. But the authority of

45 *EppIgn,* 132; see *FN,* I, 194, 264, 479.
46 See below, ch. 7, pp. 160-162.

the pope over the Company was conditioned by the scope of our vocation: "we made this special promise and vow in order that His Holiness might send us on different missions for the greater glory of God our Lord *conformably to our promise and intention to go out to the whole world*" [47] (italics ours). When Ignatius felt that the orders of the pope threatened to frustrate the essentially apostolic vocation of the Company, while he obeyed the command, he used every means possible to change the mind of the pope so that the decision would be changed. This was particularly the case when Paul IV imposed monastic practices upon the Company.[48] The basic premise of the *Deliberatio primorum Patrum* (Deliberation of the First Fathers) had been the effort to arrive at the "already fixed and already known end so ardently desired" and to seek the will of God "juxta scopum vocationis nostrae.[49] The norm of discernment for all things, therefore, — even the wisdom of a papal command — was the apostolic end of the Company, the "scope of our vocation." [50]

The other specific characteristic of the apostolic vocation of the Company is mobility. Ignatius and his companions were convinced from the beginning that their vocation was to go anywhere in the world where the pope would send them to aid souls. This conception of the vocation of the Company was in accord with yet another trait in the mental structure of Ignatius traceable to his first years at Loyola. From his earliest youth Ignatius had lived in a milieu enthused by the grand ideal of crusade: to carry the cross of Christ to the infidels and the New World. Granada, the last Moorish redoubt in Spain, fell to the Catholic Kings in 1492, the very year Columbus discovered America. A whole new world was opened to the zeal of the

---

47 *Cons*MHSJ, I, 160.
48 For a summary of the most notable instances of Ignatius seeking to change a papal decision, see C. Palmes de Genover, *La Obediencia Religiosa Ignaciana* (Barcelona, 1963), pp. 302-319. Palmes provides the documentation and also a curious and tortured commentary.
49 *Cons*MHSJ, I, 2.
50 It is interesting that in the account of his election as general, Ignatius seems to give priority to the confessor in discerning the motions of the Holy Spirit with regard to the personal vocation of his penitent (*FN*, I, 19). The passage seems to suggest that the confessor is a more reliable interpreter of the divine will for an individual than is the juridical-hierarchical authority of the Holy See, except when this invokes its

crusaders, and it inflamed all Spaniards with the desire to conquer it for Christ and Spain. The family of Loyola had a tradition of going anywhere to fight for their king. The oldest brother of Ignatius fell in battle at Naples in 1496. Another died for the conquest of Mexico, and a third brother gave his life fighting the Turks in Hungary. Romantic stories of the Crusades, of the New World and of the liberation of the Holy Sepulchre must have been retold often in the castle at Loyola. The child Iñigo must have dreamed of signalizing himself as a *caballero* on crusade, carrying the banner of his king and the cross of Christ to the infidel in far away lands. Though Divine Providence would transform this ideal into a worldwide spiritual crusade under the vicar of Christ, it would build upon this natural foundation laid at Loyola in the soul of the little Basque *hidalgo*.

Indeed, the sense of universal mission was already clearly present in Ignatius' presentation of the call of the King in the meditation on the Kingdom of Christ in the Spiritual Exercises: "My will is to conquer the whole world and all enemies and, so, to enter into the glory of My Father." [51] It is not surprising, therefore, to find throughout the preliminary documents and in the Constitutions themselves many expressions of this essential mobility of the Company. The very first condition laid down for admission to the Company was to pronounce the vow of obedience to the pope "to offer themselves to go to any provinces or regions whatsoever." [52] The Formula of the Institute and the papal bulls following it specify that Jesuits must obey the pope with no hesitation or excuse, "whether he sends us to the Turks or the New World or to the Lutherans or to any other infidels or faithful." [53] The most characteristic word in the documents for the mobility of the Company is *discurrir*,

---

plenary Christ-given mandate; for Ignatius adds that he would follow the confessor over the pope unless it would be clear that there would be sin in not following the pope. It is impossible here to pursue the possible implications of this passage; but it would be interesting to reflect upon the suggested tensions between "spiritual" and "hierarchical" authority in finding the will of God for an individual, especially in view of contemporary problems.

51 *SpEx,* [95].
52 *Cons*MHSJ, I, 10.
53 Ibid., 17, 27, 83, 377.

which implies constant movement.[54] The end of the Company demands: "moving about from some regions to other regions of the world" at the command of the vicar of Christ on earth, so that all the companions must be ready to go and work "to the very ends of the earth." [55]

The Scope
of
Our Vocation

The program conceived by Ignatius for the Company of Jesus, thus, was very concrete. The praise and glory of God was to be realized through the ever greater service of His Divine Majesty, a service which, existentially, would be the service of Christ carrying out His universal redemptive mission through the Church under the leadership of His vicar on earth. The Company of Jesus would be a corporate instrument of this mission through placing itself under a vow to go anywhere in the world for the aid of souls. The scope of the vocation of the Company of Jesus is, therefore, essentially apostolic, and everything else, including the pursuit of personal perfection is a means to this apostolic end. This is clear in the ultimate reasons listed in the Deliberation for the choice of obedience. Significantly the document does not mention an ascetical motive for obedience. This motive had been developed, it is true, in the random list of four reasons Codure had given as examples of the arguments proposed in favor of obedience by various ones of the companions;[56] but of these reasons, only the second — conservation of the Company in unity — and the fourth — the fact that the pope, to whom they had consecrated themselves in total obedience, could not possibly pay attention to the particular contingencies in their lives — appear in the ultimate motives adduced for the decision.

In the First Sketch of the Institute of the Society of Jesus (*Prima Societatis Jesu Instituti Summa*) presented to Paul III in September, 1539, to seek confirmation for the Company, we have the initial reflections of Ignatius on the life of the Company in the light of the Deliberation. Here, for the first time, he indicates the manner of obedience of the companions: they are obliged to obey the superior in all matters pertaining to the

---

54 *Cons*MHSJ, I, 49, 60, 159, 160, 161, 162, 181; II, 66, 74, 169, 192, 206, 210, 211, 214, 222, 223, 378, 560.
55 Ibid., I, 49, 51.
56 Ibid., I, 6-7.

institute of the Company, both because of the great usefulness of order and for the attentive practice of most praiseworthy humility.[57] It is significant that the first motive given is utility, which, in view of the unifying role of the superior, refers to obedience as the means to the most effective corporate apostolic service of Christ. The second motive is ascetical, but is explicitly ordered to the apostolic end of the Company. The official confirmation of the new religious order did not occur until the promulgation of the papal bull *Regimini militantis Ecclesiae* on September 27, 1540. This document repeated almost textually the First Sketch of the Institute, adding only certain "edifying" remarks. For example, in the passage concerning the vow of obedience to the pope, which previously had referred only to the apostolic end of the Company, an ascetical motive is now added: "for the greater humility of our Company, and the perfect mortification and abnegation of our wills of each one." [58] This language is almost certainly the result of curial pressure, since Ignatius had become conscious of the necessity of adducing additional motives for the special vow to the pope, which Cardinal Guidiccioni had called "superfluous" in his critique of the First Sketch in 1539.[59]

To understand the place of personal perfection in the scope of the vocation of the Company, one must never forget the personal evolution of Ignatius and the first companions, which finally reached its term in the foundation of this order. Each of them began with the truth, so succinctly expressed in the Principle and Foundation of the Spiritual Exercises, that the final end of every individual man is the salvation of his own soul through the service and praise of God. Each of them, too, was imbued with the personal motivation of following Christ as closely as possible as was proposed as an ideal for all Christians in the Gospels and the Spiritual Exercises. For these particular men, the concrete way of serving Christ had become clear in their own "elections": it was to offer themselves totally to the apostolic service of Christ by being ready to go any-

57 Ibid., I, 18-19.
58 Ibid., I, 27.
59 See P. Tacchi Venturi, *Storia della Compagnia di Gesù in Italia*, 2 vols. in 4 tomes (Rome, 1957), II, Part I, 278-288. Also H. Bernard-Maître, "Les corrections de la Prima Societatis Jesu Instituti Summa," *RAM,* LIV (1963), 226-232.

where in the world at the command of His vicar on earth in order to aid souls to enter into the fullness off His Kingdom. All of this was the result of a gradual evolution within the souls of each of them, led by the living experience of Ignatius himself, which was clear even before they determined in the Deliberation that the best way to fulfill their vocation was by founding the Company of Jesus. The ideal of the Company — its reason for being — presupposed this personal consecration of each of them to the apostolic service of Christ in His Church. The end of the Company, therefore, was something added to and built upon this foundation of personal commitment to apostolic holiness. The end of the Company as such was to serve Christ through the aid of souls in companionship by uniting these individual vocations into one body which would be a more effective instrument of the Church for establishing the Kingdom of Christ in all mankind.

It is for this reason that in the early documents the end of the Company is always stated simply as 'to aid souls," although under curial pressure and after the arrival of Polanco as secretary some explicit references to personal perfection are added as time goes on. For example, the 1546 text of the *General Examen* for candidates to the Company states that its Institute is not only for the salvation of the souls of its members, but especially to aid and bring to perfection the souls of our neighbors.[60] It is clear from the context, however, that the recollection of the universal human end of personal salvation is introduced chiefly by way of emphasizing the end of the Company as such — the aid of souls. The first two texts of the Constitutions, text *a* (1547-1550) and text A (1550) do not mention personal perfection in their statement of the end of the Company, which is to *ayudar las ánimas;*[61] but text B, (1556) perhaps under the influence of Polanco, who wished published documents to be edifying, adds that the scope directly intended by the Company is to aid their own souls and those of their neighbors to attain the last end.[62] In a similar passage, text B alone states that the end of the studies in the Company

60 *Cons*MHSJ, II, 6.
61 Ibid., II, 169, 382.
62 Ibid., II, 382. Notice also "Sean la bullas edificativas para los que las leyeren" (Ibid., I, 296).

is to aid their own souls and those of their neighbors.[63] In the parallel passage, text A mentions only the apostolic end. This more ascetical emphasis in text B was probably the result of the gradual evolution of an educative program to form young Jesuits into mature apostles, as well as of the notions of Polanco.[64]

The end of the Company of Jesus — the "scope of our vocation" — is the service of Christ through the aid of souls in companionship. Everything else, even the pursuit of personal holiness of the individual members, is a means to this end. The role of the superior, therefore, is to achieve this end. His precise function is to unify all the companions for the fulfillment of this apostolic end.

From the study of the end of the Company of Jesus, it is possible to disengage the essential structure envisioned by Ignatius in all his future efforts to describe the role of the superior: (1) The Company of Jesus was founded in order to conserve in being the union of the companions united for fulfilling the scope of the vocation of the Company — its apostolic end. (2) The decision to vow obedience to one of their own — *"alicui ex nobis"* [65] — was taken as the surest means to preserve permanently and to increase the Company. (3) The essential role of the superior, therefore, was the constant renewal of the being of the Company, a being which consisted precisely in the mutual union of all the members of the Company for effective, unified apostolic action anywhere in the world under the direction of the vicar of Christ on earth. (4) In the concrete, this role of the superior would be carried out through making an apostolic community of love of all the companions here and now at any given historical moment. This role would involve unifying the life and action of all the actual members of the Company through: (a) incorporating new companions into the body of the Company by forming in them the spirit of the "scope of our vocation"; (b) ordering the life and action of the companions in such a way as to preserve their mutual union; (c)

63 Ibid., II, 416.
64 See R. Rouquette, "Le développement de la spiritualité apostolique de Saint Ignace de Loyola," *Christus,* no. 2 (1954), 21-45.
65 *Cons*MHSJ, I, 4.

giving unifying commands to the companions through discernment of the apostolic missions to be undertaken by the Company.

This structure provided the control, the norm, the point of reference for all of Ignatius' specific descriptions of the role of the superior given in the Constitutions, whether they touched upon his duties of forming new companions, his providence over the spiritual and the temporal lives of all, or his direction of their apostolic activities. In seeking to understand the intention of Ignatius in his remarks concerning particular duties of the superior, it is vital always to place these remarks in the illuminating context of this structure. Ignatius conceived of the superior as the living principle of unity of the Company for the achievement of its apostolic end and his fundamental intention was that the superior should always and everywhere carry out this role: making an apostolic community of love for the service of Christ through the aid of souls in companionship here and now.

APOSTOLIC LOVE
IN COMPANIONSHIP

UNDERSTANDING THE END of the Company of Jesus, the "scope of our vocation," makes it possible to disengage what is essential in the description of the role of the superior in the Ignatian documents from what is merely the accidental result of the historical and cultural epoch during which he lived. The essential role of the superior according to Ignatius was to unite all the companions in mutual love in order to accomplish their corporate apostolic service of Christ.

Through the superior, the Company is always coming into being. It constantly renews its existence in the union of the living members at any given historical moment with one another and with their head for the end of the Company: the service of Christ through the aid of souls in companionship. The apostolic end of the Company is the end of the whole Company together — in companionship. The individual members exist as "Companions of Jesus" only in function of their union with the whole body — "todo el cuerpo." Each participates in the Company's corporate achievement of its end only through his union with the others by means of their head, the living principle of union and, therefore, of unified activity. Consequently, the role of the superior is always being exercised anew: unifying the Company at each given moment, directing it towards its end as a united group of companions in every new historical situation. This is the role of the superior on every level — general, provincial, local.

It is the actual union of wills — mutual love — at every given moment of history which is the source of being of the Company. The Constitutions, therefore, are not the source of the being of the Company. The Company existed before the Constitutions were written and approved. Nor is the being of the Company something that exists *in* the Constitutions. They are, rather, the juridical instrument of the conservation of its being: the concrete description of the process of the coming into existence of the Company through the actual unifying of its members for their apostolic end at any historical moment. The Constitutions and the role of the superior therein outlined were entirely directed towards this conservation in being, just as the chief motive in the Deliberation for choosing obedience to an elected superior was in order to conserve the Company in being.

After the Deliberation one can follow throughout the documents preliminary to the Constitutions the experimental groping of Ignatius and the first companions to arrive at the concrete description of this ever-continuing process of giving being to the Company.[1] One can observe the actual practice of this process by Ignatius himself in the historical and cultural circumstances of the Company under his generalate through his letters and the memoirs of his contemporaries.[2] But the essential structure of the process was already given in the Deliberation and it is this process of constantly bringing the Company to be which gives meaning to the final Constitutions.

A study of Ignatius' description of the union of all the companions is necessary in order to gain a fuller understanding of his conception of the unifying role of the superior. How did Ignatius conceive of this union? What was the essential bond which would unite all the companions in one apostolic com-

---

1 *Cons*MHSJ, I, 1-7.
2 Among the most useful documents for studying Ignatius' own practice of government are the *Memoriale* of Gonçalves da Câmara (*FN*, I, 527-752), and three works of Pedro de Ribadeneyra: *De Actis P. Ignatii* (*FN*, II, 317-393); *Dicta et facta S. Ignatii* (*FN*, II, 772-798), and *Tractatus de ratione quam in gubernando tenebat Ignatius* (*FN*, III, 606-633). All of these texts, however, must be read in the light of the character and the circumstances of the author at the time of writing them. Father de Certeau has pointed out that the evolution of a man brings him to perceive in a different way the true meaning of his memories; and, precisely, he refers to the fact that Da Câmara, after several difficult years as a superior in Portugal, added to the *Memoriale* new "memories" which particularly manifested the strictness of Ignatius as a superior ("L'épreuve du temps", *Christus*, no. 61 [1966], 315, n. 2). In the first chapter of his *Le gouvernement spirituel selon Saint Ignace de Loyola* (Montreal, 1961), Jacques Lewis

munity? What were the means necessary to realize this union and which, therefore, the superior should employ and insist upon in fulfilling his role?

The being of the Company consists in the profound interior union of all its members — "unión de los ánimos" (*a*, 236).[3] Since the vocation of the companions is precisely to be dispersed throughout the whole world on apostolic missions confided to them by the vicar of Christ on earth, the essential union which is the very existence of the Company could not be the physical union of members of a community living together; although, as will be seen, such community living is of primary importance in the genesis of this interior union of spirit.

The mutual aid with which the companions would sustain one another in the accomplishment of their corporate apostolic service of Christ was seen principally as help on the level of deep interpersonal comprehension and spiritual support. This is evident from the fact that the companions determined to conserve their union permanently precisely because they knew that the fulfillment of their apostolic vocation would entail physical separation from one another. The profound reality of interior strength resulting in the more effective aid of souls which a companion derives from his consciousness of being sustained by the true companionship of others — even though working alone and far away from them — is nowhere more manifest than in the missionary life of St. Francis Xavier.

Although his mission from the vicar of Christ through Ignatius put enormous physical distance between Xavier and his beloved companions, it is clear from his letters that it was his deep awareness of union with them and his knowledge that they were aiding him spiritually which gave him the psychological force

has studied the practice of government of Ignatius as presented in the memoirs and letters. One could wish for a clearer situating of the practices of Ignatius in the cultural patterns of his own epoch. Ignatius was a man who had his own temperament, which was sometimes difficult in spite of his sanctity, and his own manner of exercising the role of the superior in terms of his own historical and cultural formation.

3 *a*, 226, i.e., text *a* of the Constitutions, in *Cons*MHSJ, II, on page 226. Henceforth, to avoid excessive multiplication of footnotes, the references to text *a* will be cited thus within parentheses in the running text.

to carry out his heroic and lonely apostolate. Writing to his companions in Europe, Xavier often gave thanks to God that, in spite of their physical absence, they had gained for him the "strength to walk among the infidels" by their prayers and constant remembrance of him.[4] Although God had separated him from them in such distant lands, he felt that this bodily absence could not cause a lack of love or care for one another, since they were all "so identified in one love and spirit." Their love and union were "founded in Christ" and made up for the lack of physical presence. Xavier wrote that he felt the "continual spiritual presence" of all the companions. By their prayers and sacrifices for him, "you, my dearest brothers in Christ, have imprinted within my heart the constant remembrance of you"; and he testified that there was always "an awareness marked upon my soul of the great obligation I am under to all the members of the Company."[5] He avowed that if he could ever forget the Company of Jesus, "I would forget my own right hand, since in so many ways I am conscious of how much I owe to all of the Company." [6] Xavier prayed that God "who has united us in His holy Company" in this life, would unite them in His glorious Company in heaven, "since in this life we are so separated from one another for His love." [7] In a letter to Ignatius written at Cochin in 1549, Xavier used the famous expression that for him "the Company of Jesus means the Company of love and of identity of spirit." [8]

The very being of the Company, then, is the profound interior union of companions who are identified in spirit through commitment to the same vocation. Ignatius wrote that there could be no separation of those whom the Lord "has joined together into one," and that the foundation of this union was that "all of us share one and the same spirit in Our Lord." [9] But this interior union of spirit is mutual love: "the bond of the wills which is the charity and love of one another" (*a*, 255). Consequently, the conservation in being of the Company — the constantly renewed act of bringing the Company to be here and

4 *EppXav,* I, 175, 259, 330.
5 Ibid., I, 272-273.
6 Ibid., I, 395.
7 Ibid., I, 394-395.
8 Ibid., II, 8.
9 *EppIgn,* I, 210.

now — consists in the continual renewal of this union of love.[10] This is why the essential role of the superior is to make an apostolic community of love.

Now since the bond of union — of being — of the Company is mutual love, and since the role of the superior is to bring the Company to be, it is of vital importance to understand Ignatius' conception of the nature of this mutual love. The Eighth Part of the Constitutions is entirely devoted to the consideration of means to "unite the dispersed companions with their head and with one another" (*a,* 226).[11] In a key text Ignatius points out that the foundation of the mutual love of the companions is their love of God, which is the source of the individual vocation of each member to join himself to this Company for the

10 In a hortatory communication sent from Rome to the companions "dispersed at Cologne" in 1544 (written in such execrable Latin that one feels assurance that it must have been composed by Ignatius himself), the structure of the interior union of love which is the being of the Company clearly appears. Although the companions are separated physically ("tecto sitis corporibusque seiuncti"), with the help of God their union of spirit will be conserved. This union is manifested by their free commitment to the same way of life ("voluntario disciplinarum studio") and is grounded in their common vocation ("in vitae proposito"), which they have sealed by vows of religion that have established them in profound unity ("tam arcto inter vos nexu ad Jesu Christi gloriam"). A final image identifies this interior union which overcomes all physical separation with the love of Christ ("cuius veluti glutino caritatis totam hanc conglutinari familiam et copulari par est") (*EppIgn,* I, 295-296).

11 In his introduction to *Constitutions de la Compagnie de Jésus,* II (Paris, 1967), F. Roustang has pointed out that the first section of the Eighth Part is concerned with union of hearts (*unión de los ánimos*), while the second section treats of the effective union of persons (*la unión personal en congregationes o capitulos*) (*Cons*MHSJ, II, 226). Roustang notes that to call together the congregation is to call together the Company. The first companions experienced the difficulty of calling together all the members. Consequently, the Company decided to send certain ones to the general congregation and to recognize itself in their decisions. If the apostolate permitted it, all would attend. The delegates, therefore, do not represent their own provinces, but the universal Company. The congregation is identified with the Company (p. 100). In his analysis of the first three chapters of the Eighth Part, Roustang has shown that each one has the same structure of means for union: (1) self-abnegation; (2) right use of authority on the part of the superior and obedience on the part of the companions; (3) mutual love. To universal subordination responds the unique source of authority. Finally, union, viewed first in a negative manner through the source of division, changes into communication in the following chapters (pp. 96-97).

service of Christ through the aid of souls in companionship. The text is divided into two parts, the first identifying personal love of God as the ground of the mutual love of the companions, and the second indicating both the fundamental means to foster this union and the greatest danger to its existence, the divisive thrust of self-seeking and self-love. The force of his thought is clearer if his balanced sentence is schematically arranged:

(1) "For the union of the members with one another
and with their head,
the principal bond is the love of God our Lord,
since,
being united with the divine and highest goodness,
the superior and the companions will very easily
be united with one another by the same love,
which will reach out to all men,
especially to the body of the Company;

(2) so that charity, and in general all goodness
will help to union of the one with the other
and to complete freedom from the worship
of temporal values,
wherein self-love,
which is the principal enemy of this union,
leads to deordination" (*a,* 229).

The union of spirit or of wills or of love which is the being of the Company results, therefore, from the personal love of God of each of the companions, a love which is concretized in a common vocation: the service of Christ through the aid of souls in companionship in the Company of Jesus. That which holds together all the members of the Company in effective union with one another and with their head is the profound commitment of each individual man to this vocation which is the existential realization of his love of God. Each member discovers his own vocation, his own personal identity in the common vocation of all. This discovery results in a profound, interior awareness of union, of "identification" with all the companions who find their own personal identity in the same vocation. Their love of God grounds their love of all mankind, which is expressed in their apostolic vocation and it grounds their love for one another which enables them to realize this vocation in companionship, bringing the Company of Jesus to

44

be here and now. Their mutual union of love for one another issues from the conscious sharing of the same life-ideal which is embodied in a common life-form. The living principle of union for the exercise of this common vocation is the superior, which is why the love of God must unite all the members "with one another and with the head." It is also the reason that Ignatius saw a quasi-identity of "love and obedience and mutual union." [12]

The second part of the text explains that this mutual love which is grounded in the love of God, "the highest goodness" will be expressed through "charity and in general all goodness" and, thus, will help the "union of the one with the other." The dynamic mental structure of Ignatius is evident in this conception of the mutual union as constantly increasing through charity and goodness, rather than as an abstract union established once and for all by incorporation into the Company. Ever deeper mutual love uniting the companions in ever greater service of Christ through the aid of souls in companionship can prepare the individual member for the sometimes terrible demands of self-sacrifice for the accomplishment of the corporate vocation of the Company. Thus, personal love of God must be so intense in each one that it will purify his soul of self-seeking and self-love and, so, remove the greatest obstacle to the union which brings the Company to be and enables it to carry out the "scope of our vocation."

The richness and density of the Ignatian text can be penetrated more fully through an analysis of his meaning of love. In the Contemplation for Obtaining Love in the *Spiritual Exercises,* Ignatius states his conception of love, in which he finds two essential characteristics: (1) Love should be expressed in action; and (2) love consists in mutual *communication*: the lover gives and communicates to the beloved all that he possibly can of everything he has, and the beloved responds with equally total self-giving. [13]

In his development of the contemplation of the love of God for man, Ignatius makes it clear that this gift of all that one possesses signifies the gift of one's own being, in so far as this is

12 Text A of the Constitutions (1550), in the *Cons*MHSJ, II, 616.
13 *SpEx,* [231].

possible: "and, consequently, the same Lord desires to give Himself to me in so far as He can according to His divine ordering of things"; and man's response to this divine love should be to give to God "all my liberty, my memory, my understanding and my whole will, all that I have and possess." [14] Love is essentially unitive, therefore. It moves through mutual self-communication to *communion*.

Given this conception of love, it was natural for Ignatius to state that the members of the Company all should be "of one same will and love one another and communicate their affairs to one another in true companionship (*conviadamente*) for greater union" (*a*, 162). The union of wills of the members of the Company, realized in their obedience to the unifying commands of one superior, is the interior mutual love originating in their communion of self-giving in the service of Christ through the aid of souls in companionship.

In order to grow in the love of God in which the mutual love of the companions of Jesus is grounded, it is necessary to overcome that other love which would close a man in upon himself, the "carnal and worldly love", [15] which causes him to love "what the world loves and embraces." [16] The Ignatian vocabulary of love manifests his anthropology, which was based upon his experience of the conflicting motions of divine love and self-love in his own heart: "high love against low love." [17] The Spiritual Exercises are intended to form a man's desire to seek only God and His will and to bring him to true spiritual liberty, freedom from "self-love, self-seeking and self-interest." [18] Because of the thrust within every man to love himself for himself and to follow his self-will, the final probation of the Company consists of spiritual and corporal exercises which will cause "greater humility and abnegation of all sensual love and self-will and judgment" (*a*, 199). Such profound interior liberation is essential within the members of the Company in order to overcome "self-love which is the principal enemy of this union" (*a*, 229). The role of the superior in forming members

---

14 Ibid., [234].
15 Ibid., [320].
16 *Cons*MHSJ, II, 84.
17 *DirSpEx,* 72, 76.
18 *SpEx,* [390].

of the Company preparing for full incorporation into it is ordered entirely to his essential role of making an apostolic community of love, which requires that he help each companion to arrive at the liberation from his own self-love which the mutual love and union of all the members demands.[19]

The love of God to be expressed in action identified itself in the mind of Ignatius with the praise and glory of God through apostolic service.[20] The aid of souls was an act of universal love reaching out to all men to accomplish in them the redemptive mission of Christ.[21] Once more, it is clear that for Ignatius love on every level was the communication of one's goods and of oneself — here, the mission of the members of the Company to *discurrir* throughout the world in order to aid souls through sharing with them the good news of God's saving love given to them in Christ through His Church. The love of God which grounds the mutual love of the companions and constitutes the union — the being — of the Company is also the source of its corporate action to accomplish its apostolic end. Love is the being, the life, and the activity of the Company of Jesus.

The essential role of the superior, then, is to bring the Company to be by making an apostolic community of love wherein all the companions are united with one another by "the bond of charity." [22] Since the being of the Company consists in the profound interior union of its members, the most important means to conserve its being is the ever-growing mutual love of the companions here and now. The deep spiritual union grounded in each one's personal love of God and in their common vocation to serve Christ through the aid of souls in companionship must be fostered in its human realization through mutual comprehension and help.[23]

The mutual love of the companions of Jesus, therefore, exists on two levels: (1) the profound spiritual level of personal love of God concretized in the common scope of our vocation; (2) the level of their human relationship with one another. Their

---

19 See below, ch. 4, pp. 95-100.
20 *SpEx*, [238, 428, 554]; *Cons*MHSJ, I, 61; II, 171, 353, 484.
21 *Cons*MHSJ, I, 15, 18, 25, 26, 29, 82, 183, 296, 374, 376; II, 203, 218, 256, 282, 470, 540, 546.
22 Ibid., I, 72, 374; II, 220.
23 Ibid., I, 3; II, 162.

shared life-ideal is incarnated in a variety of persons — the existing companions here and now in a house, in a province, in a larger region, in the whole world. The degree of intimacy in this human relationship depends upon factors of time and space, of human temperaments, of different cultures and languages, of all that enters into the structure of any inter-personal relationship. In their genesis these two levels cannot be split. The second is grounded in the first: the basis for the progressive intimacy of human companionship is the identify of shared vocation.[24] But the profound interior union is embodied and made humanly actual through the living experience of growing human love and mutual help.[25]

This human love of the companions is a special love different in quality than that within a family or among friends having different vocations. It should lead each member to his own human affective fulfillment, to the strengthening results of a unique kind of friendship. The members of the Company of Jesus are companions not casually, but in their common dedication to the unifying scope of our vocation. They are bound together here and now on both levels of love through the identity of their life-ideal lived and carried out through mutual love and aid. This is a true, concrete human love, not abstract "charity," not formalistic "fraternal charity," but a total way of being-in-companionship which permeates all their lives and enables them to realize their own identity in the service of Christ through the aid of souls in companionship. Because of the vocation of the companions to be dispersed throughout the world, the level of concrete, human companionship often must be absorbed into the profound spiritual union of wills which is the essential being of the Company. In a house of formation or residence, however, the unifying role of the superior must be exercised in leading the companions to the human relationship of mutual love and guarding against all that might cause dissension or disunion.

---

24 Any Jesuit who has had occasion to visit houses of the Company in many different lands has experienced the depth and solidity of the basic mutual union with his new and hitherto unknown companions, which is already established because of their identical vocation to the Company. This profound union provides the firm foundation for building a warm human relationship.
25 See above, pp. 41-43.

Ignatius was well aware of the difficulties for union which could be caused by the difference of backgrounds of the companions and their various temperaments, idiosyncrasies and spontaneous likes and dislikes.[26] He insists that all that would cause misunderstandings and anger be avoided and that, should these occur, there be an immediate reconciliation.[27] Those who cause disunion and division should be dismissed from the Company.[28] The superior should see to it that differences of character and temperament and degree of virtue should be a source of mutual help, rather than of division.[29]

Ignatius considered one of the most important aids to the conservation of union to be uniformity or conformity of life and doctrine among all the companions, embracing, therefore, both their style of life and their will and judgment, inasmuch as this might be possible according to the different qualities of persons and places and other circumstances.[30] The never-failing respect of Ignatius for the teaching of living experience and the exigencies of concrete situations is manifest in the qualifying phrases. He was insistent upon interior and exterior uniformity not because of a wooden adherence to some a priori conception of the religious life, which would have been entirely out of accord with his essentially dynamic and experience-oriented mental structure, but because he considered this uniformity and conformity to be a powerful aid to mutual love and interpersonal communication among the companions. Companionship, living in community, is nothing more than abstract theory supported by physical continguity, unless this companionship is humanly embodied somehow in some form of a common style of life and a common understanding of fundamental issues. Text A of the *Constitutions* provides a clarifying explanation of this

---

26 The sometimes caricatured rules of "religious modesty" (*Cons*MHSJ, II, 157-158) which, as is only natural reflect the cultural patterns of the time of Ignatius in their concrete details, might better be called "rules of conversation and courtesy" in relations with others, both in the Company and in apostolic work. They are entirely ordered to foster true personal relationships.
27 *Cons*MHSJ, II, 350.
28 Ibid, II, 227.
29 Ibid., II, 220, 227.
30 Ibid., II, 162, 229.

insistence upon uniformity of doctrine and shows certainly that Ignatius valued uniformity only as a means to union:

> Even in the judgment of practical affairs, differences should be avoided, as much as possible, since they are the mother of discord. For differences of understanding are naturally the enemy of the union of wills. This union and conformity with one another must be diligently fostered, and the contrary must not be permitted, in order that, united with one another by the bond of fraternal charity, they can better and more effectively carry out the service of God and the aid of the neighbor.[31]

As always, the underlying principle from which all legislation flows is the preservation in being of the Company through the mutual love and union of all its members for the ever greater service of Christ through the aid of souls in companionship. The essential role of the superior is again clear. In order to make an apostolic community of love, he has the responsibility of fostering union and conformity and not permitting discord, the destroyer of union. If today, in an epoch of theological pluralism within a cultural structure of much more unity in diversity, the particular provisions for union given in the Constitutions are no longer indicated as necessary or desirable, nevertheless, the underlying principle of using all possible effective means to establish unity and to embody community among the members of the Company remains true and essential to the being of that body and to the role of the superior.

Ignatius considered that another essential means to conserve the mutual love and union of the members of the Company was that of much interpersonal communication.[32] If the self-giving which is love is to bring about true communion among the companions, it must be actualized through mutual communication at all levels of the life of the Company. This is why Ignatius insists upon much communication by letters among the companions and the superiors all the way to the general.[33] It is the responsibility of the superior to preserve the union of the companions by seeing to it that all effective means are used to this end. The love and union of the Company of Jesus is not some

---

31 Ibid., II, 356.
32 Ibid., II, 255.
33 Ibid., II, 229.

sort of abstract ideal, but the actual mutual love of the concrete persons constituting the Company here and now; and this
love can be realized only through true interpersonal communication, especially when the companions are physically dispersed
on apostolic missions. The reason Ignatius gave to Pierre Favre
in December, 1542, for threatening to command him under
obedience to write letters as directed to Rome was "for the
greater union, charity and edification of all." [34] He was so
conscious of the practical need of frequent communication
among the persons in the Company for the preservation of true
mutual love and union, that it is certain that Ignatius would
have utilized to the full all modern techniques of communication.

To conserve the union which is the being of the Company it
is necessary that the superior and all the rest of the companions
be bound together by the bond of mutual love. The Ignatian
documents frequently treat of the love of the superior for the
companions and of their love for him. In the chapter of the
Eighth Part of the Constitutions consecrated to the means which
will aid the superior to be united with the companions, Ignatius
describes the personal qualities of the superior which will facilitate this union: that he love the companions and inspire their
confidence; that he give orders with moderation and respect
the liberty and personal initiative of the companions when possible, and that he guard the hierarchical subordination of lower
superiors to the general, because the more this hierarchical
order is followed, "the better love and union will be conserved
among them." [35] It is for the sake of mutual union, rather
than for ascetical purposes, that Ignatius is so insistent upon
the hierarchical principle of subordination in the Company,
because "this subordination will maintain union with the help
of the grace of God" (*a*, 227).[36]

The Bond of Love between the Superior and the Companions

Ignatius often specifically refers to the love which the superior
should show towards the companions: "the kindness and meekness of the charity of Christ," [37] giving them commands with

34 *EppIgn*, I, 237.
35 *Cons*MHSJ, II, 228.
36 See below, ch. 3, pp. 79-83.
37 *Cons*MHSJ, I, 18.

"all love, modesty and charity." [38] Love should be manifest in his manner of ruling and correcting and even in the dismissal from the Company of those unfitted for it.[39] The superior's love for the companions should issue in prayer and sacrifices and a holy vigilance to aid them to become true servants of God.[40] Just as the love of God should always be the fundamental norm of all discernment,[41] so the love of the Company in all of his companions should guide the superior in making decisions concerning their lives and action: "discreet charity,"[42] "charity and discretion filled with the Holy Spirit" (*a*, 326). On the other hand, Ignatius insists that the companions should love their superiors: "showing greater love and confidence in those whom they have to govern them." [43] All should strive for perfect observance of the Constitutions, proceeding "with the spirit of love and not disturbed by fear." [44]

The mutual love which is the bond of union that gives being to the Company must be embodied in the personal relationship of the superior and the companions living here and now. Ignatius considered obedience the most important aid to actualize the mutual love, the "bond of the wills," which constitutes the union and being of the Company (*a*, 226; 227; 255-256). From this love issue the unifying commands of the superior and the correlative obedience of the companions which bring the Company to be through "the love and obedience and union among them." [45] Obedience, the concrete act of self-giving which is true love accomplishes the living communion of all the companions in their common commitment to the "scope of our vocation." The end of the Company of Jesus is to aid all men to the knowledge and love of God who sent His only Son into the world to carry out the universal redemptive mission of divine love, continued in history through His Church under the unifying direction of the vicar of Christ on earth. The Company has its origin in the love of God; it comes to be in the

38 Ibid., II, 616.
39 Ibid., II, 161, 193.
40 Ibid., II, 165.
41 Ibid., II, 248, 251, 255.
42 Ibid., II, 316, 326, 336, 365, 546.
43 Ibid., II, 74, 94, 106, 118.
44 Ibid., I, 216, II, 208.
45 Ibid., II, 616.

mutual love of its actual members, which issues from their love of God; and it achieves its end in accomplishing an ever greater communion of all men in this same divine love.

Since the very being of the Company consists in the union of all the companions for the service of Christ through the aid of souls, it was natural for Ignatius to have the imaginative conception of the Company as one organic body composed of all its members integrated into a dynamic unity through their union with one another and with their head. Thus, the head, the superior, was for Ignatius the living principle of union within the body. The unique head of the entire body of the Company is Jesus Christ acting through His vicar on earth who, in turn, is vicariously represented by the superior of the Company and his subordinate vicars who, consequently, give commands "in the place of Christ." [46] Thus, the image of the body — a living unity composed of head and members — is a key metaphor in the Ignatian vocabulary of images. Expressions such as "the whole body of the Company," "the universal body," "the head with his members," and "incorporation in the Company" abound. There were obvious scriptural sources for this image (cf. I Cor, 12: 7; Col, 2: 14). It was also current in the Castilian tradition which had formed the notions of authority of Ignatius during his youth as a *caballero*. The *Siete Partidas*, taking up the ancient image of the king as head of the kingdom of which the people are the members, developed the metaphor of the state as one body: "The king, therefore, is the heart, the soul, and head of the kingdom; and his subjects, as its members, should be united to him," (II, 172).[47]

46 See below, ch. 3, pp. 58-60.
47 *Las Siete Partidas*, compiled and edited with an introduction by Don José Muro Martínez, 2 vols. (Valladolid, 1875), II, 172. The first codification of Castilian law was the *Siete Partidas*, begun by King Alfonso X (1252-1284), in 1256, and after a long period of development, officially proclaimed by Alfonso XI in Ordenamiento de Alcalá of 1348. After circulating for many years in manuscript, *Las Siete Partidas* were first printed at Seville in 1491. They remained the basic principles of law until the legislation of Charles V. The *Partidas* present a system of law which is entirely theocentric. They sum up and give expression to a world view which reflected the conceptions that men had of authority and obedience and the relation of men in society to God. Although Ignatius undoubtedly never read the *Partidas*, his mentality was formed in Castile according to their principles and, as will appear in later chapters, he echoed these in the Constitutions.

Apostolic Love in Companionship

The metaphor underwent more and more development in the writings of the later ecclesiastical and political writers.[48] Thus, this image was an integral part of the notion of authority and the language expressing it within the cultural background of Ignatius, and it was quite spontaneous for him to imagine the Company as a unified body integrated into the universal body of the Church and serving it.[49] The richness of the body image is especially revealing for the role of the superior. All government of the Company comes from the general "as from its head" (*a,* 131, 132). He must possess the personal qualities needed to exercise "his office of head with all the members of the Company" (*a,* 228). From the general "as from the head" flow all authority of subordinate superiors and all apostolic missions of the Company (*a,* 228). It is vital to elect the best man available as general, because "the good or evil condition of the head affects the whole body" (*a,* 255).

The Role of the Superior   Study of the Ignatian conception of the being of the Company of Jesus reveals his extremely rich synthetic vision of the scope of our vocation. The Company was made up of a group of companions called by God to form themselves into one dynamic body for the service of Christ and the praise and glory of God through the aid of souls anywhere in the world where the vicar of Christ might send them. Because their apostolate would be more effective if exercised in companionship, which would make possible a fruitful division of labor as well as mutual spiritual and corporal help, it was necessary to conserve their union and to increase the number of companions. To stabilize and make permanent their union, in spite of dispersal to all regions of the world on apostolic missions, the bond of obedience to one head was forged as the means to integrate all the members into one living body. That which would overcome all physical separation and sustain their profound, interior union was mutual love: the love of God and of one another

48 For examples see A. García-Gallo, *Manual de historia del derecho español,* 2 vols., 2nd ed. (Madrid, 1964), II, 723, 903, 984.
49 In a letter written to the Emperor of Ethiopia in 1555, Ignatius develops the head and body image with respect to the Church in terms very similar to those used in the Constitutions for the Company (*Epp Ign,* VIII, 460-467).

54

which would make them always one among themselves and with their head. This union would enable them to undertake effective, integrated missions in the service of the Church as they would be sent to aid souls at the command of Christ through His vicar and their superior.

The essential role of the superior, therefore, would be to bring the Company to be at every new moment in history. The language of Ignatius in the Constitutions describing the role of the superior necessarily reflects his Basque-Castilian background and the cultural patterns of Catholic Europe in the early sixteenth century. That which animates this language and which remains valid transhistorically is the notion of the essential role of the superior: to bring to be the apostolic community of love which is the Company for the fulfillment of the "scope of our vocation." The truest fidelity to Ignatius in any epoch is the translation of this essential role into the language and cultural patterns revealed by the "signs of the times."

THE LIVING PRINCIPLE
OF APOSTOLIC LOVE

WHEN IGNATIUS in preparing the Constitutions began the task of delineating the concrete manner in which the superior should carry out his essential role of making an apostolic community of love, his conception of the role itself was already formed. He saw the superior as the living principle of union of the Company, bringing it to be anew at every moment by uniting all the companions for the service of Christ through the aid of souls in companionship.

Cultural Patterns In detailing the various functions and duties of the superior, Ignatius reflected the cultural and linguistic patterns of his own time. He selected and rejected practices discovered through observation of older religious orders or study of their rules. Curial pressure had an effect on his language and legislation. Finally, the evolution of the Company itself, especially its rapid growth in far away places and the increasing necessity to form young Jesuits properly for full incorporation into the Company, determined many specific prescriptions for the conduct of superiors. A study of the language which Ignatius used in describing the various "roles" of the superior must be balanced with the realization that he always conceived these roles in function of the essential role of the superior: to form an apostolic group of companions united in mutual love.

Ignatius' conception of the nature of the authority of the superior in the Company of Jesus shows the influence of his Basque and Castilian formation. As a member of the seignorial class of Guipúzcoa, Ignatius was born into a world shaped by an age-old tradition of independence from any profoundly marking outside influences. The regions of Spain had experienced over the centuries a gradual evolution from tribal laws of custom to legal formulations and organized structures of au-

56

thority because of the successive influences of the Roman occupation and the growth of Christianity, the Visigothic inva-
sions with their contribution of the *Liber judiciorum* or *Lex
visigothorum,* the Moorish occupation which under the impulse
of Arabian philosophy elevated jurisprudence to a science sub-
sidiary to theology, and the growing influence of Church law in
the shaping of secular laws.[1] This last influence began with the
Libri poenitentiales and developed through the reform of Canon
Law instituted by Pope Gregory VII (1073-1085), to the
monumental Decretals of Gratian (1140), which became authoritative rapidly. As the science of jurisprudence developed,
a flood of codices, institutions, summas, digests and glosses
flowed from the pens of ecclesiastical writers. Universities were
founded which formed jurists who were sent all over Spain as
counsellors to kings and judges, bringing about a wide diffusion
of organized law. As the jurists gained influence, the ancient
territorial laws based on custom gradually were overridden by
Roman Law as modified by Canon Law.[2]

During this long period of evolution of law in the rest of
Spain, the Law of Custom continued to prevail in the Basque
country. The hardy peoples in these rugged mountains were
never conquered by the Moors and during the Roman and
Visigothic periods they had been influenced only marginally
by the forces so important in shaping the culture of the rest of
the peninsula. Even after 1379 when the Basque territories were
politically under Castile, each region kept its own public and
private law, which remained principally the Law of Custom.[3]
The customary laws of the peoples had been in conflict with
the coded laws imposed by the kings through all the centuries of
the development of structures of authority. This struggle between the ancient law of custom and the new law had a different history in the various kingdoms. In each case, the final
structure of law which evolved from this struggle was shaped

1 Alfonso García-Gallo, *Manual de historia del derecho español,* 2nd.
ed., 2 vols. (Madrid, 1964), I, 27-58 (abbreviated hereafter as GG).
For historical data about the development of law in Spain, I rely
heavily upon this magnificently documented synthesis. The first volume
is a true cultural analysis of the evolution of Spanish law. The second
is an invaluable collection of documents.
2 GG, I, 61-94.
3 GG, I, 72-76.

by the forces in conflict. Where a king was powerful enough to establish uniform laws throughout his kingdom, these would differ from the laws in another kingdom where the Law of Custom had been stronger. As a result the juridical areas of the late Middle Ages were redrawn according to the political frontiers of the various kingdoms.[4] Leon and Castile united in 1320 under Ferdinand III. Alfonso VIII had already joined Alava and Guipúzcoa to the kingdom of Castile in 1200, although the bonds of the latter were only nominal until they were strengthened by Alfonso XI in 1332. Viscaya became a part of Castile in 1379 under Juan I. The integration of Navarre into the kingdom was much more complex and would touch upon the personal life of Ignatius at the siege of Pamplona. It was the marriage of Ferdinand and Isabella in 1479 that finally united Castile and Aragon. In Guipúzcoa, then, Castilian influences were felt only gradually; the law was purely customary until the end of the fourteenth century, when laws finally began to be codified into writing.[5]

As a Basque *hidalgo* Ignatius was part of a social structure which was above all familial, wherein the father as the *Señor* had exercised an absolute power of discipline over the persons of his family and of all those who lived under his protection.[6]

---

4 GG, I, 80-90.
5 These laws which were codified into writing were: *Fuero de Guipúzcoa,* 1397, *Fuero de 147 Leyes,* 1457, and *Fuero de 207 Leyes,* 1463. All these *fueros* were confirmed by the kings (GG, I, 262). See the *Nueva recopilación de los fueros, privilegios buenos usos y costumbres, leyes y ordenanzas de M. N. y M. L. Provincial de Guipúzcoa* (San Sebastian, 1919). Some Castilian notions of law had been introduced into Guipúzcoa as early as 1348, by the Ordenamiento de Alcalá. In practice, nevertheless, the traditional laws of custom based upon strong family structures prevailed when conflicts arose with Castilian law; and these customary laws greatly influenced the final *fueros* (GG, I, 403-404). Cf. C. Echegaray, *Las provincias vascongadas a fines de la edad media* (San Sebastian, 1895). An interesting document dating from 1505 proves that Ignatius himself was involved in an application of the *fueros* of Guipúzcoa when he was called as a witness in a trial at Azpeitia. In 1515, he himself was the accused at another trial (FN, I, 21*-22*).
6 See A. Coster, *Juan de Anchieta et la famille de Loyola* (Paris, 1930), p. 40. For indications of the authority and responsibility of the chief of the family, see the letters of Ignatius to his brother Martin García de Oñaz (*EppIgn,* I, 77-83), and to his nephew Beltrán de Loyola (ibid., 148-151).

By right of birth, Ignatius was a member of a seignorial family, and it was as natural as breathing for him to form his first notions of social order and authority along these lines.[7] The weight of the familial structure in the social order is attested by an interesting bit of the Loyola family history, still vivid in the incongruous brick crown of toy-like Moorish towers atop the old grey stones of castle Loyola. Some thirty-one years before the birth of Ignatius, a league of towns had declared war on twenty-four seignorial families, including the Loyolas at Azpeitia, because of their oppressive privileges. The king, Henry IV, made a declaration in favor of the towns on April 21, 1457. He not only demanded that the fortress castles of the families be denuded of defenses, but also commanded their lords to go off to fight the Moors. Among those ordered to the crusades were Ignatius' great-uncle, Lope García de Lascana, and his son, Juan Pérez de Loyola. The striking thing on reading the list of those sentenced is the fact that the king respected the bonds of family and in no instance separated a son from his father or a son-in-law from his father-in-law.[8] On the other hand, the incident shows the depth of respect for the authority of the king, who could not have effectively forced his will upon the seignorial families had they chosen to disobey him. Obedience to recognized authority, even in painful matters, was a profoundly rooted cultural pattern even among the independent minded Basques. These cultural patterns entered into the consciousness of Ignatius from his earliest days.

When at the age of thirteen or fourteen Ignatius went to Arévalo to be formed into a *caballero,* he entered into a milieu where the notion of law and authority was much more developed than in Guipúzcoa. Without ever studying the theory of law, he entered into and lived its royal organization and he inevitably heard and unconsciously absorbed its basic assumptions and its conventional expressions. He made his own the theory of the limitations of authority which would mark his future conduct and shape his notion of the role of the superior

7 In interpreting the "absolutist" statements of Ignatius concerning the role of the superior or in his own exercise of this role, his cultural formation must always be kept in view. It is necessary to grasp his profound intention for the role of the superior and to discover how to realize this intention within an extremely different culture.

8 Coster, *op. cit.,* p. 48.

in the Company of Jesus. Here too he absorbed the principles of authority and obedience codified in the *Siete Partidas* which formulated these Castilian notions.[9] The purpose of the *Partidas* from the beginning had been to establish a uniform rule of law throughout the kingdom, withdrawing from the nobles ancient and sometimes contradictory rights and privileges. Because of the resistance of the nobles and the abstract idealism of many of the laws in the *Partidas,* they never were followed completely, but they do contain the basic assumptions of the Castilian view of authority. An almost lapidary sentence in the fourth *Partida* situates the essential duties of a man: "A man owes much to God who created him, to his father who engendered him, to the nurse who nourished him, the master who taught him, and to the lord of the land of his birth." [10] This maxim sums up well the system of values of the Basque and Castilian mentality.

All of these cultural influences — the historical epoch of political and ecclesiastical development into which he was born, the traditions of the Basque *hidalgo,* the ideals of the Castilian *caballero,* and the structures and expressions of authority in the midst of which he lived — entered into the formation of the mental structure of Ignatius, which would ground his conception of the role of the superior in the Company of Jesus. All of these influences, nevertheless, passed through the personalizing alembic of Ignatius' own experience, his spiritual evolution,

---

9 See above, ch. 2, n. 47. A curious and rather frightening indication of the extent (only theoretical!) of the power of the father of a family, as well as of the necessity of absolute loyalty to the Señor, is given in the law of the *Partidas,* coldly entitled: "Cases in which the father may sell or pawn or eat his son." Underlying the law is the old Roman notion of the father's power of life and death over his children. The rights are specifically denied to the mother. It reads:

When it happens that a father is suffering from great hunger and that he is so poverty-stricken that he has no other recourse, and this fact is well known to everyone, he may sell or pawn a son who is in his power, in order to buy something to eat, since, by so doing, both the father and the son will be spared the death which otherwise could not be avoided. If the father finds himself surrounded in a castle which belongs to his Lord, and if he is so tortured with hunger that he can feel nothing but the need of eating, he may eat his son with no guilt before he may surrender the castle without the command of his Lord (II, 64-65).

10 *Siete Partidas,* II, 75.

which gradually led him to the foundation of the Company.[11]

In the Deliberation it was decided that one of the companions — "alicui ex nobis" — should be elected whom all would obey in order to preserve and increase the Company as a unified group of men exercising the apostolate in companionship. From the beginning, therefore, the superior was conceived as a kind of "emanation" of the Company, the unifier who at the crucial moment of apostolic action would assure that all the combined force of the companions would be brought to bear in united, efficacious activity for the Kingdom of Christ. That a man happened to be elected superior did not, in this view, place him outside the companions as one having some mysterious kind of inspired role. He is simply one of the companions to whom the others have given the responsibility (at least through the hierarchical structure) of being the living principle of union through which their companionship would realize its end of the corporate aid of souls.[12]

Special light is thrown upon the origins of this notion of the role of the superior within the cultural formation of Ignatius by a study of the Castilian theory of the authority of the king. The *Siete Partidas* presented the power of the king as much more absolute than it ever became in practice in Spain. The

---

11 See above, ch. 1.

12 There is need of an historical and cultural study of the development in the Company later on of an exaggerated exaltation of the person of the superior. Such a study would undoubtedly show that this was a reflection of a general tendency to absolutize the power of monarchs and ecclesiastical authorities, just as Ignatius' conception of the superior reflects the *pactista* notion which was a part of his Castilian heritage. Probably it would also reveal strong influences in the Company for exalting the superior as a result of the almost illuministic apotheosis of Ignatius after his death by the early Jesuits and also of the character and background of St. Francis Borgia. In modern times both the definition of papal infallibility during the First Vatican Council and the very strong and authoritarian character of Fr. Wlodimir Ledochowski, whose generalate spanned a generation of the early twentieth century, would seem to have been powerful factors in strengthening a conception of quasi-infallibility and rather absolutist authority as belonging to the superior — a conception often extended to include even local superiors. Not negligible either would be the defensive mentality in the face of modern political upheavals and theological modernism, which tended to make religious and Catholics in general seek security in a particularly blind dependence upon authority.

"Prince" first appeared as truly powerful during the Reconquest. Great military chiefs in the struggle against the Moors, such as Cid, were chosen as princes by the people. These rulers were in a true sense "emanations" of the people. Without being a representative of the people in the strict juridical sense, the prince appeared as their natural chief rising from the people themselves and not coming from afar to dominate them.[13]

The relation of king and kingdom in Castile was considered to be the result of a pact between them. The ecclesiastical theory had stressed from the beginning that God gave the power to the community which designated the king. The king, therefore, received his authority through a pact with the community. This notion became more general and was the subject of theoretical reflection during the fourteenth century, and at the beginning of the fifteenth century Alvaro Pelayo and Alfonso de Madrigal called the *pactista* theory the common doctrine. Indeed, Madrigal defended the idea that the community should always keep the power to elect and correct the prince; and in 1521 Alfonso de Castrillo held that rulers should be subject to removal by the community. The doctrine was most clearly expressed at the Cortes of Ocaña in 1469, and of Valladolid in 1518. Ignatius was quite possibly present at the latter.[14] These Cortes explicitly stated that the king received his power from the kingdom through a tacit contract binding him to exercise his authority for the good of the community as its *mercenario*. Neither Henry IV nor Charles V ever questioned these declarations.[15]

The influence of the *pactista* theory would be found in the Ignatian legislation on the general, viewed as an emanation of

13 In the theory of kingship developed by the ecclesiastical writers, the king did not have power for his own benefit, but as the means to govern his people for the common good and the *salus totius regni*. Kingship constituted a ministry, a service, a duty exercised for the community. It conferred upon the king more obligations than rights. The power of the king was intrinsically limited by the doctrines of religion and Christian morality. It was subject to the conditions imposed by existing customs, laws and privileges and also by the constantly observed norm that the king governed with his *cortes* — his council — and that all important decisions should be taken in accord with it (GG, I, 611-622, 636).

14 *FN*, I, 27*. See the map of the Castilian travels of Ignatius given by I. Iparraguirre, *Obras Completas de San Ignacio de Loyola* (Madrid, 1963), p. 36.

15 GG, I, 742-743.

the Company. The language in the earlier documents often makes the superior and the Company equivalent, referring to the whole Company as the authority in cases where later organization and structuring will have the superior acting in the name of the Company, or referring to the Company and/or the superior as practically identical.[16] The power of acting in the name of the Company gradually became more and more centered in the person of the general because of the dispersal of the companions and the pressures of the rapidly expanding numbers of the Company.[17] It is not surprising that in the later papal documents all privileges are given to the Company through the general and that explicit statements of his personal authority are greatly multiplied in the Constitutions.[18] But his powers are clearly limited from the earliest documents, and he cannot make important and permanent decisions without submitting them to the Company in a general congregation.[19] His exercise of his authority is always subject to the judgment of the whole Company whom he should obey in the place of Christ.[20] Four chapters of the Ninth Part of the Constitutions are devoted to the authority of the Company over the general.[21] The Company must provide spiritual and corporal help to him for the exercise of his role and, if necessary, it must correct him and even remove him from office or expel him from the Company. In the legislation in these chapters echoes of the *pactista* tradition are evident. Ignatius had no conception of a magical elevation of the superior to infallibility or moral in-

---

16 *Cons*MHSJ, I, 11, 12, 18, 39, 40, 47, 53, 55, 56, 57, 58, 59, 83, 84, 165, 166, 254, 271, 288, 289, 307, 384; II, 32, 82, 92, 94, 102, 104, 106, 107, 108, 110, 112, 116, 118, 120, 122, 136, 137, 145, 149.
17 Until 1551, there were only three provinces of the Company: Portugal (1546), Spain (1546), and India (1549). Each of these had its own provincial, while all other houses were governed directly by Ignatius. In 1551, when the number of colleges began to increase rapidly, it became necessary to form new provinces: Tuscany in 1551, Sicily in 1553, Brazil in 1553. Spain was divided into three provinces in 1554, and two provinces were created in Germany in 1556. See *EppIgn*, V, 269.
18 Eg., *Cons*MHSJ, I, 167, 173; II, 240-244. See below, pp. 65-74.
19 Ibid., I, 13, 14, 17, 18, 34, 39, 41, 42, 46, 198, 245, 308; II, 172, 174, 193, 229-230, 243.
20 Ibid., I, 210, 215, 217, 303, 325, 385; II, 240, 244-252. See below, ch. 7, pp. 159-162.
21 *Cons*MHSJ, II, 244-252.

vulnerability. He was far too realistic a student of human experience for this. The general is elected by the Company to unify all the companions for the apostolic service of Christ, and he is always responsible to the Company in carrying out his role. If for the sake of more effective realization of this union for the fulfillment of the "scope of our vocation" most authority is centralized in the general, he always acts "in the name of the whole Company." [22]

The idea of authority expressed by Ignatius in the Constitutions is Castilian. While it is morally certain that he never read the ecclesiastical and juridical theories, at least before doing his studies, it is equally certain that during his years of royal service he often would have participated in discussions about kingship. Even more important, he lived at the core of the system. Consequently, his mental structure and his language to express the role of the superior were cast in the Castilian mold.

The gradual evolution of Ignatius' vocabulary of titles for superiors reflects his developing awareness of the necessity of using curial language as well as the traditional terminology in the rules of older religious orders which he studied with Polanco. In the beginning, Ignatius' spontaneous term for superiors was the general Castilian term for them: *perlado*. The preponderance of the term *perlado* in the earliest preliminary documents indicates the lack of a juridical background and orientation in Ignatius. He simply used the word which arose most spontaneously in his consciousness because of his cultural background. During his struggle to receive approbation for the Company in 1539, he became aware of the necessity of finding classical curial forms of language.[23] From this time, the traditional, juridical term for the religious superior — *praepositus* — appears with increasing frequency, although *perlado* continues to be the normal term in informal documents. Ignatius in no way changed his notion of the role of the superior, but he adapted his vocabulary to the concrete circumstances in which he found himself. In March, 1547, Ignatius called Juan de Polanco to Rome and named him secretary and procurator general of the

22 Ibid., 390.
23 See J. Urrutia, "Regimen de las órdenes religiosas a mediados del s. XVI y aportación de San Ignacio," *Miscelanea Comillas*, **XXXVI** (1961), pp. 91-142.

Company. Within a few months Polanco had begun industriously to collect and to put order into the various papers which Ignatius had prepared, with a view to final redaction of the Constitutions. Polanco also began to search in the older, classical religious rules for formulae and vocabulary. The notes on his discussions with Ignatius concerning the Constitutions are contained in the document entitled the "Sex Dubiorum Series." [24] Directed by the more juridical spirit of Polanco, these notes contain a more organized and curial vocabulary than the strictly Ignatian documents.

As a result of this gradual evolution of terminology, by the time the texts of the Constitutions were composed, the vocabulary concerning superiors was well-established. The common term in generalized contexts is *superior*. *Prepósito* tends to be used in more formal and juridical passages and in chapter titles. It occurs alone or with a qualifying "general," "provincial," "local," etc. Text B, as the final text and the one most structured by Polanco, continues the same vocabulary pattern but adds numerous instances of these terms, especially in the Declarations. While this gradual evolution of terminology reveals the progressive structuring of the Company as it grew and became more organized as well as the influence of curial and traditional language, it does not imply any change in the original conception of Ignatius of the essential role of the superior. Rather it indicates an effort on his part to make it possible to carry out this role in the actual situations in which it was necessary to assure the preservation and growth of the Company for the accomplishment of the "scope of our vocation." It is significant that in adopting the traditional terminology, Ignatius never used titles such as "abbot," "prior" or other monastic formulae, a reflection of his insistence upon disassociating the Company from the orientation of monastic, otherworldly directed orders for the sake of forming a totally apostolic group dedicated entirely to the service of Christ through the aid of souls in companionship.

From his living experience as a *caballero* in the service of the king, Ignatius had received as part of his cultural formation a notion of the relationship between a good king and his sub-

24 *Cons*MHSJ, I, 268-355.

jects which would be reflected in his conception of the relationship between the superior of the Company and the companions. The traditional Spanish doctrine on kingship was summed up in the second of the *Siete Partidas,* and subsequent theories echoed its language as would the Constitutions of Ignatius. Once more, it is morally certain that Ignatius never read the *Partidas,* but a comparison of the language of the second *Partida* with that of Ignatius treating of authority in the Company shows that he had received its ideas and its language through living in the culture which it expressed. The law entitled: "The love of the king for his people" remarkably anticipated Ignatius' description of the manner of action of the superior towards the companions:

> The king should have much love for his people and he should show this love, being merciful to them as necessity demands, punishing with kindness, sometimes pardoning delinquents, granting to each person and place favors corresponding to its degree of nobility or to the services rendered to him, praising good actions, not failing in justice, not demanding so much from his subjects that afterwards, when it might be necessary, they cannot aid him, defending them from all harm which they might do to each other or that outsiders might cause. The king who in this way loves, honors and guards his people will be loved, reverenced, and served by his subjects. He will be considered a good king in this world; and, thus, he will gain the eternal good of the other world. To the king who does not act in this way, God will give exactly the contrary.[25]

The ruler and his subjects must be united above all by the bond of love. "The emperor has the greatest power and the most complete authority when he loves his people and is loved by them." [26]

The Ignatian notion of the essential role of the superior as the living principle of union of the Company is best expressed in the texts specifically treating of the father general. These are the second chapter of the Eighth Part of the Constitutions concerning what actions on the part of the superior will aid the union of the dispersed members with one another and with

---

25 *Siete Partidas,* II, 207.
26 Ibid., II, 168.

their head and the Ninth Part which is entirely devoted to a discussion of the general and his government.

Text *a* in the Eighth Part points out that for the sake of union with the companions, the general must have their trust in his authority; therefore, he must have and manifest love and care for them, so that they will be convinced that he has the knowledge and good will and capability to rule them well. To establish this confidence in the companions, the superior should have well-qualified advisors to aid him in making decisions. Furthermore, he should be aware of human psychology, encouraging obedience by giving commands moderately with modesty and charity. Recognizing that man is a free being inclined to rule himself, the superior should leave personal initiative to the companions when possible, that is to say, when doing so will not lead to serious mistakes.[27] Ignatius knew that what was involved in the union of the superior and the companions was a very delicate personal relationship of free men which would require great discretion on the part of the superior.[28] Only thus could the end of authority in the Company — making a community of love for the service of Christ through the aid of souls in companionship — be achieved.

In defining the role of the general at the beginning of the Ninth Part, text *a* remarks that in all well-ordered communities it is necessary to have not only authorities to seek the particular ends of such communities, but also those responsible for the universal good. Consequently, in the Company, which is dispersed throughout the whole world for the aid of souls, it is necessary to have not only local superiors, but also one who

27 Ibid., II, 228; see also II, 616.
28 An interesting Ignatian technique for fostering the personal relations between the superior and the companions is given in an undated document entitled *De Mensa Praepositi*. This provides that the superior (general, provincial and local) ordinarily should eat in a dining room apart from the companions, rather than in the community refectory. The reason given for this is that it will enable the superior better to aid his subjects with his authority when necessary and will reduce the occasions "to disturb the companions by him whom they should consider to be their refuge in their troubles" (*Cons*MHSJ, I, 389). This document was not included in the Constitutions, but was placed among the rules of superiors by the First General Congregation. It reflects cultural patterns of Ignatius' own time, rather than modern ones; but the underlying preoccupation with seeking techniques to aid the personal relationship of superiors and companions is significant.

has authority over the whole body; and his role will be to assure "the good government and conservation and growth of the whole body of the Company" (*a*, 236). The conception enunciated here simply repeats the extremely dense but remarkably integrated notion of the role of authority in the Company for the achievement of its end and the "scope of our vocation" originally expressed in the Deliberation. The reasons given for electing the general for life are all in function of this end of the good government of the Company.[29]

The Second Chapter details the personal qualities which the general should possess. First of all, he should be united with God — a true man of prayer, so that from him "as from a fountain of all good," the entire body of the Company will receive the gifts and grace of its head for the efficacy of the means it uses apostolically (*a*, 238). This very rich image of mutual participation of all the members of the body of the Company in the spiritual vitality of its head for its apostolic end reveals the power of the metaphor of the living, unified head and members in the thought of Ignatius. Text B would add in the Eighth Part another striking expression of this image; the general is head of all the members of the Company and from him "the influx descends to all which is necessary for the end they pursue." [30] There is a constant "circulation" of apostolic grace in the Company between the superior, who is an emanation of the Company, and all its members wherever they go in the world for the aid of souls. This union of love and participation in the same apostolic grace overcomes all physical separation. Through their profound, interior union with their one head, all the companions are united with one another and are enabled to realize their vocation to aid souls in companionship.

The Second Chapter continues the list of the ideal qualities of the general. He should have no vices and be an example of all virtues for the help of his companions. Most especially, he should splendidly manifest love of the neighbor, love of the Company and true humility (*a*, 238). It is noted in a remark suppressed in texts A and B that ambition and the desire to

29 In judging today whether or not the generalate should still be retained for life, the norm of discernment must still be the good government of the Company rather than wooden adherence to the decision reached by Ignatius during his own time.

30 *Cons*MHSJ, II, 614.

command are opposed to love and humility. Therefore, the general should have no desire to rule others; and anyone who seeks the office directly or indirectly cannot be validly elected. The general should be free from all passions so that they may not trouble his judgment. Since he must make the final unifying decisions concerning the lives and apostolic action of the companions, it is vital that he possess complete spiritual liberty in order to practice discernment without being blinded by subtle self-love and self-seeking. Even here, then, the Ignatian ordering of ascetical perfection to the apostolic end of the Company is clear.

The external comportment of the general, and above all his manner of speaking, must be such as to give edification not only to the members of the Company, for whom he should be a mirror and a model, but also to all men outside the Company whom it was founded to aid (*a*, 238). In his personal relationships with the companions as their superior, he should temper any necessary severity with kindness and meekness. On the one hand, he should not falter in insisting upon what he judges most pleasing to God; but on the other hand, he should not fail to have compassion for his sons, so that even those who have been reprehended will recognize the justice and charity of his actions, even when they go against the grain.[31] In his direction of the Company for the aid of souls, the general must have great magnanimity and courage and never lose heart even in the face of powerful opposition from great personages. He must be capable of maintaining his equilibrium in both prosperity and adversity; and, if necessary for the good of the Company in the service of Jesus Christ, he should be ready to accept death (*a*, 239).

Since the general often will be confronted with both speculative and practical problems, he should have great intelligence and sure judgment. One obvious reason indicating that he should be well educated is the fact that many of the companions will be exceptionally learned men. Ignatius was well aware of the stresses that could be laid upon personal rela-

---

31 It is interesting that this is the only time in the Constitutions that the companions are referred to as sons of the general. The monastic notion of paternal government is notably absent from the Ignatian conception and vocabulary. See below, ch. 4, pp. 100-104.

tions if an erudite companion were called upon to obey decisions of a superior not qualified in the matter under discussion. Nevertheless, of far greater importance is prudence and the ability of discernment in order to make correct judgments in interior matters, as well as common sense in ordering external affairs and the capability of establishing good personal relations with the great variety of human beings within and without the Company. The general must also possess all the qualities necessary for the practical execution of decisions, so that projects will not be left unfinished (*a,* 239).

The general should be endowed with good health and the strength required to fulfill his responsibilities and have the age and appearance which will inspire respect for his authority. Ignatius had a preoccupation with bodily appearance which undoubtedly stemmed from his formation as a *caballero* and, perhaps, from the fact that he was left with a permanent limp from his wound at Pamplona. This is reflected in his legislation as well as in his vocabulary and imagery. Concerning the age of the general, texts A and B add a declaration explaining that he should not be too old to carry out his duties, nor too young to possess the authority and experience demanded by his office.[32] For the sake of the service of God and the aid of souls, the general should also be a man of excellent public reputation and possess the qualities which help to establish personal authority. Finally, the companion elected general should be among those most outstanding in every virtue and most widely known for his efficacious work in the Company. The passage closing the Second Chapter remarks that if the general lacks some of these characteristics, he must at least have much goodness, love of the Company and good judgment. In the other matters, many of his limitations can be made up for by the aids given to him by the Company. But he absolutely must possess the basic qualities required to carry out his essential role of making a community of love for the service of Christ through the aid of souls in companionship.[33]

---

32 *Cons*MHSJ, II, 666.
33 To this final list of essential qualifications, texts A and B add that his good judgment should be accompanied by a good academic education, which perhaps reflects the evolution of the intellectual apostolate of the Company (*Cons*MHSJ, II, 668).

The authority of the general over the Company is outlined in the Third Chapter. For good government, he must have "all authority over the Company for building it up, not for tearing it down" (*a,* 240).[34] His role is to bring the Company to be in the actual circumstances of each historical moment. The fundamental principle underlying all exercise of his authority is that the general must unify the Company at all times for the service of Christ through the aid of souls in companionship. This principle is clearly enunciated in the last sentence of the Third Chapter:

> Generally speaking, he can give commands under obedience to all with respect to everything which is done for the end which is sought by the Company. Although he communicates his authority to other subordinate superiors or visitors, he has the power in all things to order and to approve or revoke what they do. He should be obeyed in all things and reverenced as one who takes the place of Christ Our Lord (*a,* 243-244).[35]

The Sixth Chapter details the means which will help the general to carry out his role. His specific function is to "govern the whole body of the Company that its well-being and its action for the glory of God our Lord is conserved and increased with the help of divine grace" (*a,* 247). The first means to carry out this function will be the example of the life of the general

34 These powers include all authority for admission into the Company, receiving a member into his final grade, dismissal of those unfitted for this vocation; sending scholastics to study or recalling them or changing them from one place to another, the government of all colleges and universities through the officials he names, dispensing from the Constitutions when necessary, all authority in the missions: sending or recalling men and determining the work they should do, though never encroaching upon papal authority, distribution of all offices in the Company, communication of all privileges given to the Company by the Holy See and their revocation or limitation, punishment or giving penances when necessary, calling general congregations, deciding whether a Jesuit should accept a dignity outside the Company, naming all subordinate superiors and communicating to them as much or as little authority as he judges good and also confirming or rejecting appointments made by provincials, admitting houses, colleges and universities and their professors, although as noted in the Fourth Part, he may not renounce them without the authority of the general congregation (*a,* 241-243).

35 The fourth and fifth chapters of the Ninth Part treat of the authority of the Company over the general. See above, pp. 62-64.

manifesting his love of the Company and continual prayer and desires and sacrifices for it. Secondly, in fulfilling the duty of guarding the Constitutions, he must be in constant communication with all the provincials and have full knowledge of the life and activity of the Company everywhere. Granted that, according to the principle of hierarchy, he should communicate wide powers to subordinate superiors, he is responsible for their manner of carrying out their role; and he must be informed of their actions, even by consulting with the companions under their authority, in order to aid them or, when necessary, to correct them and to make up for their defects (*a*, 248). The general must have at hand all authoritative documents and full statistics of the Company. He must be "informed of all things so that he can better provide in everything" (*a*, 249). Ignatius was profoundly aware that good government and actual union require complete and concrete knowledge of all existing circumstances and persons as a sine qua non condition. Finally, the general must not occupy himself with affairs not concerning the Company, since his office "requires more than the whole man." For this reason, he must appoint excellent and trustworthy provincials and other helpers to whom he can commit much of the concern over particular matters, in order that he can devote himself to "the matters of universal import which he alone can take care of" (*a*, 249).

The role of the general would, indeed, demand more than the whole man. The companion elected to this office, nevertheless, would always be merely a man subject to all the limitations and weaknesses of the human race. With all his profound trust in Divine Providence and reliance on grace, Ignatius never forgot this fact, however much in later times and under the influence of different cultural patterns there might be a tendency to quasi-divinize the superior and endow him with almost magical powers of discretion and clairvoyance concerning the intentions of God. In the Seventh Chapter on the various persons required to aid the general to carry out his role properly, Ignatius three times eloquently expresses the weakness of human nature before such a responsibility. The general will require help not only for particular affairs, but even for "those universal affairs proper to his office," because one who must have comprehension of so many persons and consider so many matters of great importance "will carry an insupportable burden

which, even with great discretion and shortening of his life, he
will not be able to sustain" (*a*, 249). The general, therefore,
will need men to help him attend to all the affairs of his office,
to help him with their advice to order these affairs and to aid
him in accomplishing them:

> For it is certain neither the memory of one man is sufficient
> to remember so many things; nor, even if it were sufficient, would
> his intellect suffice to reflect upon them and order them well;
> nor, even if this were sufficient, would his strength be enough to
> accomplish them (*a*, 250).

Specifically, the general must have advisors to help him arrive
at decisions in ordering the affairs of the Company because of
"their multitude and of the weakness of human understanding
which is not capable of paying attention to so many different
matters" (*a*, 250). Ignatius, whose master was always living
experience and who had grown up in the Castilian tradition of
cortes to aid the king in his government, adds that the example
of all those who have great responsibilities proves the necessity of
having advisors (*a*, 251).

Shortly after the redaction of these texts, Ignatius gave very
striking personal testimony of how deeply he was convinced of
the terrible weight of responsibility of the general. At the end
of 1550, he called the available fathers of the Company to
Rome to examine and approve the text of the Constitutions. In
an autograph document dated January 30, 1551, he offered his
resignation in terms of unmistakable sincerity.[36] No matter how
earnestly a pious hagiographer might endeavor to interpret this
action as simply the extraordinary humility of a saint, close
reading of the language of the document, coupled with knowledge of the great realism and total dedication of Ignatius to the
universal good of the Company, can leave no doubt of the reality of his conviction that another companion should replace him
as general. After revealing that his judgment is the result of
months and years of reflection in complete tranquility of
spirit, he states in language which is typical of his vocabulary for
a final election after discernment of spirits, that his conclusion
is that which he "feels (*sentir*) and understands to be to the
greater praise and glory of His Divine Majesty." [37] Consider-

36 *EppIgn,* III, 303-304.
37 See below ch. 5, pp. 111-116.

ing with no passion whatever what he feels within himself, he judges that because of his many sins, imperfections and infirmities, "I really do not possess — as if infinitely not — the qualifications required for this responsibility of the Company." He is so convinced of this that he desires that the companions elect a successor as general who will fulfill the role better than himself, or not so badly or even only equally well. Should the companions not be in agreement concerning this request, he beseeches them to commend the matter to God in prayer "in order that His most holy will may be done in all things to His greater glory and to the greater universal good of souls and of the whole Company." His request was denied by all but Oviedo, and Ignatius was obliged to carry until death the responsibility of the Company which he had endured from the beginning "because it was imposed upon me."

The general is an emanation of the Company who is responsible to it for his government according to the *pactista* notion. Because of the great difficulty of the role of the general and the limitations of human nature, the head of the Company is subject to its authority "in order that no disorder be permitted him," and he can be removed from office or dismissed from the Company if his actions warrant it. Just as the general is the vicar of the vicar of Christ for the members of the Company, so too all other superiors are his vicars, all of whom have as their essential role the unifying of the companions committed to their care with one another and with their one head, so that the entire body of the Company is made into one community of love of companions acting together for the aid of souls. In concluding the Ninth Part of the Constitutions, therefore, Ignatius points out that all that has been stated about the qualities and duties of the General also applies, *mutatis mutandis,* to provincials and local superiors (*a*, 252).

Qualities and Duties of Rectors   Throughout the Constitutions Ignatius makes specific references to subordinate superiors as these seem necessary.[38] Since the essential qualities and duties of all superiors are included in

38 The term *provincial* occurs in the preliminary documents 27 times, in text *a* of the Constitutions 51 times, in text A an additional 4, and in text B an additional 34 times. *Rector* appears only 7 times in the preliminary documents. Of the 38 times it occurs in text *a* of the Constitutions, 31 are in the Fourth Part concerning colleges. Text A adds

remarks about the general, he does not detail these for lower superiors except in the case of the rectors of colleges discussed in the Fourth Part of the Constitutions. Since rectors were responsible for the formation of young Jesuits, Ignatius may have felt that it was important to emphasize the requirements of this office, even though these echo the description of the general given in the Ninth Part.[39] The rector must be Catholic, virtuous, discreet, talented for government, and of pleasing external appearance. He must also be experienced in temporal and spiritual affairs, well-educated, and have spiritual liberty from his passions, being especially proved in obedience and humility. He must know how to be severe when it is necessary, while remaining kind. A conscientious hard-worker, he must be so trustworthy that the provincial and the general can communicate great authority to him, since the effectiveness of his government will be in proportion to the extent of his personal power to rule. Even if he is not outstanding in the other desired qualities, at the least he must have goodness, prudence, and concern for his charges. His essential role is to make a community of love of the various individuals committed to him; consequently, he must have the human qualities required for establishing personal relationships with them as the foundation for carrying out all his other duties of government (*a,* 194).

The text goes on to enumerate the specific duties of the rector: (1) to support the whole community with prayer and holy desires; (2) to guard the Constitutions; (3) to watch over all his companions with great care, protecting them from troubles from within and without the house — heading them off, or, if they occur, finding a remedy as dictated by the good of the individual or of the whole community; (4) seeing to the progress in virtue and in learning of his subjects; (5) conserving their physical health and managing well the material affairs of the house; (6) appointing well-qualified subordinate officials and observing their performance, retaining them in their func-

---

4 instances, but text B adds 31, chiefly in the additional passages in the Fourth Part on universities.

39 *Colleges* in the preliminary documents and in the Constitutions means residences for students who attended lectures at the university. At first these students were exclusively Jesuits. See George E. Ganss, *Saint Ignatius' Idea of a Jesuit University* (Milwaukee, 1956), pp. 20, 31-33.

tions or changing them as is seen to be necessary; (7) and, finally, carrying out all the duties detailed in the Fourth Part for the administration of colleges, always entirely respecting the hierarchical subordination to the provincial and keeping him informed of all important matters, following all orders which he might give (*a,* 194).

Making a community of love for the service of Christ through the aid of souls in companionship demands attention to the actual individuals who make up this community in the concrete, material circumstances in which they live. The role of the rector is precisely to bring this community to be in these individuals and to guard their unity with the whole body and its one head. In detailing the essential duties of the rector, Ignatius carefully included the basic requirements imposed by the concrete exigencies of forming and conserving an apostolic community of love. The specific methods of carrying out these duties will depend upon concrete circumstances, but all are directed towards the accomplishment of the apostolic end of the Company anywhere in the world.

The Collateral   A special aid was provided by Ignatius for subordinate superiors such as the rector. He established the office of *collateral* to help them carry out their essential role of realizing the union of mutual love within their communities.[40] It is highly significant that the office of collateral is described in a Declaration on the First Chapter of the Eighth Part of the Constitutions concerning those things which will help to interior union of the members of the Company with one another and with their head. The being of the Company consists in this union, and Ignatius was always seeking effective means to preserve this union. In fulfilling his essential role of making a community of love, a superior is always faced with the need of creating true personal relationships between all the various concrete individ-

---

40 Shortly after the completion of text A of the Constitutions, a preliminary document entitled *De Praeposito et Collaterali* was composed (*Cons*MHSJ, I, 387-389). This text was taken over into text B where it appears almost verbatim, although its order is reversed (ibid., II, 608-612). For a history of the gradual development of this office and its rules, see J. M. Aicardo, *Commentario a las Constituciones de la Compañía de Jésus,* 6 vols. (Madrid, 1902-1925), V, 831-835.

uals in his community and himself, also a concrete individual with his own temperament and character and limitations. Ignatius, whose master was always living experience, knew quite well that pious exhortations and lofty spiritual theories were insufficient to bring about a true community of love among specific concrete persons. He had had his own difficulties with members of the first small group of companions such as Bobadilla and Rodrigues. In the idea of the office of the collateral we have one of the finest examples of his practical genius at work on the problem of personal relations in a community.

The essential role of the collateral is to foster the union of mutual love of the companions with one another and with their superior. Such a union requires mutual understanding, and the collateral must always seek to bring about this common accord, "walking among them as an angel of peace" and inspiring in the companions true comprehension of and love for their superior "whom they have in the place of Christ Our Lord." [41] In order to fulfill this role effectively (and here the originality and the insight of Ignatius are particularly striking), the collateral is not under the authority of the superior, nor does he have any authority over the companions. Thus, a climate of liberty is established for the companions, for the superior and for the collateral himself, which can be of great value in removing misunderstandings and smoothing away the rough obstacles to personal relations. The means which the collateral is to use with respect to the companions in fulfilling his role are to bring them to understand and love the superior and to give them an example of reverence for him, even though the collateral himself is not bound to obedience to him. This supposes that the collateral will listen to the difficulties of the companions and through interpersonal dialogue will help them to solve their problems with the superior. Further, the collateral has the duty of pointing out to the superior with all liberty and modesty his deficiencies in carrying out his role and to advise the provincial or general if through indisposition, overwork, or other reasons the superior is failing to fulfill the duties of his office. Obviously, much of the evidence for such a judgment would come to the collateral through his dialogue with the companions.

41 *Cons*MHSJ, II, 610.

With respect to the superior, the collateral is his close helper, and he must love and reverence the superior and seek ways to help him to carry out his role of making a community of love. The collateral must be the most useful instrument of the superior in bringing about this union of love and, through his observations and advice, in freeing the superior from the limitations of his subjective point of view.[42] The superior's attitude towards his collateral should be one of special love and respect, encouraging him to speak with freedom and frankness. In his difficulties the superior should seek the advice of his collateral in order to have the help of another's judgment in arriving at his own decisions. In governing his community, he should use the collateral "as a faithful instrument" in more important matters, whether they concern the common good of all or the particular good of one of the companions. In short, "he must consider him and confide in him as he does in himself, not subject to his authority, in a union of spirit in Our Lord." The greatest human risk of a superior is that he might unwittingly close himself within his own judgment and preconceptions, and nothing would be more fatal to true union with the companions in his community. By having "another self" with him at all times, he is given the means to attain the spiritual liberty necessary for truly making a community of love.

The office of collateral disappeared from the practice of the Company within a century. Indeed, it rather quickly became confused with the office of superintendent in the colleges and universities, an office which is not mentioned in the Constitutions, but for which St. Francis Borgia composed a set of rules in 1567.[44] It is possible that the tendency to quasi-divinize the superior, which was a result of cultural patterns of the epoch, gradually made the office of collateral seem not quite fitting. The Declaration in the Constitutions notes that the collateral would be useful particularly in two cases: (1) when a superior

---

42 F. Roustang, *Constitutions de la Compagnie de Jesús*, 2 vols. (Paris, 1967), describes the collateral as "une sorte de miroir sans autorité, permettant au supérieur de s'exprimer et de se découvrir lui-même dans l'elaboration des décisions et dans les effets de son gouvernement auprès de ses subordonnés" (II, 90).

43 *Cons*MHSJ, II, 612.

44 See A. Coemans, S.J., "Collatéral et surintendant," *AHSJ*, V (1936), 293-295.

needed greater aid because he was not very experienced in his office or for other reasons, even though his life and desires were most praiseworthy; (2) when the qualities of a subject were such that he could best function in the role of collateral.[45] Possibly, the phrase "or other reasons" did not attract sufficient attention, and the impression grew that a collateral should be given only to an inadequate superior.[46] Nonetheless, it is clear from the text itself that for Ignatius the reason for having a collateral was above all to help a superior to fulfill his role of making an apostolic community of love.

As has been noted already, with the growth of the Company, it became necessary to give an hierarchical structure to the Company, providing regional and local superiors as the living principle of union of the companions working in a particular province or house and as the instrument of union of all the members with the one head of the whole body and through him with all the companions dispersed throughout the world. These subordinate superiors were vicars of the general who was himself the vicar of the vicar of Christ on earth for the Company and who, therefore, ruled all the companions in the place of Christ.[47] It is possible to trace the evolution of the hierarchical organization of the Company and to follow within it its never-changing essential function of achieving the union of the companions for the aid of souls.

The decision had been made in the Deliberation to elect a superior, because nothing would be more effective in preserving

Hierarchical Union for Apostolic Love

---

45 *Cons*MHSJ, II, 612.
46 Even the First General Congregation seemed to feel ill at ease with the role of the collateral, as it suppressed the words *en algo* in the passage concerning the collateral's duty to *suplir* for the superior, calling to his attention any failures noted in his manner of fulfilling his role. The explanation given for this suppression was that it did not seem that the collateral should *supplere vices Rectoris sponte sua* in any other way than in writing (*Cons*MHSJ, II, 610, n. 14). One has the impression that even the fathers of the First Congregation had missed the point, and thus this very astute contribution of Ignatius to aid the superior to carry out his role of making a true community of love gradually fell into desuetude.
47 For a very clear presentation of Ignatius' notion of the role of the subordinate superior as a vicar of the general who must realize the loving union of all the companions committed to his care for the sake

79

the union of the companions than obedience.[48] In the Formula of the Institute it had been provided that all discretion and distribution of offices would be in the hands of the superior, "so that the right order necessary in every well-established community may be guaranteed." [49] The papal bulls and briefs after 1546, gave all privileges to the Company through the general.[50] Ignatius had requested this as an effective source of the union of all the members of the Company with their one head.[51]

The Constitutions insist upon guarding this hierarchical subordination for the sake of unity. On the other hand, the general should amply communicate his authority to lower superiors, because "in as much as it is more ample, the better they can govern" (a, 194). The rector should guard entire subordination to the provincial; and in his own community he should name competent officials and see to it that one does not interfere in the office of another. The clearest texts concerning the unifying function of this hierarchical structure occur in the Eighth and Tenth Parts, which are entirely directed to the conservation of the union of the members with one another and with their head and, so, to the being of the Company. Interior union will be aided by "the well guarded subordination of one to the other," namely, of the companions to their local superior, of members of a province to their provincial and of provincials to the general, with no exceptions; because this carefully maintained subordination "will maintain union with the grace of God" (a, 227). Union will be aided on the part of the general, because there flows from him, as from the head, all the authority of the provincials and from them all that of local superiors and from them all that of particular persons of the Company. Similarly, all the missions of the companions flow from the one head or, at least, with his approval and communicated authority. Furthermore, all the privileges of the Company come through the General, "for the more the companions depend upon the su-

of the apostolic end, see the letter to Gandía of July 29, 1547 (*EppIgn,* I, 551-561).

48 *Cons*MHSJ, I, 6.
49 Ibid., I, 16.
50 Ibid., 172, 356-371.
51 See *Cons*MHSJ, I, *Prolegomena,* ccxxi-ccxxii, n. 5.

periors, the better will love and union be conserved among them" (*a*, 228; cf. 242). For the genuine good of the being of the Company, it is not only essential to elect the best man possible as general, but also that "the particular superiors have great authority over the companions and, on the other hand, the general over these superiors and the Company over the general, so that all possess all power for the good, and if things are done badly, they are entirely subject to authority" (*a*, 255). The primary means to effect the union of love among the companions is the bond of obedience, "which unites the companions with their superiors and with one another, the local superiors with the privincials and these with the general, so that the subordination of the ones to the others is diligently maintained" (*a*, 255-256).

Concerning the communication of authority to admit candidates to the Company, text B enunciates the basic practical reason for the multiplication of subordinate superiors: "Because the general cannot be everywhere, he may communicate to others of the Company as much of his authority as seems indicated for the good of the whole body of the Company." [52] This recalls one of the reasons given in the Deliberation for electing one of the Company as the superior whom all would obey: because the pope, to whom they had committed themselves in entire obedience, could not pay attention to the particular, concrete details of their lives together. The unique superior of the Company is its head, the general, who is the vicar of the vicar of Christ. All subordinate superiors are vicars of the general for the life and union of the members of the Company with one another and with their head. What appears through a study of the evolution of the hierarchical structure of authority in the Company as the body organized itself for the preservation and growth of its union of members for the service of Christ through the aid of souls in companionship is, once more, the end of all authority in the Company: to bring the Company to be here and now.

The language of the Ignatian documents often was borrowed from older religious rules as, at times, were the descriptions of specific duties of superiors and subordinate officials. Ignatius,

---

52 *Cons*MHSJ, II, 496; cf. 702.

with his usual suppleness before the exigencies of concrete circumstances, adapted these offices to the needs of the Company of Jesus in the pursuit of its apostolic end. The fundamental structure of authority in the Company as conceived by Ignatius is one of great simplicity. The one head of the Company is Jesus Christ. His will is communicated to the companions through His vicar on earth. The general acts as vicar of the pope and, therefore, of Christ for the members of the Company. All subordinate superiors receive their authority from the general and act as his vicars in communicating the will of Christ to their companions.

It is remarkable that in all these texts concerning subordination, dependence and obedience, the emphasis is not ascetical. Obedience is aimed at union for apostolic action in companionship.[53] The structure of hierarchy is always directed towards achieving the union of the companions — bringing the Company to be — for the apostolic service of Christ. Its particular structure as described in the Ignatian documents obviously was erected in function of the concrete, actual exigencies which existed in the historical and cultural situation for achieving this union: the number of companions, their stage of formation, their ministries, their physical dispersal, the available means of communication, etc. One can legitimately discuss whether or not this vocabulary of dependence is truly expressive in modern times, but the essential purpose of this hierarchical structure remains actual and vital to the life of the Company for the service of Christ through the aid of souls. Adaptation of this structure to any other epoch requires the weighing of all these factors as they exist here and now and the determination of the particular forms of hierarchy demanded by these conditions for the Company to fulfill its one purpose of accomplishing the "scope of our vocation." In the contemporary period, it is evident that the achievement of this unifying structure is much more complex and difficult. On the other hand, the means are available to create an effective hierarchical structure if the essential aim of Ignatius is grasped and translated into modern times and techniques. It is through this hierarchical structure that the union of all the companions in one body is

53 See below, ch. 7.

achieved and that each individual Jesuit is commissioned to aid souls by his superior "in the place of Christ." True fidelity to this vision of Ignatius and to his own practice demands a constant openness to the teachings of actual experience concerning the structural organization required at any given time in order to facilitate the one essential role of all superiors in the Company: to make an apostolic community of love.

EXERCISING AUTHORITY
FOR APOSTOLIC LOVE

THE ESSENTIAL ROLE OF THE SUPERIOR according to Ignatius is to make an apostolic community of love: to unify all the members of the whole body of the Company with one another and with their head for the greater service of Christ through the aid of souls in companionship. The union is effected when the superior after the process of mutual discernment makes the final decision and issues a command which all the companions obey. The Company comes to be in this moment of perfect union of wills directing the activity of the whole body towards its one apostolic end. In the concrete, the realization of this union in mutual love and corporate apostolic action supposes the exercise of authority on the part of the superior.

What appears from an analysis of the word authority in the vocabulary of Ignatius is that in his conception all authority in the Company is derived vicariously from Jesus Christ and is directed towards the conservation and growth of the Company in its well-being through the ever renewed union of all its members with one another and, through the structure of hierarchy, with their one head for the apostolic service of Christ. It was entirely natural for Ignatius to think of legitimate authorities, whether secular or religious, as speaking "in the place of Christ" to whom had been given all authority in heaven and earth.[1] Thus all legitimate authority came from God and in the deepest sense was vicarious. Ignatius' notion of authority was not philosophical, although he had undoubtedly studied the scho-

---

1 An excellent history and analysis of the vicarious conception of authority is given by J. M. Cameron, *Images of Authority — A Consideration of the Concepts of Regnum and Sacerdotium* (New Haven, 1966). See especially pp. 1-16.

lastic writers on the subject at Paris, but it was rooted in his Castilian background and was taken for granted rather than analyzed. The whole social order of his early formation had been supported by a structure of hierarchical authority: in the family, the state, and the Church.

The will of God in the concrete was communicated by the commands of duly constituted superiors at the moment that these commands had to be executed. Nevertheless, this view was always nuanced and controlled by the *pactista* notion that the superior ultimately was responsible not only to God, but also to his subjects for his manner of exercising his authority. Authority, consequently, involved a power or right communicated by God to those who were His vicars on earth,[2] but this divine communication of authority was given through the community itself.[3]

The word authority for Ignatius, then, corresponded to a concept of the responsibility to govern others in the name of Jesus Christ.[4] The source of this authority was Christ Himself, and those who exercised authority, whether popes or kings, did so as His vicars. In the vicarious representation of God there were degrees of authority, a structure of hierarchy. The powers and rights of those placed higher within this structure could be communicated by them to other subordinate authorities, which implied, therefore, granting permission to exercise these powers and rights.[5]

Since all authority in the Company is directed toward its conservation in being, most of the explicit discussions in the Ignatian documents of the exercise of authority concern the admission and formation of new members and their final incorporation in the Company, the dismissal of those who cannot or refuse to unite themselves with the whole body in mutual love

---

2 *Cons*MHSJ, 347.
3 See above, ch. 3 pp. 61-64.
4 *Cons*MHSJ, I, 315; II, 211.
5 Communication of the authority of the pope to the general: *Cons*-MHSJ, I, 17, 27, 163, 317, 376, 395; of the authority of the general to lower superiors: Ibid., I, 276, 279, 319, 322, 347, 350, 394; II, 52, 72, 132, 143, 144, 160, 162, 167, 176, 194, 198, 199, 215, 228, 243, 244, 248, 255, 282, 284, 290, 312, 314, 316, 324, 434, 496, 552, 612, 666, 670, 672, 674, 694.

Exercising Authority for Apostolic Love

and common apostolic activity, and the sending of members on apostolic missions. The being of the Company consists in this union of all its members with one another and with their head for the aid of souls. This explains the insistence in the juridical structure of the Constitutions that all authority is derived from the one head of the whole body whose essential role, therefore, is always to be the living principle of union of all its members. That in his person and in his office the superior should have personal and external characteristics which would support and manifest his authority is simply a realistic human aid for carrying out his role.[6]

The Exercise of Authority   The concrete exercise of authority implies various actions directed towards achieving the end of this authority. Concerning the superior's exercise of authority, Ignatius' vocabulary consists of words of command (*mandar*): giving orders (*ordenar*), governing and ruling (*gobernar, regir*); words of giving permission or approval (*licençia, approbaçión*); and words of providing and caring for the needs of the companions (*proveer, cuidado*). As will be seen, these various duties of the superior in the concrete order are all conceived by Ignatius as simply the practical exercise of his essential role of making an apostolic community of love.

The word command was a privileged term in the vocabulary of Ignatius for the exercise of authority.[7] He tended to use it chiefly in contexts indicating the full exercise of divinely founded authority: in references to the commandments of God,[8]

---

6 *Cons*MHSJ, I, 300, 389; II, 228, 237, 240, 251.
7 S. de Covarrubias' extremely useful *Tesoro de la lengua Castellana Española según la impressión de 1611, con las adiciones de Benito Remigio Noydens publicadas en la de 1674* (Barcelona, 1943), defines *mandar* as giving an order to another to do something. It means to *govern* and should be exercised only towards those who are under one's legitimate authority. *Mandamiento* means that which is commanded and should be carried out, and it is used especially of the commandments of God, p. 784. J. Corominas, *Dicionario critico etimologico de la lengua Castellana*, 4 vols. (Madrid, 1954), adds that *mandar* often means to give a person a responsibility or *dar una misión* (III, 20). Hereafter, these works will be referred to as *Covarrubias* and *Corominas*.
8 *SpEx*, [18, 39, 238, 241, 365]. *EppIgn*, I, 72, 102, 105, 139, 162.

86

or of Christ,[9] and of the Church;[10] in speaking of the invocation by the vicar of Christ, either immediately or through the superior of the Company, of the special vow of the professed to go on missions anywhere in the world;[11] and in passages explaining the plenary use of the superior's authority to command in the name of Christ or under obedience,[12] or exhorting the companions to the practice of perfect obedience.[13] The word used for the ordinary exercise of authority in the daily requirements for making an apostolic community of love, amidst all the practical exigencies of living and working together, is not to "command", but to "order": to establish an order of community life and action, putting order into the apostolic union of the companions. In the Castilian of the epoch of Ignatius, the basic notion of the word order was physical. It signified the proper situation of things in relation to one another, each being in its own place.[14] A community exsits only in the mutual relations of the persons who compose it through their common commitment to one life-purpose. To give an order is to put persons into their proper place in the dynamic situation of life and action — to organize their mutual relationship for the attainment of their end. Those things which are ordered are unified and placed in their proper mutual relationship for acting together; that which is disordered is out of its proper place, and, so, disunited and out of step.

Ignatius conceived the act of ordering the lives of the members of the Company or of giving orders to them as always directed towards unifying them for the accomplishment of the "scope of our vocation." To order the lives and action of the companions, unifying them in the interrelation of mutual love

9 *SpEx*, [280, 283, 306].

10 *SpEx*, [229, 344].

11 *EppIgn*, I, 138, 141, 144, 153, 155, 159, 174, 184; *Cons*MHSJ, I, 11, 49, 161, 162, 164, 301, 395; II, 8, 68, 74, 169, 211, 212, 215, 508.

12 *EppIgn*, I, 237, 247, 280; *Cons*MHSJ, II, 207, 209, 243. That this solemn invocation of the superior's authority was repugnant to the temperament of Ignatius is shown by his remark to Bobadilla that he will be forced to give a command under obedience in view of common spiritual progress and of his own conscience "although this runs deeply counter to my feelings." (*EppIgn*, I, 280).

13 *Cons*MHSJ, I, 392; II, 70, 71, 98, 167, 207, 524.

14 *Covarrubias*, p. 838. An Ignatian triplet reflects this physical basis of the word order. In a letter of 1536, he reminds Cazador that God has placed "order, weight and measure in all things" (*EppIgn*, I, 98).

and corporate work for the fulfillment of the end of the Company, requires that the superior constantly exercise discernment which leads to decisions which will enable the companions to carry out their vocation in tranquillity and without conflict.[15] Consequently, on his own level — general, provincial, or local — the superior must guide the companions by giving them unifying orders and pointing out to them the corporate apostolate to be exercised.[16] This ordering must not remain purely theoretical, but must constantly be carried out in practice.[17] The superior gives orders in the concrete circumstances of persons, places, historical times and the exigencies of particular forms of apostolic endeavor. The Ignatian vocabulary of orders looks to the physical ordering of the companions' lives: bodily health, intellectual formation and all the administration of colleges and universities involved — clothing, food and housing, etc. It looks to the spiritual ordering of their lives of union with God and to their formation as true companions ready to unite themselves with one another and with their head to accomplish the "scope of our vocation," to which they are totally committed.[18] Finally, it looks to the ordering of the life of the whole Company in its ever-evolving hierarchical organization as it grows and develops: a life of ordered union consisting in the subordination of the general to the Company, in the subordination of all the members to the general, and in the ordered communication of the authority of the general to lower superiors.

The notion of order was extraordinarily central in the mental structure of Ignatius. During the Basque and Castilian periods of his early formation, he had lived in tightly ordered familial, ecclesiastical, and political structures. Through concrete experience he had come to see that the coherence of the universe and the lives of men required order and that the source of all order is the perfect wisdom of God "who is the principle of all

---

15 *SpEx,* [213]; *EppIgn,* I, 106, 149, 154, 159; *Cons*MHSJ, I, 78; II, 188, 250, 616, 644.
16 *Cons*MHSJ, I, 217, 377; II, 66, 122.
17 Ibid., II, 255.
18 *Cons*MHSJ, I, 1, 16, 17, 19, 52, 53, 59, 78, 175, 176, 252, 384; II, 100, 208, 209, 226, 236, 250, 410, 420, 470, 474, 478, 486, 506, 546, 702.

order." [19] He saw the universe as ruled by God "our universal Giver, Governor and Lord." [20]

Thus the great principle underlying all authority and obedience in the Church is the truth that between Christ and His Church "is the same Spirit which governs and rules us"; and by the same Spirit who gave the Ten Commandments, the Church "is ruled and governed." [21] In the concrete, God rules the members of the Company through their head.[22] All human potential should be developed to cooperate with divine grace "according to the order of the supreme providence of God our Lord" (*a*, 253). Thus those admitted to the Company should trust that God is ruling them through the mediation of the superior;[23] while it is the duty of the superior to "rule them in the place of Christ our Lord as the interpreter of His divine will." [24] The Company itself is "ordered to the greater divine glory and the greater universal good and the greater spiritual progress of souls." [25]

The content of the word "order" in the Ignatian vocabulary, therefore, is rich and complex. It does not signify the simple giving of commands in a military sense for the sake of insuring external discipline. Rather, it is concerned with directing all the life and action of the companions toward the apostolic end of the Company. In his mind there was a quasi-identity of the notions of union, good government, and the conservation of the being of the Company. Indeed, he expresses the identity of union and order in the Constitutions when he insists that persons who do not possess spiritual liberty in their passions and judgments must not be admitted or retained in the Company, since they will not "endure order and, thus, also union" (*a*, 226).

The giving of orders described in the Constitutions is entirely directed to bringing the Company to be in the union of all the

19 Ibid., II, 264.
20 God's ordering of the universe and of events: *SpEx,* [234]; *Epplgn,* I, 74, 83, 98, 99, 104, 115, 119, 193; *Cons*MHSJ, I, 122, 123; II, 253, 264. Man's ordering of his life and action to God: *SpEx,* [23, 40, 46, 63, 135, 169, 171, 173, 199, 214, 317]; *Epplgn,* I, 116, 198; *Cons*MHSJ, I, 247; II, 122.
21 *SpEx,* [365]; see *Cons*MHSJ, II, 22.
22 *Cons*MHSJ, II, 140, 380, 522.
23 Ibid., II, 140.
24 Ibid., II, 574.
25 Ibid., I, 247, 250, II, 280, 348.

companions at each historical moment for the apostolic service of Christ. Government for Ignatius always was an essential means to this end of constantly bringing the Company to be and never the wooden application of static, a priori rules. If in his concrete working out of this dynamic principle of government during his own historical and cultural epoch Ignatius formulated specific rules, it would be totally false to his own profound intention to consider that these rules were intended to be imposed formalistically in other times and places independently of the basic, dynamic principle of authority as always renewing the being of the Company for the service of Christ through the aid of souls here and now.

The extreme density and profound unity of the mental structure of Ignatius underlying his conception of the being of the Company and the role of the superior is once again clear. Authority, government, rule, commands are directed to and quasi-identified with the conservation and growth of the Company in the union of mutual love which constitutes its being and its dynamic ordering to the achievement of the scope of our vocation.[26] The dynamic structure of the mentality of Ignatius is reflected in this vision of authority in the Company as always being "on the move" — ever renewing the being of the Company in the union of all the members of the whole body for its apostolic end.

Giving commands and orders in an organized, hierarchical structure of government logically involves granting permissions. The usual terms used by Ignatius are permission (*liçençia*) and approval (*aprobaçión*).[27] The initial groping of Ignatius toward an ordered form of community life through the teach-

26 In the Ignatian vocabulary of authority the words govern and rule are practically synonymous. *Covarrubias,* pp. 652, 900, gives these words as definitions of each other. He states that the person who has the role of administering justice has the office of *govierno,* which is often equivalent to *mantener y sustentar,* reflecting the Ignatian notion of preservation in being as the end of government in the Company. The lexicographer goes on to note that good government results in the peaceful union of all subjects, while bad government causes dissension. As a Castilian who knew his *pactista* theory, he adds that *cortes* should watch over the one who governs.

27 *Covarrubias,* p. 885, notes that to approve signifies accepting something as good. Its opposite would be reproval. *Licentia,* rather, means the granting of permission to perform an action that would otherwise be forbidden.

ing of experience and the study of older religious rules is shown by the fact that the words permission and approval, or their equivalents, occur nearly twice as often in the preliminary texts as in all three Ignatian texts of the Constitutions. Throughout the early documents, the use of the terms reflects a developing awareness of the need to order the temporal and spiritual lives of the companions in their communities. The words would appear less frequently in the Constitutions because Ignatius came to distinguish between Constitutions and more ad hoc rules, and the instances of permission tended to fall into the latter category.[28]

In the final Ignatian legislation, therefore, the notion of granting permissions is well-integrated into his fundamental, dynamic principle of authority. The granting of permissions and the approval of the actions of the companions enable the superior to guard their union in all the practical exigencies of community life and action. Many of the specific instances of permission and approval in the texts are directed toward the formation of the younger companions into fully incorporated members of the body of the Company who are united with one another and with their head for apostolic action. The unity of this apostolic action itself is assured by the superior's responsibility for directing it. That these specific instances of permission and approval might well require modification in different times and places in order to be faithful to the dynamic principle of authority of Ignatius is evident.

28 See *ConsMHSJ*, III, especially *Regulae S. Ignatii*, pp. 135-211. J. F. Gilmont, *Les écrits spirituels des premiers Jésuites* (Rome, 1961), has shown that the terminological distinction between the words rules and constitutions became current during the sixteenth century. Before this, Rule had been what defined a religious order. It contained above all spiritual principles. In addition to the Rule, there were customs books, statutes, and constitutions, which were more juridical and which specified the essential directives of the Rule. The distinction between rules and constitutions was made clear by the Fourth Lateran Council in 1215, when it obliged founders of new orders to adopt one of four Rules: Basil, Augustine, Benedict or Francis. The first exceptions to this directive were made during the 16th century when the Holy See permitted the Clerks Regular to define their new institutes by "Constitutions." "Cette décision explique que, depuis cette époque, les constitutions, et notamment celles de la Compagnie, continnent à la fois des principes ascétiques et des dispositions juridiques" (p. 73).

Very frequent terms in the Ignatian vocabulary of authority
are the words to provide (*proveer*) and care (*cuidado*) for the
companions.[29] These words connoted much more to Ignatius
than mere attention to the necessities of community life. Ignatius' idea of companionship was that of a profound interpersonal relationship of mutual love grounded in the love of God
realized in the common "scope of our vocation." [30] Nothing
could have been farther from his mind than the merely func-
tional organization and administration of an impersonal group
unified in action merely for the sake of efficiency. For him all
authority and government were founded on the reality of divine providence, the active love of God caring for the spiritual
and temporal needs of his creatures.[31] In the Company the
providence of God rules the companions through the mediation
of the superior.[32] The superior, therefore, should reflect the
loving providence of God in his care for the companions, and
they should leave all the care of themselves to their Creator and
Lord and in His name and for His love and reverence to the
Company or the superior.[33]

It is interesting that as the life of the Company evolved in the
growth of numbers of members and of houses, the instances of
these words in the texts increased.[34] This progressive employment of the words provide and care by Ignatius manifests his
increasing awareness of the need to attend to an ever greater
number of sometimes banal spiritual and temporal details due
to the rapid growth of the Company and the need to govern
many houses, to form new members and to care for the ever
expanding missions of the Company. Once more, it is evident
that to be true to Ignatius the specific manner of attending to
these matters should be adapted to the circumstances of dif-

29 *Covarrubias,* p. 885, defines *proveer* as the act of foreseeing in good
   time what will be necessary and taking care of it. He notes that in
   the Castilian military there was an officer called the *Proveedor,* who
   was responsible for providing the needs of his unit.
30 See above, ch. 2.
31 *Cons*MHSJ, I, 122; II, 203, 253.
32 Ibid., II, 380, 522.
33 Ibid., II, 120.
34 In all the preliminary documents (*Cons*MHSJ, I) they occur twenty
   times and in the General Examen eight times. But in text *a* of the
   Constitutions alone they occur thirty-eight times, to which text A
   makes nine additions and text B twenty more.

ferent times and places.[35] The making of an apostolic community of love, to which all government in the Company is directed according to Ignatius, requires in the concrete the unification of the real human beings composing this community with all their spiritual and bodily strengths and weaknesses. Only by caring and providing for the actual exigencies of these men living together in pursuit of their common vocation here and now can the superior carry out his essential role of uniting them with one another and with their head for the service of Christ through the aid of souls in companionship.

One of the most revealing indices of the mental structure of a man is the imagery which he employs in the effort to communicate his thoughts and feelings. Without undertaking an analysis of the nature of this imaginative code from the viewpoint of depth psychology, it is clear that the metaphorical grasping of reality and the expression of this conception through images manifest a particular subject's manner of structuring experience in the interiority of his own consciousness. Contrary to popular misconceptions about the dry and unpoetic temperament of Ignatius, he often expressed himself through images. In the effort to understand the notion of the role of the superior underlying Ignatius' language of authority, it is helpful to notice his vocabulary of images of authority.

A scriptural image for the power and providence of God, who rules all things, which often occurs in the writings of Ignatius is that of the hand of God.[36] It was only natural that Ignatius would extend the hand image to expressions of the authority and providence of the superior. Vicar of the vicar of Christ on earth, the general rules and governs the Company as the instrument of the "hand" of divine providence. The unity of life and action of the members of the whole body of the Company is assured because all authority is in the "hand" of their one head.[37]

A rich image particularly dear to Ignatius is that of the downflowing of goodness from above — from God.[38] He imagines

---

35 See below, ch. 6, pp. 149-150.
36 *SpEx* [91]; *EppIgn,* I, 84, 118, 149, 150, 194; *Cons*MHSJ, II, 171, 252, 253, 650, 654.
37 Ibid., I, 10, 16; II, 193, 245, 350, 526, 680.
38 *SpEx,* [235]; *Cons*MHSJ, II, 650.

the general as the head of the whole body of the Company from whom, as from a fountain of all good, there descends the vital force which animates the members in their unified, corporate apostolate.[39] Ignatius insists that the general must be a "mirror and model" of virtue for the companions.[40]

The dynamic mental structure of Ignatius is reflected in his special predilection for what might be called his "pilgrim" imagery. The word road (*via*) occurs with great frequency, as do moving along the road (*caminar*) and walking (*andar*). The process of life — and the being of the Company of Jesus — was always "on the way" for Ignatius, moving towards its divinely ordered end. His own experience as a *caballero* shows itself in this imagery in several references to journeying on horseback.[41] The superior must lead all the companions along the "way of the Lord," pointing the way to all of them to achieve mutual union for the apostolic service of Christ. Although the unction of the Holy Spirit should teach the companions, nevertheless, authority can at least "open up the road" with useful advice and direction (*a*, 192). The superior must be aware of the temperament and character and strength and weakness of each of the companions, reining them in or spurring them on, giving them dynamic leadership down the direct path to the apostolic end of the Company (*a*, 161, 166, 187, 227).

Forming Companions in Apostolic Love As a part of his role of unifying all the companions into an apostolic community of love, the superior must exercise a pedagogical function. The preservation of the Company requires its constant growth through the incorporation of new members. The superior has the responsibility of incorporating these new members into the life of the Company, forming each and all of

39 *Cons*MHSJ, II, 238, 614.
40 Ibid., II, 238.
41 A word Ignatius used often for the superior's guidance of the companions on the way of the Lord was *enderezar* (*Cons*MHSJ, I, 188; II, 74, 124, 147, 148, 161, 208, 217, 484, 572, 594). *Covarrubias*, p. 507, says that *enderezar* means to correct and turn in the right direction that which is going in a "squint-eyed" manner, outside the rule of order. A reason Ignatius gives for the manifestation of conscience is that all members of the Company should have the pure intention *to be endereçado* wherever they are turned, not seeking in anything *yr por su cabeça* (to go according to their own head) (*Cons*MHSJ, II, 161). Here, the horsemanship image is clearly implied.

94

them into men who are totally committed to the scope of our vocation. The process of this formation is described in the General Examen and in the Constitutions, Parts I, II, IV, and V. This process requires on the part of the superior a concern for the progress in personal perfection of Jesuits in formation and on the part of the companions a deep personal motivation to achieve sanctity. In the mind of Ignatius, of course, personal perfection is always ordered to the final end of the whole Company — the apostolic service of Christ.[42] Consequently, the introduction of motives of personal perfection is intended as a stimulus for individual Jesuits to fulfill all the exigencies of their apostolic vocation.[43]

The "ascetical" role of the superior is to help all the individual members to make progress in the virtues required to achieve mutual union and the most effective apostolic activity possible. The Ignatian vocabulary for this function of the superior consists of the expressions "to aid spiritually" (*ayudar en spíritu*) and "to lead to spiritual progress" (*aprovechar*).[44] Because mutual corporal and spiritual aid had enabled the first companions to be more effective apostles, the spiritual aid of the companions quite naturally became one of the primary duties of the superior. The dynamic mental structure of Ignatius made the word progress (*provecho*) a constant in his vocabulary.[45]

That the ideal of personal perfection is presupposed as the foundation of the pursuit of the apostolic end of the Company is

---

42 See above, ch. 1, pp. 34-37.
43 Ignatius states what he means by perfection in a passage in the Spiritual Exercises concerning swearing. The perfect rather than the imperfect may swear by creatures, because "the perfect by daily contemplation and by the illumination of their understanding reflect and meditate and contemplate God present in all creatures through His own essence and presence and power" (*SpEx,* [39]). For Ignatius, perfection meant to find God in all things. The superior must lead the companions in formation to this perfection, teaching them "to seek God our Lord in all things . . . loving Him in all things and all things in Him" (*a,* 168).
44 *Aprovechar: Cons*MHSJ, I, 133, 206, 251, 257, 258, 275; II, 72, 106, 133, 150, 155, 165, 166, 177, 192, 199, 260, 338, 354, 370, 382, 420, 544, 546, 602. *Ayudar en spíritu:* ibid., I, 385; II, 11, 37, 74, 76, 133, 147, 149, 156, 159, 165, 192, 208, 238, 350, 360, 382, 416.
45 It is interesting that in defining the opposite of this word — *desaprovechado* —, Covarrubias stresses that it means to be of no fruit or *servicio* (p. 885).

brought out by the insistence of Ignatius that very few men be admitted and only those who already demonstrate a high degree of virtue.[46] Persons who have no self-control are not for the Company, which is not so much directed towards training the undisciplined as to use those who already have self-mastery "for the divine service and the good of souls." [47]

To make certain that candidates for membership in the Company have the qualities demanded by the service of Christ through the aid of souls in companionship, Ignatius placed three "experiments," each lasting one month, at the beginning of the probation period. The first experiment consists of making the Spiritual Exercises in order to discern (or perhaps awaken) in the candidate the desire to follow Christ as closely as possible and "to be outstanding in every service of his eternal King and universal Lord." [48] The Exercises are precisely a school for the training of desire: liberation from "disordered affections" — the turning of one's desire in upon self and his own egotistical ends — so that he may be completely open to hear the word of God to him, desiring only His greater honor and glory.

Evidently presupposing that the candidate has made his election during the Spiritual Exercises to request admission into the Company, he then passes on to the other two experiments, intended to form his desire to serve Christ according to the particular end of the Company.[49] These experiments consist of spending one month in a hospital for the poor, doing the most

---

46 *Cons*MHSJ, II, 133, 139. But see also ibid., 226, and *Cons,* [657, 658] about those whom Ignatius' term "a large crowd" does not exclude.
47 Ibid., I, 139.
48 *SpEx,* [97].
49 In the preliminary document "De Collegiis et Domibus Fundandis" of 1541, Ignatius explains the reasons for the specific "experiments" chosen. Whereas in a monastic vocation a newcomer would be separated automatically from many occasions of sin through the tranquillity of life in a cloister, he will find no such protection in the Company, where he must "discurre de una parte en otra." Thus, while a person of bad habits and no perfection might eventually become perfect in the stable religious regime of a monastery, in the Company it is necessary to begin with candidates already "bien experimentado y mucho probado" before their admission. This is so because besides going everywhere, they will be required by their apostolic vocation to have relations with many people, good and bad; and such a vocation requires greater strength, wider experience and richer graces from God (*Cons*MHSJ, I, 60).

lowly work in order to become humble and, thus, to conquer the desire for worldly honors; then, a month of pilgrimage taking no money and having the living experience of bad food and uncomfortable lodgings, because one who cannot endure these could hardly persevere in the Company, which is committed to go anywhere in the world for the aid of souls.[50] It is through their personal perfection — their ability to find God in all things — that the companions will be enabled to carry out the scope of their vocation.

The means which Ignatius considered essential for the achievement of personal perfection was the continual abnegation of all self-seeking and self-love.[51] To express in modern language the profound intention of Ignatius, it would be more accurate to translate these words as liberation or interior freedom. Ignatian abnegation is not a negative concept; it is wholly positive. A man can achieve the spiritual liberty to find God in all things and to be totally open to His love only if he can break through the barriers of "unlove," of being turned in upon himself and imprisoned in self-love. Liberated from self-centered needs, the companion of Jesus can convert his whole being into the unique desire to serve Christ apostolically.[52]

But it is impossible to form an apostle truly able to serve Christ in the corporate apostolic work of a group of companions, unless he is led to spiritual freedom through profound

---

50 *Cons*MHSJ, I, II. This reason is developed in a Declaration in text A of the Constitutions which advises the superior that when at the beginning of probation it seems that a candidate may be lacking in the qualities required for the end of the Company, the experiments and trials should be increased (with the discretion of charity); because, unless candidates have great magnanimity and are prepared to suffer any extremes, they will not be apt for the work of the Company (*Cons*MHSJ, II, 300). The General Examen adds three more experiments: doing lowly work in the house; preaching and confessing and teaching catechism to children and to the poor (*ibid.*, 52-56).

51 *Cons*MHSJ, I, 6, 7, 50, 79, 286, 301; II, 64, 66, 167, 170, 178, 183, 194, 226, 238, 382. For a discussion of Ignatian ascetical practices and, especially, the negative meaning of *mundo* and *seculo* in his vocabulary, see J. Solano, "El carácter de 'oposición' en el seguimiento de Christo," *Gregorianum*, XXVII (1956), 484-506. In view of the contemporary concern with "secularization," a study in depth is needed of the vocabulary of Ignatius concerning secular values.

52 For a brilliant discussion of the "passage from need to desire," see D. Vasse, "Le temps du désir: Du besoin de la prière à la prière du désir," *Christus*, no. 54 (1967), 164-183.

liberation from self-seeking. When thus liberated, the companions are united in love with one another and with their superior
and are ready when the moment of execution has arrived to
obey perfectly the unifying command of the superior. For
Ignatius such spiritual liberty was identified with humility, the
condition for following Christ in the accomplishment of His
universal salvific mission.[53] Indeed, his coupling of humility
with other virtues in triplets and doublets manifests the intimate
relationship in the mind of Ignatius between the spiritual freedom achieved through the abnegation of self-love (identified
with humility) and spiritual progress,[54] personal perfection,[55]
obedience,[56] and love.[57]

Humility traditionally has been related to lowliness.[58] It requires breaking down the barriers to love of God and of others
thrown up by self-love and pride. Ignatius was convinced that
the effective way to achieve the lowliness of humility was
through the experience of poverty and humiliations, as he pointed
out repeatedly in the Spiritual Exercises. The particular examples
which Ignatius gives of humiliations and lowly occupations are
the result of his own cultural formation and in most instances
would no longer be effective.[59] His ruling intention to form the
desire of the Jesuit in formation so that he is truly totally committed to the scope of his vocation remains completely valid,

---

53 *SpEx,* [167]; *Cons*MHSJ, I, 27, 191, 254, 301; II, 68, 100, 167, 183,
194, 195, 199, 227.
54 *Cons*MHSJ, II, 66, 159.
55 Ibid., II, 94, 106, 118.
56 Ibid., I, 191; II, 68, 86, 100, 120, 167, 182, 194, 227.
57 Ibid., I, 18; II, 76, 166.
58 The first definition of *humilde* given by Covarrubias is "a son of common parents." He remarks that the word is derived from *humus*
— of the earth. So, as the earth is the most humble of the four elements, turned in on the center and turned away from the high
heaven, in like manner the humble man must hold to his condition
and walk along bowed toward the earth (p. 705). The image given
here perhaps suggests the cultural underpinning of the Ignatian rule
of "modesty" to keep the eyes lowered when speaking to high personages.
59 Many things found humiliating in Asian cultures today, for example,
carry no vestige of embarrassment in Western culture and conversely.
It is possible that the concrete experience of self-sacrifice in the
service of others would be the most effective means in the contemporary world to achieve the end sought by Ignatius through
humiliations and lowly occupations.

however. To be true to this intention today effective means to
the formation of this desire must be found in terms of the
"signs of the times."

In the Ignatian schema, a companion, through humiliations
and the performance of lowly occupations, is freed from *amor
baxo,* the love of self, in order to be completely open to *amor
alto,* the love of God.[60] In his legislation for the formation of
the companions, he provided for begging from door to door "for
greater humiliation and spiritual progress," [61] and for wearing
poor clothing "for greater humiliation." [62] Revelatory of the
conditioning of Ignatius' mental structure by his cultural formation is his preoccupation with clothes as a means of practicing mortification and humility.[63] The Castilian *caballero* had
undoubtedly been something of a dandy and just before his
period at Manresa, the renunciation of his knightly garments
in exchange for a beggar's rags was an important experience in
his spiritual evolution.[64] For all of the first companions too, the
experience of actual poverty in food and drink, clothing and
lodging had been of great influence in their spiritual development. Naturally enough, they felt that those who came after
them in the Company would best be formed as true companions
of Jesus by passing through the same trials.[65]

Ignatius often couples the word humility with lowliness
(*baxeça*) or with those lowly occupations (*officios baxos*)
which bring about the humiliation which can lead a man to
true interior humility.[66] The ascetical principle underlying the
performance of lowly work is stated clearly in the remark of the
Constitutions that companions in formation "should exercise

60 *DirEx,* 72.
61 *Cons*MHSJ, II, 66.
62 Ibid., II, 158, 163.
63 See ibid., II, 205, n. 14.
64 *FN,* I, 384-388.
65 *Cons*MHSJ, II, 64.
66 The manner of speaking of lowly occupations and those contrary to
the flesh must, of course, be understood in terms of the cultural patterns of the time of Ignatius. One must always balance such expressions with the humanistic principles enunciated by Ignatius in the
Principle and Foundation and the Contemplation for Obtaining
Love in the Spiritual Exercises. In his letter to Carafa, Ignatius
stated: "I hold most profoundly that God our Lord has created all
things of this present life for men and a fortiori for the best among
them" (*EppIgn,* I, 116).

themselves devotedly in lowly occupations, which help to receive the grace of God our Lord in as much as in doing them they exercise humility and charity" (*a*, 166). Ignatius was not devoted to difficult ascetical exercises for their own sake, and he recognized that if they were done out of pride or as a kind of spiritual weightlifting, they would be without true value. Rather, they should be the expression of the profound, personal love of Christ described in the Third Mode of Humility of the Spiritual Exercises, or a means to form the will of those in formation to desire only the service of Christ through the aid of souls in companionship.

Now, the being and union of the Company of Jesus can be realized here and now only in the moment of perfect obedience of all the companions to the unifying command of their superior. Thus, in the Ignatian documents the formation of humility in the companions through exercising them in humiliations and lowly occupations often is explicitly ordered to disposing them to perfect obedience. Obedience is grounded in humility — in the recognition of one's creaturely duty to submit to the will of God. On any level, obedience demands the conquest of the proud thrust to make oneself the center of his world and the arbiter of all his actions, through the humble recognition of his place in relation to God and to other men. In the Company this humble obedience is the sine qua non condition for the conservation in being of the union of the members with one another and with their head for the apostolic service of Christ. The finality of Jesuit obedience is union — mutual love.[67] It is clear then that by leading the companions to interior freedom from their own self-love to the true humility which unites them with Christ, the superior can unite them in an apostolic community of love.

Paternal
Government
In bringing to a close this chapter on exercising authority for apostolic love, it is necessary to consider the notion of paternal government. Many commentators have insisted that Ignatius' conception of the role of the superior was notably paternal.[68]

---

67 This must always be understood in studying Ignatian texts on obedience. See below, ch. 7.

68 For instance, Archbishop Roberts in his *Black Popes — Authority: its Use and Abuse* (London, 1954), p. 11, writes: "The key to Jesuit

An analysis of Ignatius' use of the words father (*padre*) and son (*hijo*) shows that this is a false interpretation.[69]

It is striking that the superior is never directly called the father of the companions. The word is used in a few of the preliminary documents in addressing Ignatius personally,[70] and in the formal address, "to you, reverend Father," in the vow formula.[71] The nearest Ignatius comes to thinking of the superior as a father to the companions, however, is in what might be termed an hortatory comparison. At the end of the Sixth Part of the Constitutions, he describes at length the attitude that the companions should maintain towards their superiors: great reverence for them, especially interiorly, considering and rever-

obedience — as to all Christian obedience — is the love of a son for a father; 'Let subjects from their hearts love their superiors as fathers — not from the motive of fear but in the spirit of love.' Many have said that before and since; nowhere better than in the Ignatian system of government is effect given to that principle of obedience." It is clear that the Archbishop's reflections were based more upon a personal conception of obedience and upon "classical" commentaries on Jesuit obedience, rather than upon a close study of the Ignatian vocabulary. The notion of paternal government entered into the terminology of the Company during the post-Ignatian period, as did other monastic terms. Research would probably show that reverence for "our father Ignatius" also had an effect on developing a "paternity" notion of the superior, especially the general. Claudius Aquaviva, fifth general of the Company (1581-1615), in his "Industriae" for superiors (found in *Thesaurus Spiritualis Societatis Iesu* [Vatican City, 1948], pp. 338-413) devotes his preface and first two chapters to a description of a paternal superior (pp. 338-355). The notion of paternal government, therefore, has long existed in the Company. Properly understood, this notion need have no overtones of "paternalism" and can even be interpreted in a way true to the intentions of Ignatius. Nevertheless, Ignatius' own vision of the superior was that of one of the companions (*alicui ex nobis*) given the responsibility of being the living principle of union of all, and his vocabulary and imagery is expressive of companionship rather than of paternity.

69 The word father in the Ignatian vocabulary most often refers to God the Father, and the great majority of its uses occur in the passages of Trinitarian mysticism in the *Spiritual Diary* (*Cons*MHSJ, I, 86-158). The pope is referred to as father six times in the preliminary documents, but always in a curial context (*Cons*MHSJ, I, 21, 70, 181, 182, 183, 184). The expression "our holy Father" is used only once in speaking of Paul III in texts A and B of the Constitutions (*Cons*MHSJ, 676).

70 *Cons*MHSJ, I, 77, 198, 220, 247, 302.

71 Ibid., I, 68; II, 200, 201.

encing Jesus Christ in them and loving them "as fathers in Christ" ("como a padres en el mesmo").[72] This one comparative phrase is hardly sufficient as a foundation upon which to erect the theory that Ignatius had a paternal notion of government.[73] That such a theory did develop in the Company was due rather to historical evolution in the Company after the death of Ignatius. The tremendous reverence felt by his companions towards him as the founder of the Company and, therefore, as their father in Christ was evident even during his lifetime.[74]

Ignatius, on the other hand, did not want members of the Company to call each other father or brother, as Gonçalves da Câmara recounts, adding that the custom of calling one another by personal names is *"muy antiguo"* in the Company.[75] It is true that he would allow companions to call their superiors "Father," [76] but the reason given for this is that they were priests.[77] It seems that the normal appellation for Ignatius himself in the house was "Iñigo." [78] He definitely did not wish to be addressed as "Paternity" and went so far as to give penances to poor Father Olave who did it out of forgetfulness and great reverence for Ignatius.[79] In the more formal context of letters the use of father was normal. However, it is clear

---

72 Ibid., II, 208.
73 Cf. J. M. Le Blond, "Obéissance et autorité dans l'église", *Études*, (Juillet-Août, 1966), pp. 100-114. "Une affection quasi filiale pourra colorer la rapport des sujets au chef; ce n'est pas en tant que Père que le chef sera chef" (p. 103).
74 For instance, Gonçalves da Câmara once wrote to Ignatius: "V.P. es mi Padre y mi Dios en la tierra" (*EppMixt*, II, 708). Cf. J. F. Gilmont, "Paternité et médiation du Fondateur d'Ordre", *RAM*, XL (1960), 393-426. He shows that the early Jesuits, in general, did not speak of Ignatius as having "fathered them in Christ" (pp. 397-398), but that the image of paternity gave way rather to the image of mediation of a divine mission (p. 403).
75 *FN*, I, 612-613.
76 Ibid., 729.
77 Ibid., I, 613, n. 33.
78 When Ignatius' nephew, Antonio de Araoz, arrived at the house in Rome to seek admission into the Company, he told the lay brother who was the porter that he wished to see his uncle. This must have been before the use of call-bells, because the brother turned and shouted, "Iñigo, Iñigo" (*FN,* I, 613).
79 Ibid., 738.

that the idea of paternity did not enter into the conception Ignatius had of the role of the superior as such.

This fact is verified by an analysis of the Ignatian use of the word son.[80] The companions are spoken of as sons of their superiors only four times. In the preliminary document "Constituta et Annotata," it is stated that according to his greater or lesser doubts concerning decisions that he must make, the superior should have greater or lesser "recourse to those who are his brothers and sons in the Lord." [81] In the Third Part of the Constitutions, treating of the pedagogical role of the superior with respect to those in formation, he is told that he must love his sons and pray and make sacrifices for his sons.[82] In the chapter on the qualities of the general in the Ninth Part, it is stated that he must combine necessary stric†ness with kindness and meekness and have fitting compassion for his sons.[83] Once more, these expressions indicate an implicit metaphor in contexts of exhortation to practice the love of a warm human relationship, rather than the presence in the mental structure of Ignatius of a paternal conception of government.[84]

A close study of the Ignatian vocabulary forbids one to conclude that the superior's role was paternal according to him. Rather, as has been demonstrated already, the general is an

---

80 Generally, the word son refers to Christ as Son of God, especially in the Trinitarian texts of the *Diary*. It appears in a consecrated curial use in many of the papal documents which call the companions the Pope's "beloved sons." In the preliminary documents the spiritual son of a confessor is mentioned twice (*Cons*MHSJ, I, 14, 58).
81 Ibid., I, 218.
82 Ibid., II, 165.
83 Ibid., 239.
84 It would be interesting to investigate the reasons why the notion of paternity was of such insignificance in the mental structure of Ignatius, but this would go beyond the scope of this study. One can at least conjecture that the death of his father when Ignatius was relatively young may have been an unconscious psychological influence. Furthermore, his integration into court life at an early age, where the relationship among *caballeros* was more that of companions may have counterbalanced the childhood formation in the paternalistic Basque culture. More important in determining his notion of the role of the superior as not being paternal was probably his profound awareness of the need to construct a new and non-monastic form of the religious life for the apostolic end of the Company.

emanation of the Company. He is a companion — "alicui ex nobis" as stated in the Deliberation[85] — to whom the other companions commit the responsibility of unifying all of them in a community of love in order to serve Christ more effectively through the aid of souls in companionship. Their obedience is offered to him not as is that of sons to their fathers, but as members of the whole body of the Company to their head who unites them all in community living and corporate apostolic action. This obedience is motivated not by the filial reverence of monks for the abbot, who is their father in Christ, but by the recognition that he who is the vicar of the vicar of Christ on earth commands them in the place of Christ.[86]

The Role of the Superior

The study of Ignatius' language describing the exercise of authority by the superior illuminates the mental structure underlying his notion of the role of the superior in the Company of Jesus. In the mental structure of Ignatius, authority, order, government, providence all were integrated in his notion of the love of the superior for his companions, a love which would reflect the active love of God ruling the universe through His providence and ruling the members of the Company of Jesus through the mediation of their head. Through the loving exercise of his authority, the superior would fulfill his role of being the living principle of union of all the companions, forming them into an apostolic community of love for the achievement of the "scope of our vocation" here and now. The Company as a whole is dynamic in the vision of Ignatius. It is a living body at the disposal of the Church, always on the way, always open to every appeal of the vicar of Christ, ever ready to go anywhere at anytime for the aid of souls. Similarly, Ignatius' conception of the role of the superior and of the exercise of authority was entirely dynamic, never fixed. All is ordered always to the ever greater apostolic service of Christ through the constantly renewed being of the Company at every new historical

85 *Cons*MHSJ, I, 4.
86 Gilmont, *op. cit.*, p. 408, argues that in spite of the difference of terminology, the essential vision of the superior in the minds of both St. Benedict and St. Ignatius was the same: "le supérieur tient la place du Christ médiateur".

moment, realized through whatever specific form of government and rule are demanded by the actual situation. The superior and the Company must be engaged in the never ending process of discernment of the will of God for the Company in the concrete circumstances here and now. In order fully to understand the role of the superior according to St. Ignatius, therefore, it is necessary to turn in the following chapter to an analysis of his language of discernment.

DECISIONS FOR APOSTOLIC LOVE—I:
THE VOCABULARY OF DISCERNMENT

BRINGING THE COMPANY TO BE HERE AND NOW by making a community of love to serve Christ through the aid of souls in companionship requires a constantly continuing discernment of the actual will of God according to the scope of our vocation in each new situation which confronts the Company. As has been shown in the study of the exercise of authority according to Ignatius, this discernment essentially bears upon three aspects of the life of the Company: (1) the determination of the will of God for the apostolic missions of the Company; (2) the determination of His will for conserving the union of all the members with one another and with their head; (3) the determination of His will for achieving the personal good and spiritual progress of each individual member in relation to the universal good of the whole body for the accomplishment of its apostolic end. Each determination is the result of a process of discernment issuing in the decision of the superior.

The Vocabulary of Discernment   In describing this process of discernment, Ignatius employs a vocabulary which reveals a definite structure of moving from the sometimes very laborious search for the will of God in the concrete to the moment of final determination of what His will

---

1 This structure was the product of Ignatius' own experience of making the Spiritual Exercises in order to find the will of God for him, and it is expressed throughout the manual of the Exercises, especially in the Rules for the Discernment of Spirits. See J. Clemence, "Le discernment des esprits dans les 'Exercices Spirituels' de saint Ignace de Loyola," *RAM,* XXVII (1951), 347-375; XXVIII (1952), 64-81, for an analysis of the psychological structure of these rules. For a discussion of the most significant modern commentaries and an effort to interpret them in terms of kerygmatic theology, see M. A. Fiorito,

seems to be in actual situations.[1] Certain words constantly recur in the Ignatian documents to refer to the psychological states involved in the discernment process. By far the most common term employed in this context is *pareçer: to have an opinion.* This is undoubtedly because of Ignatius' awareness, derived from living experience, of the extreme difficulty of arriving at complete certitude about the will of God, especially in the sometimes baffling complexity of concrete circumstances. *Pareçer* fundamentally means an opinion resulting from one's personal assessment of "appearances" — the particular aspects one sees in a concrete situation requiring discernment.[2]

By employing this term Ignatius emphasizes the fact that in many cases, especially in decisions concerning practical, contingent matters, the superior's final determination is not a position of objective certitude, but merely an opinion.[3] Since the

---

"Apuntes para una teología de discernimiento de espíritus," *Ciencia y Fe,* XIX (1962), 401-417; XX (1964), 93-123. See also J. C. Futrell, "Ignatian Discernment," *Studies in the Spirituality of Jesuits,* II (April, 1970), 47-88.

Little has as yet been published in English on discernment. Of particular value, however, are Rahner, Karl, S.J., *The Dynamic Element in the Church* (New York, 1964), and a résumé and commentary on Rahner's treatment by Avery Dulles, S.J., "Finding God's Will," *WL,* XCIV (1965), 139-152. Worth noting, also, are H. Coathalem, *Ignatian Insights,* trans. C. J. McCarthy (Taiwan, 1961), pp. 243-278; W. W. Meissner, "Psychological Notes on the Spiritual Exercises," *WL,* XCII (1963), 349-366; XCIII, 31-58, 165-199. The most complete treatment and bibliographies are in the articles on "Discernement" in the *Dictionnaire de Spiritualité,* compressed in the *New Catholic Encyclopedia,* X, 893-895; see also XIII, 580. There are some very fine articles on discernment in *Christus,* especially in no. 4 (1954). Innumerable other articles have been written in French and Spanish, but many of them are of little value. A work of considerable value and notable difficulty is G. Fessard, *La dialectique des Exercises Spirituels de Saint Ignace de Loyola* (Paris, Vol. I, 1956; Vol. II, 1966).

2 See *Covarrubias,* pp. 853-854.

3 *Cons*MHSJ, I, 40, 41, 44, 45, 47, 162, 164, 178, 189, 213, 215, 218, 219, 245, 254, 273, 275, 276, 314, 320, 321, 388, 391; II, 14, 19, 54, 66, 80, 112, 120, 152, 153, 156, 160, 162, 176, 178, 179, 183, 185, 186, 187, 188, 189, 204, 208, 212, 224, 227, 241, 242, 244, 250, 294, 300, 412, 418, 426, 464, 478, 488, 614, 616, 618, 622. *Pareçer* is employed also, however, for decisions in more important matters: *Cons*MHSJ, I, 51, 55, 57, 58, 161, 162, 165, 219; II, 4, 5, 14, 72, 110, 130, 132, 136, 145, 146, 147, 160, 214, 241, 242, 243, 288, 290, 312, 464, 466, 610, 612, 628, 678.

degree of certitude depends upon the clarity with which the various aspects of the situation appear as well as upon the lucidity and objectivity of the persons forming opinions, the possibilities of difference of opinion and of risk of error exist.

It is for this reason that Ignatius insists upon the necessity for the superior to seek the opinions of others before arriving at his decision and so much the more so in difficult or important matters, although for the sake of unity the final decision must depend upon his determination.[4] Ignatius saw the need in discernment to ground opinions solidly on evidence, rather than upon merely superficial impressions or feelings. For example, the preliminary document "Constitutiones de Missionibus" states that when the choice of missions requires consideration, the superior should consult those of the Company present, because he can make a better decision "hearing and reacting to (*sentiendo*) many different opinions based on reasons."[5] An interesting passage in the Constitutions remarks that the rector should choose theological commentaries to be studied by the scholastics after consulting "the opinion of intelligent persons" (*a*, 186). Ignatius was quite aware that a superior did not become an expert in all fields by right of office and that he must make up for his own limitations by seeking the advice of competent persons.

Ignatius saw also the necessity of the superior's conditioning the acceptability of his own opinion by the opinions the companions themselves would form when confronted with the evidence on the spot. In an instruction written for Broët and Salmerón concerning their conduct as nuncios to Ireland, Ignatius offered his own opinions, but he always left the final decision up to them.[6] Ignatius knew that from the distance of Rome he could easily be mistaken about the concrete circumstances of a situation which would condition discernment. As a matter of fact, his opinions in this instruction were based upon

---

4 *Cons*MHSJ, I, 39, 41, 163, 210, 215, 219, 245, 291, 292, 321, 337, 388; II, 186, 216, 464, 610, 624, 680, 690. The *pareçer* of others than the superior is sometimes invoked, also, in treating of the many situations requiring discernment in the concrete life of the Company: *Cons*MHSJ, I, 300, 383, 387, 395; II, 37, 135, 152, 153, 161, 195, 235, 236, 251, 650, 654, 684.

5 Ibid., I, 163.

6 *EppIgn*, I, 176-178.

his observation of relations of Church and state and monarchical structure in Spain and Italy and were quite false as regarded Scotland and Ireland.

The frequency of the word *pareçer* in the Ignatian vocabulary of discernment and decision manifests the true reason why the final opinion of the superior must be fully accepted by all the companions with perfect obedience. It is not because the superior's opinion is the best nor even necessarily correct. When, however, at the end of the time for discernment it becomes imperative to act now and there is no longer time to weigh and compare the various opinions concerning the action to be taken, the moment has come when the superior must carry out the responsibility given to him by the Company: his role of uniting his companions in an apostolic community of love as a corporate instrument of the universal redemptive mission of Christ acting in His Church. It is only through this final perfect obedience of all the companions in a house or in the whole world to the decisive opinion of their superior or the general expressed in his unifying command that the Company comes to be in the union of wills and of action which alone can enable the whole body to achieve its end of the service of Christ through the aid of souls in companionship here and now.

The repeated occurrence of the word *pareçer*, with its fundamental content of appearances, in the vocabulary of Ignatius reflects the strongly visual orientation of his mind. A basic element in his mental structure underlying his approach to discernment was an intense psychological drive always to seek more light or clarity for seeing the will of God in concrete situations. His whole life after his conversion could be described as an effort to seek more and more light in order to see clearly how to accomplish the will of God. The great illumination at the Cardoner is presented as a tremendous enlightenment of his understanding, and the mystical experiences of the *Spiritual Diary* are very often expressed in terms of light. The terms "to see," "light," and "clarity" frequently occur in contexts of discernment, both in the Spiritual Exercises and in the Constitutions.[7] The function of light and clarity in the discernment process of the superior is to enable his mind to see clearly all the

7 *SpEx*, [2, 176, 334, 363]; *Cons*MHSJ, II, 133, 134, 136, 137, 153, 166, 207, 214, 247, 249, 260, 272, 306, 650.

elements involved in coming to a decision. This involves a constant effort to overcome the obscurities and doubts which cloud clarity of judgment and to illuminate the concrete details of a situation in order to decide correctly.

This Ignatian thrust to more and more clarity manifests, once again, the dynamic structure of his mind. In order to arrive at a valid decision through the discernment of the will of God for the Company here and now, the superior must use all possible means to see clearly all the elements of a complex situation. He must strive for true spiritual liberty in order not to be blinded by prejudice or subtle self-love in forming his opinions. He must seek the help afforded by listening to the opinions of his companions. He must always be open to sometimes disconcerting and unexpected clarifications provided by living experience. A command of the superior delimits a field of action for the companions. The superior must "clarify the contours" of a situation through true discernment before declaring what the companions should do in ordering their life and action to the fulfillment of the "scope of our vocation."

Another basically visual word which Ignatius often employs in his vocabulary of discernment is *mirar*. The term radically means to look at, to regard attentively.[8] It has several nuances in the Ignatian documents, but it especially signifies the act of considering the evidence carefully in order to arrive at a correct decision.[9] Ignatius knew well that coming to a decision through discernment of the will of God demands deep reflection on all the elements in the actual situation: "observing attentively the circumstances," "reflecting upon the particular situations of times, places, and persons."[10] His language here again shows the very practical mental structure of Ignatius which excluded all a priorism and which remained open to the teaching of living experience indicating the will of God. Often, too, the word *mirar* signifies looking to the norms of discernment: "the greater service and honor of God and the good of the Com-

8 *Covarrubias,* p. 806. Cf. *Corominas,* III, 382.
9 *Cons*MHSJ, I, 45, 89, 90, 91, 94, 95, 96, 100, 117, 124, 255, 258, 387; II, 48, 104, 171, 174, 195, 196, 216, 217, 235, 236, 251, 302, 484, 490, 542, 616, 674, 688, 708.
10 *Cons*MHSJ, I, 45, 195, 248, 258, 387; II, 149, 152, 154, 196, 222, 490, 542.

pany," "the greater spiritual help of souls." [11] Ignatius' use of *mirar* once more manifests his great consciousness of the difficulty of discernment. It is necessary to pass from appearances — what first leaps to the eyes — to reflection in the light of the scope of our vocation.

A word of special importance in Ignatius' vocabulary of discernment is *sentir*. Due to the importance of this term, especially in the Spiritual Exercises and in the description of the mystical experience of Ignatius in the *Spiritual Diary*, it has been much discussed by the commentators.[12] The limitation of these commentaries is that they are one-sided or incomplete, chiefly being concerned with the use of *sentir* in a highly spiritual sense, but not with the specific purpose of trying to understand Igantius' use of the word in contexts concerning the superior's role of discernment.

---

11 *Cons*MHSJ, I, 162, 163, 195, 218, 219, 245, 248, 251; II, 104, 136, 174, 214, 215, 218, 221, 241, 242, 254, 268, 278, 400, 440, 454, 458, 472, 542, 566, 602, 682, 684.

12 P. Leturia, *Estudios Ignacianos,* 2 vols. (Rome, 1957), II, 153, states that in the spiritual life *sentir* is a kind of instinct which is not merely knowledge, but knowledge a thousand times relished and assimilated in such a way as to fill and satisfy the soul. H. Pinard de la Boullaye, "*Sentir, sentimiento, sentido* dans le style de saint Ignace", *AHSJ*, XXV (1956), 416-430, basing his analysis chiefly on the Spiritual Exercises, the *Spiritual Diary* and some of the letters, concludes that *sentir* gives primacy to intellectual, rational perception even in mystical experiences. In discernment contexts the word means that the intelligence clearly sees what corresponds to the will of God (p. 429). Analysis of Ignatius' use of the term shows that this rationalistic interpretation cannot stand. M. Giuliani, *Saint Ignace Journal Spirituel* (Paris, 1959), states that *sentir* refers to a properly spiritual knowledge which is neither purely intellectual nor purely affective (p. 45). Cf. his "Les motions de l'esprit," *Christus*, no. 4 (1954), 62-76. J. Lewis, *Le gouvernement spirituel selon saint Ignace de Loyola* (Montreal, 1961), pp. 50-53, insists upon the mystical content of the term and, while granting a role to intelligence, says that in *sentir* this role is played by what one may call a spiritual emotion. He calls it an experience of the soul infused by divine intervention surpassing the normal operation of human intelligence, while including it. F. Marxer, *Die inneren geistlichen sinne* (Freiburg, 1963), in his extensive treatment also stresses the mystical quality of *sentir*. M. Hernandez, "*Sentir* en el estilo literario de Ignacio de Loyola," *Manresa*, XXXVIII (1966), 349-370; XXXIX (1967), 5-18, using a method of vocabulary analysis similar to that employed in this study, concludes that previous commentators all failed to take into consideration the extreme density of the content of the word *sentir* in the vocabulary of Ignatius. His conclusions are similar to

Decisions — I: The Vocabulary of Discernment

The many nuances of the content of the word *sentir* in the vocabulary of Ignatius are grounded in its root meaning of sense experience.[13] He often uses the term, especially in the Spiritual Exercises, to refer to the five bodily senses and their sensations or their imaginative representation. Frequently, also, he employs *sentir* to describe emotional or spiritual states or reactions, a sense of the word which is heightened to an intense degree in Ignatius' use of the word in the *Spiritual Diary* to describe his mystical states. Here, *sentir* means a profound spiritual feeling endowing him with an intuition of deeper truths than can be expressed in clear concepts or words but which, nevertheless, often are guideposts for discernment.[14] The most common meaning of *sentir* in the vocabulary of Ignatius is that of understanding, but always with the stress upon affective, intuitive knowledge possessed through the reaction of human feelings to exterior and interior experience.[15] A triplet in the *Spiritual Diary* offers a clear example of this. God the Father had granted such a marvellous visitation to Ignatius that, like St. Paul, he did not know how to express it: "I knew, I felt or I saw, the Lord knows" (*conoçía, sentía o vía, Dominus scit.*).[16] Here, in a context of mystical experience, Ignatius expresses a unity of knowing, feeling and seeing, an experience of felt-knowledge so rich and integrated in consciousness that it is impossible sharply to distinguish the different psychological states involved. This intermingling of states in the ordinary process of discernment is expressed in the doublets "to feel or to form an opinion" (*sentir o pareçer*),[17] "to feel and know" (*sentir y cognoscer*)[18] and "to feel and judge" (sentir y juzgar).[19]

those presented in this chapter, although they concern interpreting the closing rubric of Ignatius' letters rather than his language of discernment.

13 *Covarrubias,* p. 933.
14 *Cons*MHSJ, I, 87, 90, 93, 94, 95, 96, 97, 98, 99, 100, 102, 103, 104, 105, 106, 107, 108, 109, 111, 112, 114, 115, 116, 119, 123, 124, 125, 127, 129, 130, 137.
15 *SpEx,* [2, 62, 263, 320, 322, 330, 334, 351]; *EppIgn,* I, 79, 81, 88, 92, 94, 103, 113, 115, 140, 167, 170, 171, 173 180, 190, 191, 195, 228, 278, 280, 281, 282.
16 *Cons*MHSJ, I, 102.
17 Ibid., I, 102, 108, 219; II, 32.
18 Ibid., II, 218, 289.
19 Ibid., I, 158, 384; II, 210, 640.

In human experience the act of forming opinions or of attaining knowledge or of making a judgment carries with it an emotional resonance; and, at times, the different psychological states are so intermingled as to become one — a kind of felt-knowledge. Ignatius' use of *sentir* in contexts of discernment signifies a concrete, psychological movement of personal consciousness involving at the same time the continuity of thoughts during reflection, the concomitant feelings constantly reacting to these thoughts (feelings which confirm or call into question the ideas arrived at through consideration) and the act of understanding which involves both the thoughts and the feelings.[20] The felt-knowledge resulting from the reaction of human feelings to evidence and reflection plays a determinative role in the formation of decisions. Ignatius' use of the word *sentir* manifests the remarkably concrete quality of his mental structure. Knowledge was not for him a merely intellectual adherence to abstract propositions, but a total human experience of understanding with all its emotional resonance.[21]

An analysis of the use of the word *sentir* in various contexts in the Ignatian documents makes clear that its meaning ranges in degree from ordinary human feelings reacting to a situation where these involve a minimum of understanding and could be inordinate, through the felt-understanding which accompanies and issues from careful reflection and prayer, to that aroused by mystical experience. Consequently, the meaning of *sentir* as used in the directly personal and mystical vocabulary of Ignatius should not be too rapidly read into contexts concerning the discernment of the role of the superior, where his intention is considerably more modest.[22]

---

20 *SpEx,* [6, 8, 10, 88, 130, 179, 184, 213, 235, 243, 313, 339, 536]; *EppIgn,* I, 82, 88, 101, 105, 107, 113, 122, 144, 146, 169, 171, 229; *Cons*MHSJ, I, 34, 39, 124, 159, 201, 204, 218, 219, 289, 290, 321, 384, 388; II, 32, 60, 110, 133, 151, 152, 163, 167, 172, 210, 216, 231, 234, 235, 245, 292, 316, 464, 488, 500, 525, 574, 590, 594, 596, 610, 626, 632, 640, 680, 686.

21 This awareness of Ignatius of the intimate intermingling of judging, feeling and willing underlies his insistence that there can be no perfect obedience unless the "will and feeling" (*querer y sentir*) of the obedient companion is conformed to that of the superior (*Cons*MHSJ, II, 167, 524, 290). See below, ch. 7.

22 The defect of J. Lewis's otherwise very useful study *Le gouvernment spirituel* . . . is precisely his effort to give an overly "mystical" in-

The validity of the *sentir* as felt-knowledge depends upon the validity of the reaction to evidence (*pareçer*) and of the prayerful reflection (*mirar*) which accompanies it, and therefore upon the completeness of the evidence as well as upon the spiritual liberty of the discerner.

Ignatius knew from experience that the *sentir* manifests a certain orientation, which may be more or less fluctuating. It is this orientation of *sentir* which is the object of discernment — to what does it finally lead: the love of God or self-love? [23] In exercising his role of discernment, then, the superior must pay close attention to the orientation of his feelings. Through the spiritual liberty gained from making the Spiritual Exercises the superior should have formed within himself the unique desire to praise and serve God so that his feelings will react spontaneously according to the norms of discernment of the Company. This fundamental orientation of *sentir* to the service and glory of God as the affective ground of discernment is sometimes expressed by Ignatius as "to feel in our Lord" (*sentir en el Señor nuestro*).[24] For example, a passage in text A of the Constitutions states that the superior may send more than two companions on the same mission "as the unction of the Holy Spirit inspires him, or as he feels in the divine majesty would be better or more fitting." [25] This text is particularly interesting for the apparent distinction it makes between divine inspiration and the felt-understanding — even "in the divine majesty" — which is the normal process of discernment. The *sentir* supposes a prayerful reflection resulting in the feeling that this

terpretation of the role of the Holy Spirit in the government of the Company.

23 This need to discern the orientation of *sentir* is clearly expressed in the Spiritual Exercises: *SpEx*, [179, 183, 213, 313, 336, 338]. Ignatius describes this analysis of the orientation of feelings in the *Spiritual Diary*. He remarked that he felt (*sentía*) that it would be more pleasing to God to conclude his election immediately; but at the same time he felt a contrary orientation in his will (*sentía en mi volición*): that he wanted God to give in to his desire to finish at a time of great consolation. Discerning the contrary orientation of these feelings — self-seeking and desiring only to please God (*en sentir mi inclinaçión y por otra parte el plazer de Dios nuestro Señor*) — Ignatius began to seek only to please God (*ConsMHSJ, I, 124*).

24 *EppIgn,* I, 101, 122; *Cons*MHSJ, I, 204, 219; II, 245, 316, 594.

25 *Cons*MHSJ, II, 596.

course of action is better and will be more effective for the divine glory and the universal good, the norms which are mentioned in the phrase immediately before the citation. The *sentir* is not conceived by Ignatius, therefore, as a direct result of inspiration from the Holy Spirit, though he admits the possibility of this, while distinguishing it from the *sentir* way of discernment.[26]

In the vocabulary describing the superior's role of discernment, then, *sentir* signifies felt-knowledge based upon the reaction of human feelings to reflection on the various elements found in the concrete situation, felt-knowledge, which is integrated into a larger structure of feelings entirely oriented towards the end of the Company: the praise and glory of God through the apostolic service of Christ. This *sentir* is an affair of existence before being an affair of reflex awareness. It is a radical attitude of soul, a "bent of being," a profound, dynamic orientation of the person towards God. Rather than a conscious judgment, this radical attitude is a basic, personal commitment, more complete than ideas possessed by intellectual knowledge, more solid than the fluctuations of superficial emotions, which will lead the superior to react spontaneously according to the scope of our vocation. *Sentir* is of such enormous importance in the discernment process because it is the vital testimony of human feelings to the orientation of thoughts and considerations and judgements to the service and glory of God. The discernment issues in the felt-knowledge that the decision taken is solely for the service of Christ through the aid of souls in companionship and not for ends of subtle self-seeking. Obviously, to play its role in discernment, the *sentir* must be that of a man who has attained true spiritual liberty which must be con-

---

26 It is perhaps significant that this text is identical with the parallel passage in text *a* (*Cons*MHSJ, II, 220), except for the addition of the *sentir* phrase. Possibly, experience had taught Ignatius the danger of having superiors rely too exclusively on the unction of the Holy Spirit. The relationship of divine grace and *sentir* is indicated in the legislation that in case of a tied vote during a general congregation, the votes of the general and provincials will be given more weight, because one may hope that in view of their greater responsibilities God will give them more abundant divine aid to feel and say (*sentir y dezir*) what will be for His service (*Cons*MHSJ, II, 680). This text refers not to direct inspiration by the Holy Spirit, but rather to the "grace of state." See below, ch. 6, pp. 129-131.

stantly verified through prayer. This, too, is why the superior must control his own *sentir* by listening to the *sentir* of his companions — to confront his own felt-knowledge with theirs, and all the more so according to the importance of the decision to be made.[27] This *sentir* is, finally, the most important personal element in arriving at a decision. In the Ignatian vocabulary of discernment *sentir* does not signify supernatural illumination of understanding furnishing the content of a decision. Like *pareçer* — the opinion arrived at through mature consideration of all the aspects seen in the situation — *sentir* is subject to human error. The disposition of spiritual liberty of the superior can be perfect, but if the evidence of judgment is inadequate, the decision will not be correct. Every effort must be made to gather complete data for reflection and *sentir*. Above all, the superior, more than anyone else, is obliged to be constantly on his guard against subtle self-seeking and always to strive for that spiritual liberty which is the end of the Spiritual Exercises.

The act of determination or decision is signified in the Ignatian vocabulary of discernment by the term of judge (*juzgar*). This involves taking into consideration all the aspects in the actual situation to be judged: the *pareçer* arrived at through observation of the concrete circumstances, the *sentir* accompanying the prayerful *mirar* upon all the available evidence in the light of the "scope of our vocation," and the confrontation of the opinion and feelings of the superior with those of other companions for mutual discernment. All these help him to arrive at the final step of the discernment process: the judgment which determines the will of God here and now.

Juzgar is used by Ignatius in speaking of concrete decisions of the superior for the life and action of the Company: admission of new members, dismissal of the unfit, the ordering of the temporal and spiritual lives of the companions and determination of the apostolic works of the Company.[28] It is often

---

27 *Cons*MHSJ, I, 204, 218, 219; II, 172, 216, 488, 626, 680.
28 *Cons*MHSJ, I, 7, 37, 47, 53, 56, 163, 189, 190, 191, 195, 247, 253, 272, 284, 304, 305, 314, 323, 375, 384, 396; II, 11, 50, 64, 110, 132, 133, 143, 144, 145, 149, 151, 154, 159, 162, 172, 176, 177, 181, 185, 205, 207, 211, 212, 216, 219, 225, 234, 238, 241, 242, 243, 244, 247, 282, 290, 292, 316, 324, 332, 348, 350, 392, 394, 434, 470, 474, 478,

recalled that the superior should ask for the advice of the companions who, he judges, can help him in discernment, although after this consultation it is his responsibility to make the final unifying decision himself.[29] Similarly, the companions should represent to the superior their spiritual "motions" to go on a mission, so that he may better consider and judge for the greater service and praise of God (*a*, 216). Discernment of the will of God in concrete situations requires examination of all the evidence, and Ignatius was convinced that the workings of the Spirit in the individual person presented evidence of the highest importance for making a judgment. He saw that it is impossible to judge truly what is not completely known, and so he insisted that the superior know all his companions intimately, consult experts in matters where he is not personally competent and leave decisions in concrete circumstances to the man on the spot who knows the actual situation.

The norms of judgment involved in the scope of our vocation often are made explicit in texts speaking of the *juzgar* of the superior: the service and praise and glory of God, the personal good of individual companions and the universal good of the whole body of the Company, the greater apostolic aid of souls, and the like.[30] The term that appears most often as the norm of discernment is *conveniente*. The word signifies useful, suitable or conformable. The strongest nuance of meaning in the vocabulary of Ignatius is that of the effectiveness of means to ends and he at times employs the doublet *conveniente o necesario*. On occasion, Ignatius states the object of the term as one or other of the expressions of the end of the Company, but most frequently the word occurs without any explicit object since the service of Christ through the aid of souls in companionship is always understood. The concrete mental structure of Ignatius is evident in his constant concern that the norms of discern-

---

480, 484, 485, 490, 500, 502, 504, 546, 556, 558, 560, 618, 626, 628, 640, 642, 674, 680, 686, 720.

29 E.g., *Cons*MHSJ, I, 14, 337, 377; II, 132, 172, 324, 626, 680.

30 It is notable that in text B of the Constitutions there are many more explicit invocations of these norms than in the earlier texts. Since these norms are always implicitly understood, one wonders whether this addition might not reflect Polanco's concern that official documents be "edifying" (*Cons*MHSJ, I, 296).

ment be applied always to the real situation.[31] Judgment issues in the unifying command of the superior which brings the Company to be here and now in the moment of perfect obedience of all the companions. Judgment is the term of a process of reflection,[32] which involves a final free determination of decision, which may well be erroneous.[33] Judgment is subject to human error, especially because of the difficulty of liberating desires from self-seeking, and consequently of avoiding illusions. Good judgment requires constant openness to the teaching of living experience. It is arrived at through repeated prayerful reflection, going over judgments again and again in view of the concrete circumstances seen in the light of the norms derived from the apostolic end of the Company. The interaction of judgment and freedom underlies the insistence of Ignatius upon the necessity of conformity of the "wills and judgments" of all the companions with those of the superior for perfect obedience.[34] Otherwise, there can be no true unity, that profound, interior union which is the being of the Company.[35]

The study of the terms *pareçer, sentir* and *juzgar* in the Ignatian vocabulary shows that there tended to be considerable overlapping of their significance. The concreteness of the mental structure of Ignatius caused him to grasp the data of living experience in their inter-relatedness and to express these insights in language where the content of many words and expressions became quasi-identical. Thus, the functions of *pareçer, sentir* and *juzgar* in the discernment process often are expressed as very similar. Ignatius was aware that his own psychological experience in discerning involved a not easily distinguishable intermingling of opinions, formed from the observation of the evidence seen, with the play of human feelings reacting to these opinions and to prayerful reflection upon them, and with the formation and reformation of judgments of what seemed to be the actual will of God in the concrete situation. An examination of the texts indicates that Ignatius' use of one or the other of these terms in a passage was more likely the result of a certain

---

31 See below, pp. 149-150.
32 *Cons*MHSJ, II, 600.
33 *SpEx,* [346].
34 *Cons*MHSJ, I, 7; II, 167, 168, 199, 522.
35 Ibid., II, 229.

consciousness of which element seemed strongest at a given moment — opinion, feeling or judgment — rather than of an explicit intention to emphasize the difference of these states. Nevertheless, there is a progression from *pareçer* through *mirar* and *sentir* to *juzgar* in Ignatius' language of discernment.

In weighing all the various factors which enter into the discernment of the will of God in an actual situation, the superior is confronted with a constant tension between the personal good of individual members of the Company and the common good of the whole body in relation to its apostolic end. In the mental structure of Ignatius and in his language, this tension is expressed as a dialectic of the "particular good" (*bien particular*) and the "universal good" (*bien universal*).[36] This dialectic in the role of discernment of the superior is simply the reflection of the concrete existence of the Company made up of individual men who share the same vocation to serve Christ through the aid of souls in companionship and, therefore, to live and act as one body. The apostolic end of the Company means that its whole being and its own universal good are "ordered to the greater divine glory and the greater universal good and the greater spiritual progress of souls." [37] Consequently, the guiding principle in the choice of apostolic ministries is that "the good in as much as it is more universal is more divine" (*a*, 217). This is applied concretely in the declaration that in choosing apostolic works, all things being equal, "having certain works of more universal good which extend help to more persons, and other works which are more particular" and finding it impossible to do both, the more universal apostolate should be preferred (*a*, 219).

The end of the Constitutions is to "aid the whole body of the Company and its individual members" (*a*, 129). The basic principle of the dialectic is repeated in slightly different phras-

---

36 Ibid., I, 163, 198, 211, 251; II, 129, 144, 146, 149, 192, 199, 215, 217, 219, 236, 260, 294, 316, 348, 354, 426, 544, 558, 610.
37 The *bien universal* of the Company, of the Church and of souls is quasi-identical with the divine service, the aid of souls and the praise and glory of God in the Ignatian vocabulary expressing the end of the Company. See ch. 1.

ing in text B in the discussion of the admission of candidates:
"see to it that in admitting a person charity towards the individual does not prejudice universal charity, which should
always be given priority as more important for the glory and
honor of Christ our Lord." A member should be dismissed if
it is judged that for him to remain in the Company would be
"against the good of the one to be dismissed or against the
good of the Company or against the good of other persons outside of it" (*a,* 144). The elements of the dialectic are present
here and are made explicit in the final determination of whether
or not to dismiss a member: "always keeping before the eyes
the greater glory of God and the common good and the personal
good in as much as is possible, decide whether or not to dismiss
him" (*a,* 146). The universal good is quasi-identified with the
glory of God, while the particular good may have to be sacri-
ficed, at least in part, to the well being of the whole body for
the achievement of its apostolic end. The dialectic is explicit
once more in the provision that the general has the authority to
send members to study or recall them from it or change their
location "as he judges is most conducive to their personal good
or the universal good of the Company" (ibid., 215).[38] It is
stated in text A that the manner of giving corrections and
penances is left to the discreet charity of the superior who
should adapt them to the temperament of the persons "and
universal and personal edification of them for the divine

---

38 In cases where the common good is not clearly involved, that the
personal good alone is an adequate motive for decision is clear in the
provision in text B that a scholastic with the proper qualities may
be given a dispensation to study the languages of Scripture even before finishing the study of theology, "*quando convenga para el bien
común o particular*" (*Cons*MHSJ, II, 426). The use of the coordi-
nate conjunction is significant. The conviction of Ignatius that in
situations of conflict the universal good must always take priority
over the individual good in no sense indicates an impersonal or
mechanistic view of the persons who through their mutual love and
action form the body of the Company. On the contrary, the personal good and the universal good usually should arrive at a synthesis in the scope of our vocation. The principle of the priority of the
universal good is so far from being automatic that even in the
choice of apostolic ministries, reflection upon the concrete circumstances of an actual situation can lead to the decision to undertake
a work which is of less universal extension than its alternative
(ibid., II, 219).

glory." [39] Text B declares that the superior may give commands under obedience when he judges that this is strongly indicated "for the personal good of each one or for the universal good." [40]

The role of the superior essentially is to unify all the companions in an apostolic community of love. His role of discernment is directed to the practical realization of this mutual union in the concrete life and apostolic action of the Company. This discernment is necessary precisely to resolve the dialectic of the personal good (and judgment) of the individual members and the universal good of the whole Company in a decision synthesizing these goods in as much as possible. He is one companion to whom the others have given the responsibility of uniting them in the service of Christ through the aid of souls in companionship. His final decision at the end of the process of discernment, therefore, is the principle of union of all the companions in an apostolic community of love here and now, a union that comes to be in actual reality in the moment of perfect obedience of all the members of the body of the Company to the command of their head.

---

39 *Cons*MHSJ, II, 354.
40 Ibid., 558.

DECISIONS FOR APOSTOLIC LOVE—II: THE STEPS IN DISCERNMENT

THROUGH THE STUDY of the Ignatian vocabulary of discernment, it is possible to discover the basic structure of the discernment process. This structure, as it is manifested in the Constitutions in describing the superior's role of discernment, was arrived at by Ignatius and his companions through their years of experience of seeking the will of God together.[1] The decision of the seven companions at Montmartre to take the vow of 1534 was the result of a series of discussions which must have been analogous to a mutual manifestation of conscience, each one quite simply and openly declaring what he found to be the "motions" of the Holy Spirit within him. Through sharing their subjective interior experiences, the companions were enabled to arrive at a common judgment of the will of God for them in the objective situation in which they found themselves.

Basic Procedure in Discernment   The same method was used by the companions in 1539, when they decided to found the religious order of the Company of Jesus. As presented in the Deliberation this method consisted of four steps, which underwent further refinement when it proved particularly difficult to arrive at a decision: (1) there is a common basis upon which all are agreed: to seek the will of God according to the scope of their apostolic vocation; (2) the individual members of the group have differences of opinion about how to achieve this end, it is noted; (3) each one gives himself up to assiduous prayer and meditation, seeking divine enlightenment; (4) using all human means to find natural enlightenment also, the companions come together to share the

---

1 This method is essentially a transposition of the methods of Election of the Spiritual Exercises to communal discernment of spirits by an entire group in order to arrive at a common decision.

results of their personal discernment in the process of mutual discernment.[2] The companions arrived without difficulty at their first decision: that they should remain together in one body, taking care of one another's needs with mutual comprehension and aid, in order more effectively to aid souls. The question of whether vowing obedience to one of their number would be a necessary means to this end gave the companions much more difficulty in arriving at a common decision, and this was the occasion of further refinement of their method of mutual discernment: (1) they gave themselves even more intensely to prayer for light "to seek joy and peace in the Holy Spirit concerning obedience"; (2) during this period of personal prayer and discernment they did not talk to one another, but sought personal light from the Holy Spirit; (3) taking care to achieve as complete objectivity as possible, each one, after this personal prayer and discernment, decided in all freedom his own conclusion concerning the question of obedience as a means to the greater future service of God and the conservation of the Company; (4) during the period of mutual discernment each one with all simplicity and frankness first stated the reasons against obedience which he saw, and then outlined the reasons he saw in favor of it.[3] Through this mutual discernment the companions arrived at the decision to vow obedience to one of their number, and, thus, to found the Company of Jesus.

The structure of discernment revealed in the Ignatian documents concerning the life and action of the Company is the result of these experiences of discernment. To determine the will of God for the Company here and now a procedure is followed which involves a permanent base, three steps of discernment, and the final decision. The permanent base is the scope of our vocation, the commitment of all the individual members of the Company to consecrate all their lives and efforts to achieve the end of the whole body: the service of Christ through the aid of souls in companionship. This base provides the unchanging norm of discernment which controls all decisions concerning means to achieve this end here and now. With the increase in numbers of companions and their ever-wider dispersal, it is possible and often inevitable that there will be con-

2 *Cons*MHSJ, I, 2-3.
3 Ibid., I, 5.

siderable difference of judgment concerning these means.[4] For this reason at the end of the process of discernment it is the superior alone who must make the final decision; which all the companions must accept as their own through perfect obedience. Only in this way is it possible for the Company to come to be through the union of all its members with one another and with their head for apostolic action in companionship. It is through the exercise of his role of discernment that the superior becomes the active principle of unity in the Company and fulfills his essential role of making an apostolic community of love.

The three steps in the discernment process are: (1) prayer for light from the Holy Spirit, which involves prayerful reflection on all the aspects of the decision to be made and discernment of the "motions" experienced during this reflection: the "discernment of spirits"; (2) gathering all possible evidence for judgment, which demands not only careful observation of all the concrete circumstances (persons, places, time, etc.), but also consultation of others either because of their special competence or their particular access to the evidence; (3) effort to find confirmation of the indicated determination of the concrete will of God, sometimes through appeal for papal approval in matters of extraordinary importance, but normally through the attainment of mutual contentment of the superior and the companions in this judgment.

At the end of this process the decision is made, but it is still open to verification through living experience and, if proved mistaken, subject to further discernment. This study has revealed repeatedly the central position of the teaching of living

---

4 The companions had their first experience of inability to reach unanimous agreement during the discussions following the Deliberation. Bobadilla disagreed with the decision of the others that they should take a vow to teach catechism to children (*Cons*MHSJ, I, 12). The immediate practical solution to this difficulty was the decision that in the future important matters would be decided by majority vote (ibid., I, 13). As companions were sent far away on missions, the principle was explicated that decisions were to be left to the judgment of the majority of the companions who could be called to Rome or contacted by letter, as if the whole Company were present (ibid., I, 23-24). It was through this experience of the practical necessity of a unifying final decision at the center of the dispersed Company in order to maintain its unity that the role of the superior became more and more extended in power of decision.

experience in the mental structure of Ignatius. It was in actual life-situations and through natural and supernatural experience that he sought to discern the concrete will of God, rather than in some system of a priori principles from which he deduced practical conclusions. Nothing is more characteristic of Ignatius than this spiritual liberty, this total openness to the will of God manifested in the workings of divine providence in daily life. In the Company a major role of the superior is, with the help of prayer and the light of the Holy Spirit, precisely this weighing of the experience of all the members of the Company — the "circulation" of the whole body — in order to determine the will of God for the united life and apostolic action of all.

It is necessary to devote some consideration to Ignatius' understanding of each of these three steps of the discernment process. In practice, these are not three successive steps, but they are intermingled and progress together towards the final determination.[5] In studying the steps individually, one must never lose sight of their alternating rhythm in practice.

The tremendous importance Ignatius placed upon the role of prayer in the discernment process is clear from the entire structure of the Spiritual Exercises, which provide a complete program of meditations and contemplations aimed toward the crucial election of a person's state of life — the discovery of his vocation wherein he should serve God. It is equally clear in the *Spiritual Diary* which gives an intimate record of Ignatius' personal manner of praying for light when making an important decision. In the process of mutual discernment both the superior and the companions must pray for light and discern "spirits" with their eyes fixed uniquely upon God, so as to arrive at a judgment in true spiritual liberty, desiring only the divine service. This need to pray in discerning is frequently made explicit in the documents.[6] It is implicit in the words Ignatius often uses to express the need for careful reflection upon the evidence in order to judge in the light of the norms of divine service, the aid of souls, the praise and glory of God,

---

5 Cf. *Cons*MHSJ, I, 13-14, 218-219; II, 146, 216, 316, 324-326.
6 Ibid., I, 12, 13-14, 190, 204; II, 136, 146, 151, 164, 216, 222, 251, 316, 324-326.

etc. After *mirar,* the most common term in the Ignatian vocabulary for this prayerful reflection is discretion.[7]

In studying the role of discernment of the superior, it is important to notice that Ignatius does not assert that prayer — even highly mystical prayer — will provide a divine guarantee that the final decision taken is certainly correct. It is true that prayer holds primacy of place in the process of discernment; nevertheless, Ignatius insists upon the necessity of using natural means "to cooperate with divine grace according to the order of the supreme providence of God our Lord" (*a,* 252-253). Indeed, the whole enormous labor to frame Constitutions and to give human organization to the Company was based upon the principle stated in the *Prohemio* of text B that "the sweet disposition of divine providence seeks cooperation of His creatures."[8] An extremely tortured and complicated passage at the end of text *a* of the General Examen explains Ignatius' conception of the relation between divine grace and human means (*a,* 125).[9] He notes that were God to give equal grace to two persons, one of whom possessed great natural gifts which the other lacked, the former would be a more effective instrument for the aid of souls. While it is true that our complete good consists in the gift of grace, it is, nevertheless, true also that natural gifts are of very great service in helping others. We should, therefore, make every effort to develop our natural gifts in order better to draw people to God who helps and works in all, so that His divine Majesty may be praised and glorified in all things.

In exercising his role of discernment then, the superior must avail himself of all possible means to see all the aspects of the actual situation: discussion with competent consultors and with

---

7 Ibid., II, 148, 151, 163, 164, 166, 272, 278, 290, 332, 366, 368, 424, 426, 434, 474, 546, 700. *Discreta caritas:* ibid., II, 316, 322, 326, 336, 365, 546. *Discreto zelo:* ibid., II, 354. Other words and expressions signifying prayerful reflection are: *discernir,* ibid., I, 39; II, 222, 290, 306; *todo ponderase,* ibid., II, 4; *muy pesada y consideramente:* ibid., 294; *muy ponderada,* ibid., 314; cf., 316, *mucha consideración y peso en el Sor. Nro.,* ibid., 308.
8 Ibid., II, 260.
9 A reasonably clear English translation of this passage is given in *The Jesuits: Their Spiritual Doctrine and Practice* by J. de Guibert, translated by W. J. Young (Chicago, 1964), pp. 147-148.

those companions involved in the matter to be decided, attention to all the concrete circumstances, consideration of the teaching of living experience, and the effort to find confirmation of his judgment. Throughout this entire process he must seek divine light in prayerful reflection on all the evidence available to him. But he should not expect a divine illumination giving him infallible assurance of the truth of his judgment. Even in the *Spiritual Diary* when Ignatius records the profound "intense movement from within" never to change his election of total poverty, he adds that this is "for my part" and is subject to confirmation by the companions.[10] Indeed, his mystical experiences, like those of other saints, were characterized by great light and interior understanding which was inexpressible in ordinary human concepts and words; and he himself warned of the necessity of distinguishing an authentic divine visitation from the consequent "afterglow," when one's own *propositos y pareceres,* which are not immediately from God, come to the fore.[11]

What did Ignatius think the superior could hope for from prayer in carrying out his role of discernment? Not a "revelation" of content of a decision, but the light necessary to achieve spiritual liberty: to discern the orientation of his desires — toward subtle self-seeking or uniquely toward the praise and service of God. This, indeed, is the aim of the entire Spiritual Exercises: to arrive at interior freedom in order to direct one's life, all one's desire, uniquely toward the fulfillment of the will of God, which requires liberation from all self-oriented desire.[12] The exercitant prays for interior knowledge of Christ, of those things within him and without him which limit his liberty to find and follow the will of God, of the true life to which God calls him. This knowledge is "interior knowledge," which rejoins the Ignatian use of *sentir,* directed towards recognizing the orientation of desire, rather than toward the revelation of the Election.[13] Making the Election supposes that one has

10 *Cons*MHSJ, I, 105.
11 *SpEx,* [336]; see *EppIgn,* I, 105-106.
12 *SpEx,* [1, 23].
13 Revelation of the content of the decision is the first time of Election; but the examples Ignatius gives are the vocations of St. Paul, which involved a lightning bolt and a direct vision of Christ, and of St. Matthew who looked upon the face of Jesus and listened to His

gathered all the necessary evidence for its content and that the discernment is of his *sentir* with regard to this content. For example, if he is confronted with three specific choices, he may be able to eliminate one or all of them through prayerfully discerning the orientation of his thoughts and feelings because he sees that this choice would issue from self-love. He may also determine clearly upon one of these choices because in deciding to commit himself to it he finds that he is oriented only to the will of God in peace.[14]

The Spiritual Exercises are directed towards the election of a permanent state of life, the discovery of one's own vocation, his personal identity. If even here Ignatius looked to prayer as the source of light upon the orientation of one's desires and the formation of true spiritual liberty to choose only the greater praise and service of God, then it is clear that what the superior must seek in prayer in carrying out his role of discernment is also this light upon his desires, rather than the revelation of the content of the decisions he must make concerning the life and action of the Company. This prayer will enable him to eliminate from consideration judgments which are seen to originate in self-seeking or personal prejudice. It will not reveal to him which is the best among numerous practical possibilities nor even that his judgment is not mistaken, even though he makes it with true spiritual liberty and with the unanimous agreement of the companions. Through his prayerful reflection upon the

human voice (*SpEx*, [284]). All of Ignatius' rules and directions suppose that such a revelation is not the normal result of the Spiritual Exercises, but that the Election must be made through the discernment of the orientation of one's desires in spiritual liberty.

14 Without undertaking here the vast study of the anthropology of Ignatius which is necessary to understand his vocabulary of the "motions of the good spirit and the bad spirit," it is possible to see in this presentation his manner of expressing the difference between the thoughts which a man freely and deliberately brings to consciousness and those, whether good or bad, which arise spontaneously. Ignatius' Rules for the Discernment of Spirits are directed toward discerning the orientation of these spontaneous thoughts (*SpEx*, [313]). Thoughts (*pensamientos*) for Ignatius were not abstract ideas, but the total experiential complex of thoughts with their concomitant feelings and the desire that issues therefrom. Discernment of the orientation of these thoughts would lead one to interior knowledge of his radical attitude of soul, his fundamental desire, which structures and reveals his personal identity, his vocation from God.

evidence which he must gather from every possible source, the superior is given interior testimony that his final judgment is made in a state of true spiritual freedom and with the unique desire to serve Christ apostolically. What the superior may hope for from prayer, then, is the achievement of a basic existential attitude of total commitment to the scope of our vocation as the ground and norm of all his decisions. This is why prayer is of primary importance in the process of discernment. For the content of the decision, however, the superior must employ all the means given by Ignatius for gathering evidence.

The role of the superior is to make a community of love for the service of Christ through the aid of souls in companionship. His function is essentially ordered to the universal good of the Company. According to the "sweet dispositions of divine providence," he, therefore, may hope to receive graces ordered to this service of the Company, graces which are properly charismatic. Traditionally, this charism has been called the "grace of state." [15] Ignatius refers to this grace of state in a number of texts. However, the language of Ignatius in invoking the grace of state offers no basis for an interpretation that he believed that the superior, by reason of his office, would be given a sort of infallibility of judgment. Spiritual writers of later ages sometimes tended to suggest that the superior almost automatically declared the certainly best possible decision because of a special charism. Ignatius, on the contrary, presents the grace of state of the superior as analogous to that grace which is promised

15 The notion of "grace of state" appears clearly in the *Ordenamiento* of Olmedo (1445), which interpreted certain laws of the *Siete Partidas*. It spoke thus of the king: "whose heart is in the hands of God and which He guides and inclines to all that pleases Him" (GG, II, 988). J. Cameron, *Images of Authority* (New Haven, 1966), commenting on the widespread notion of the grace of state of temporal and ecclesiastical authorities during the Middle Ages remarks: "There is nothing strictly absurd in the idea that grace should always correspond to office. Indeed, it would seem to follow from the grounding of the Church's hierarchical structure (in its essential features) in the divine will that grace should correspond to office. If the grace that belongs to the office does not manifest itself, this can be either because its workings are hidden but nevertheless perfectly real or because the grace that belongs to the office has been forfeited by human sin" (pp. 15-16).

to each man which is sufficient to lead him to God within his state of life. God's grace of enlightenment operates in all men, "because it is proper to God our Lord ceaselessly to give understanding"; and we should always presume that "what the Lord of the whole world works in rational souls" is to give us greater glory or, at least, to keep us from evil.[16] If a man's state of life involves responsibility for others, then, indeed, this grace is ordered also to this duty and, consequently, is charismatic.

The language of Ignatius is remarkably modest.[17] Because provincials and the general have greater responsibilities, it may be hoped that God will give them more grace.[18] Ignatius' notion of the grace of state of the superior is integrated into his fundamental understanding of nature and grace. God is the source of all understanding, of all discretion — the unction of divine wisdom. He is the giver of every good gift.[19] For this reason, the superior must pray for the gift of discretion and cause others to pray for him to receive it.[20] He must seek it through spiritual exercises aimed at the achievement of true spiritual liberty and the desire only to praise and serve God. But far from expecting a divine revelation of the correct decision or an inspiration strictly so called, he must use every human means to guide his discernment of the will of God manifested in the concrete cicrumstances of the actual situation.[21]

16 *EppIgn,* I, 97-98.
17 The term *grace of state* never appears, but the notion is clear: *Cons*MHSJ, I, 215, 245; II, 136, 192, 219, 231, 235, 241, 248, 260, 264, 282, 504, 546, 640, 654, 668.
18 Ibid., II, 231; see also 282, 504, 546.
19 *EppIgn,* I, 115; *Cons*MHSJ, II, 260, 264, 668.
20 For an interpretation of grace of state which seems to demand considerably too much of divine providence in guiding the judgment of the superior, see I. Iparraguirre, "Armonia sobrenatural de la acción de Dios y del hombre en San Ignacio de Loyola", *EstEcl,* XXX (1964), 343-361. Iparraguirre cites many letters, but in a "proof text" manner rather than in their historical context and in relation to the teaching of Ignatius in the Constitutions. Cf. J. Lewis, *Le gouvernement spirituel* . . . (Montreal, 1961), pp. 35-53, 113-123, whose interpretation seems equally excessive. An extremely complicated discussion of the action of divine providence in the decisions of the superior is given by Carlos Palmes, *La obediencia religiosa Ignaciana* (Barcelona, 1963), pp. 112-142. Palmes' solution involves the consequent will of God and two kinds of antecedent will (pp. 125-134)! See below, ch 7, fn. 41.
21 *Cons*MHSJ, II, 136, 192, 219, 235, 241, 248.

According to Ignatius, therefore, the superior should give primacy of place to prayer in exercising his role of discernment, trusting, too, in his grace of state. But he may not consider his decisions to be divinely revealed or guaranteed to be certainly correct. His judgments are never exempt from the possibility of error. They are always open to reform if experience should prove them wrong.[22] Despite his great confidence in grace and prayer, Ignatius was deeply aware of the dangers for true discernment of the concrete will of God which lay in the human limitations of the superior: limited intelligence, limited competence, bodily and mental fatigue, and the like. He knew, too, that even the highest superior was not made morally impeccable by the grace of state and that he might be subject to the pressures of prejudice or self-seeking in making a decision.[23] For these reasons he was extremely careful in the Constitutions to provide aids to help overcome the human limitations of the general, and he described in detail the manner to remove an unworthy general from office.[24]

To exercise his role of discernment the superior must use every possible human means to gather evidence in order to form a correct judgment of the actual situation. Ignatius, who always sought clarity in discerning the concrete will of God, knew that this could be attained only through intimate knowledge of the concrete circumstances of persons, times and places. Otherwise, mistaken decisions would be made which would result in actions not ordered to the end of the Company.

Gathering Evidence through Personal Knowledge of Each Companion

Now, since the essential role of the superior is to make an apostolic community of love, he must have as intimate a personal knowledge as possible of each individual member of this body of companions. Ignatius insists repeatedly upon the absolute necessity of this knowledge as a means of discernment, and he sought to provide efficacious means to attain it. In the preliminary documents this is already clear in the statement that

22 On two occasions Ignatius uses the word *acertar* in making a judgment as the result of the gift of divine grace (*Cons*MHSJ, II, 219, 654). At first glance this word might seem to suggest certitude. Actually it means literally to hit the mark by chance; as applied to judgment, to conjecture rightly.
23 See *Cons*MHSJ, I, 14, 39.
24 See above, ch. 3, pp. 71-74.

the professed should "give information" about candidates seeking admission, and that the first of the three experiments should be the Spiritual Exercises "in order to have some knowledge of the temperament and constancy, the talent and inclination and vocation" of the candidates.[25] The entire General Examen has as its purpose the profound mutual knowledge of the Company and the candidate. The examinations are directed to the specific persons seeking admission. For instance, those who have studied are given an additional examination to have "greater understanding and knowledge" of them.[26] At the end of his studies a scholastic is again examined so that superiors may have "more recent memory and understanding of him, so that they may more fully know his solidity and constancy or any change within him." [27] Their training and study should be observed in order to have "greater understanding and knowledge of the talent of each individual one, so that they may be better guided and directed to the greater divine glory." [28]

One specific means Ignatius provided to help the superior gain knowledge of the individual subject was the mutual manifestation to the superior of faults the companions note in one another.[29] Although this practice is presented to the candidate with the personal motivation of exercising greater humility, its true purpose clearly is to help the superior know the concrete difficulties of the companions he must unite for the apostolic service of Christ. It is a practical exercise of the mutual spiritual aid directed to the more effective aid of souls which led the companions in the Deliberation to decide to make their union into one permanent body. On an intimate and fraternal level mutual manifestation was intended to help each individual companion to overcome his personal weaknesses and to assure the individual good and the universal good. Whether in different times and cultures the practice should be followed in the traditional manner is something which must be discerned in the concrete circumstances; but the underlying principle is per-

---

25 Persons responsible for those in probation are to give testimonials about their performance of the six experiments, so that the superior can better provide in all things (*Cons*MHSJ, 62-63).

26 *Cons*MHSJ, II, 88.

27 Ibid., II, 114.

28 Ibid., I, 124.

29 Ibid., II, 54.

manently valid. A superior should know each individual subject as intimately as possible in his strengths and weaknesses if he is to be able to carry out his role of making an apostolic community of love of the group of diverse persons who make up the Company at any given time.

The Constitutions give much evidence of the deep awareness of Ignatius of the absolute importance of interpersonal relationships between companions and their superior, but nowhere more strikingly than in his employment of the manifestation of conscience. When this exercise is reduced to a mere formality without actual establishment of a relation of personal knowledge in the way that Ignatius conceived it, then it has no meaning in the Company of Jesus. The practice itself was of ancient monastic origin, but it had been ordered to the guidance of the individual monk in the pursuit of personal perfection under the direction of his spiritual father. Ignatius adapted it to the apostolic orientation of the "scope of our vocation."[30] The key text concerning the manifestation of conscience is that given in the General Examen:[31]

Reflecting upon the matter in our Lord, it has seemed to us in His divine majesty that it is of very great importance that the superiors have entire understanding of their companions. For with this knowledge they can better rule and govern them and by watching over them lead them in the way of the Lord. Thus, when the superiors have complete knowledge of everything both interior and external about their subjects, they can with so much the more diligence love and care for them and help them and protect their souls from various difficulties and dangers which may come in the future.

All rule and government in the Company is ordered to the end of the apostolic service of Christ. The personal good of the individual member is ordered to the universal good of the Company and the Church. By protecting individual companions

30 The manifestation of conscience is first mentioned in the very early document *Constituta et Annotata, ConsMHSJ,* I, 197-199. J. de Guibert, *The Jesuits: Their Spiritual Doctrine and Practice* (Chicago, 1964), p. 100, makes the end of the manifestation rather the individual good of the companion than the universal good. But in the Ignatian dialectic, attention to the particular good is always ultimately ordered to the universal good, the "scope of our vocation."
31 *ConsMHSJ,* II, 72-76.

from spiritual dangers, the superior helps each of them to in- corporate himself completely into the apostolic effort of the whole body. The passage continues:

> Furthermore, since we should always be ready, in conformity with our profession and manner of action, to go to any part of the world whenever the supreme pontiff or our own superior chooses to send us anywhere, some for one work, others for different works, it is of great importance not only for these missions, but will be a gentle help (for individual members), if the superior is fully notified of their inclinations and motions and of what defects or sins have most troubled them, so that he can give them better guidance and not appoint them to works which are more dangerous and difficult for them than they can undertake with love in our Lord.

The ordination of the personal relationship of the superior with his companions (established through the manifestation of conscience) to the apostolic end of the whole body of the Company is clear in this text and is made explicit in an addition to it in text B of the General Examen, which notes that with this knowledge "the superior can better order and provide what is required for the universal body of the Company." [32] The manifestation is to be repeated before profession or admission as a formed coadjutor,[33] and is to be made from year to year by the formed and professed Jesuits.[34] These provisions are repeated in the Constitutions.[35]

Text *a* of the Constitutions makes many explicit references to the necessity that the superior have complete knowledge of each companion: for admission of candidates;[36] for helping them spiritually;[37] for directing their studies;[38] and to enable the general to govern the whole body of the Company well.[39] The physical impossibility of the general knowing intimately each of

---

32 Ibid., II, 75.
33 Ibid., II, 76.
34 Ibid., II, 81.
35 Ibid., 153, 161, 194-195, 208; see 682.
36 Ibid., II, 132-136.
37 Ibid., II, 153, 156, 159, 165.
38 Ibid., II, 187, 192.
39 Texts A and B add numerous specific situations requiring this knowledge of the companions by the superior: *Cons*MHSJ, II, 272, 282, 294, 306, 330, 350, 486, 490, 492, 546, 590, 592, 622, 626.

the companions is overcome through their immediate relationship to his vicars, the provincials and local superiors. Although
normally the general will guard hierarchical subordination for
the sake of unity, nevertheless, at times he should communicate
directly with the companions under their authority to find out
how well these provincials or local superiors are carrying out
their role.[40] An important reason for the lifetime tenure of the
general is that he may "be known by and know all" for the sake
of good government.[41]

Through the hierarchical organization of the whole body of
the Company, each member is integrated into the entire body:
united with one another and with their head for the service of
Christ through the aid of souls in companionship. It is an obvious practical consequence that where the structure of a house
makes it morally or physically impossible for a superior to have
this personal knowledge of each of his companions, it becomes
equally impossible for him to exercise his role of discernment.
Under such conditions a man cannot be a truly Ignatian superior.[42] It is inevitable that the result of his efforts to unify
their wills and actions will be nothing more than "administration" — the ordering of an efficient, but bloodless organization,
rather than a vital, living union of companions in mutual love.
Only the personal relationship of the superior of each community with each of his companions, based upon intimate, individual knowledge of every single one, enables him to unite all
of them into a community of love.

Another Ignatian method for gathering all available evidence
in order to discern the will of God in the concrete situation is
that of dialogue between the superior and his companions. This
Gathering Evidence through Dialogue

40 Ibid., II, 248.
41 Ibid., II, 237.
42 For example, if a community is made up of too many individuals, it
becomes impossible for a superior to have the personal knowledge of
each of the companions needed to unite them in an apostolic community of love. The hierarchical structure of the Company was intended by Ignatius precisely as a means to unite all the members
with one another and with their head, no matter how dispersed or
numerous the companions might become. It would seem that this
principle could be extended in a variety of ways to overly large individual houses, as it has already been extended to provinces and to
the Company as a whole.

dialogue enables the superior to surmount his own limitations and his own prejudices through mutual discernment, paying sincere attention to the *pareçer* and *sentir* and *juzgar* of others.[43] This dialogue operates both with official consultors or persons of special competence whom the superior calls to advise him and with any and all of the companions through their use of representation. It is the extension into the organized life of the Company in hierarchical unity with its one superior of the mutual discernment experienced by the first companions in the Deliberation. It is not a dialogue leading to majority rule but to help the superior arrive at a unifying decision.[44] The superior fulfills his role of uniting all the companions in an apostolic community of love precisely through making the final judgment of the will of God here and now, which all accept in perfect obedience and, thus, bring the Company to be.[45]

This study has already had occasion to note the numerous instances when Ignatius insists upon this dialogue: the superior's consultation with others in carrying out his role of discernment.[46] Passages in the texts of the Constitutions speak specifically of consultation on decisions of admission,[47] dismissal,[48] the choice of apostolic missions,[49] the life and the studies of

---

43 Cf. J. M. Le Blond, "Obéissance et autorité dans l'église," *Études* (Juillet-Août, 1966), pp. 100-114. He remarks concerning mutual discernment and dialogue: "s'il sort de la sincérité immédiate, subjectivement vécue, c'est pour se référer à une vérité plus profonde, socialement 'interpersonellement' pensée, par quoi l'on sort du fanatisme individuel" (p. 103).

44 *Cons*MHSJ, I, 292, 321.

45 The practical principle of the conduct of all dialogue is stated in the *Presupuesto* of the Spiritual Exercises (*SpEx,* [22]). One must be more ready to save another's proposal than to condemn it. If it must be corrected, this must be done with love; and should this be ineffective, all possible means should be used to help the other come to a correct understanding. The application of this principle to dialogue between the superior and the companions would require that the superior honestly listen to their opinions, not beginning a merely formal discussion with his decision already fixed. Rather than brutally imposing his will, he must make every effort to bring the companions to understand why his final determination seems to him truly to be the concrete will of God.

46 See above, ch. 5, pp. 108, 116-117.

47 *Cons*MHSJ, II, 132.

48 Ibid., II, 146, 316, 324-326.

49 Ibid., II, 216.

scholastics in the colleges,[50] and various decisions the general must make.[51] It is clear that this list of situations where consultations is indicated was not intended to be exhaustive, even during the time of Ignatius. The principle involved is clear. Whenever the superior is required to exercise his role of discernment in circumstances demanding the clarification and liberation of his own spirit through dialogue with others, he should seek to involve his companions in the process of mutual discernment. That the extreme complication of apostolic missions of the Company in modern times, as well as the number of its members, multiply greatly such circumstances is obvious. On the other hand, a superior today has the advantage of highly developed techniques of communication and mutual discussion. There can be no doubt that Ignatius would have exploited these fully.

Another help to the superior in exercising his role of discernment is the means called representation. Representation is usually treated in studies on obedience as a right and obligation of subjects which, in a way, mitigates the rigor of submission. However, the essential function of representation in the conception of Ignatius is to play an important part in the discernment process by making vital evidence available to the superior in his search for the concrete will of God, "so that the superior may better consider and provide . . . according to what he is enabled to judge to be for the greater service and praise of God our Lord." [52]

Gathering Evidence through Representation

Ignatius practiced a form of representation during his early pilgrim years by declaring to the ecclesiastical authorities in Alcalá and Salamanca that he felt their decisions not to accord with the will of God for him.[53] In a letter of 1536 to Cardinal Carafa, founder of the Theatines, Ignatius reveals what was to remain for him the essential structure of representation. Stating boldly the dangers he has observed for the Theatines and the

---

50 Ibid., II, 186, 466, 474, 486, 488.
51 Ibid., II, 248, 250, 251, 624-626, 680, 712.
52 Ibid., I, 163.
53 *FN*, I, 442-444, 448-450, 460-462. It has already been noted in this study that Ignatius even made representations to the pope when he felt that decisions of the Holy See militated against the scope of our vocation. See above, ch. 1, pp. 31-32.

remedies he feels that Carafa should apply, Ignatius notes that before speaking out, he prayed "at various times and much to God our Lord." He then decided to write this letter "as ordinary persons are accustomed to do to persons of authority" (*como los menores à los maiores acostumbran hazer*), if they can advise or serve their superiors in the service of God so that no opportunity for divine service will be directly or indirectly missed.[54] After declaring his own *pareçeres,* Ignatius concludes that "having weighed and pondered all these things in this way," it is enough for him to represent them to Carafa "as I would to my own unique soul." In an implicit reference to his original statement that his conclusions were the result of prayerful reflections, he adds that continuously greater recourse to God cannot result in harm, but will lead to greater progress. Perhaps with a feeling that Carafa may be fixed in his own already formed ideas, Ignatius also remarks that the infinite and supreme Goodness wills to communicate new remedies to us for new works.[55] The interior liberty and constant openness of Ignatius' fundamentally dynamic mental structure is evident in this sentence.

Representation, then, is a special form of dialogue. It is initiated by those under authority and it is not unusual: *"acostumbran hazer."* In the essential structure of representation revealed in this letter (and followed in the Constitutions), there are a clear motive and three steps. The motive of making the representation, which is also the norm of discernment, is the "service of God our Lord." The sincerity of this motive is tested in repeated prayer, which is the first step. Secondly, all the evidence of the concrete circumstances is weighed and considered — submitted to personal discernment of spirits in the light of the norm of divine service. Finally, the conclusion of this discernment is presented to the superior as the sincere judgment of the subject concerning the concrete will of God, "as I would to my own unique soul." When he integrates the structure of representation into the life of the Company, Ignatius will add one further step. After having made his representation, the subject must accept the ultimate decision of the superior with

54 *EppIgn,* I, 116.
55 Ibid., I, 118.

perfect obedience.[56] Otherwise, it will be impossible for the superior to exercise his role of unifying the wills and actions of all the members of the one body and for the Company to serve Christ through the aid of souls in companionship.

Through this dialogue with any or all of his companions, the superior is enabled to share their vantage point of observation of the evidence, which is often more immediate than his own. A passage in the Constitutions states that the companions are obliged to inform the superior of their needs with respect to health, food, clothing, work, etc.[57] The use of the word *obliged* emphasizes the dependence of the superior upon the members of his community to obtain the evidence of concrete circumstances which he must have in order to carry out his role of discernment.

Not only does this dialogue bring to the superior's attention objective data affecting decisions, but also it allows him to profit from the subject's personal discernment of spirits — his *sentir* concerning the will of God. In one of the earliest documents on going on apostolic missions, it is stated that a companion who feels the desire to go to a particular place or work should "test the spirit" (*probate spiritus*) from whom this desire comes by making ten days of spiritual exercises ordered to this discernment. It is the result of this personal, subjective discernment which he presents to the Company or the superior: and, after this dialogue, he must do whatever he is commanded.[58] The objective discernment of the Company or the superior controls the subjective discernment of the individual member, as it must in order to maintain the unity of the body. Furthermore, the interpersonal communication involved in representation reveals to the superior more fully the individual character and temperament of each of the companions whom he must unite into an apostolic community of love.

Ignatius at times warns against repeating representations or seeking to bring pressure upon the superior from others.[59] This warning reflects Ignatius' tendency to fear the play of inordi-

---

56 *Cons*MHSJ, I, 11-12, 163, 201, 248, 300, 393; II, 121, 151, 154, 195, 205, 211, 216, 222, 372, 380, 458, 516, 574, 590, 594.
57 *Cons*MHSJ, II, 151.
58 Ibid., I, 11-12.
59 Ibid., II, 151, 222, 574.

nate affections, especially in material matters. However, experience seems to have taught Ignatius that due to the human limitations of superiors, repetition of representations might be indicated.[60] His practical attitude towards representation is clearly presented in his letters.[61] This is especially true of an appendix to a letter Polanco wrote to Antonio de Araoz, May 29, 1555. The late date makes it possible to consider this as the expression of the mature thought of Ignatius on the use of representation after he had much experience as general. Polanco tells Araoz that he is enclosing a copy of the "manner to discuss matters with superiors, which our Father Ignatius has ordained." [62]

This document deserves close study. The essential structure of representation is retained in the admonition that the matter should be "mulled over and reflected upon" in proportion to its importance, which, of course, means prayerful reflection. It is interesting that Ignatius here adds the explicit advice to discuss the matter with other companions before making the representation. Here, too, mutual discernment will be helpful in seeking the concrete will of God. The representation should then be made in words which reflect the openmindedness of the companion and his readiness to conform himself to the final judgment of the superior. The object here is to discover the concrete will of God according to the scope of our vocation, which requires that all the companions must be unified in will and action by the decision of the superior. It is certainly not that the companion making the representation may impose his own personal will and judgment upon the superior and, so, upon the other companions. The place of representation in the superior's exercise of his role of discernment is then made clear. Having heard the representation, the superior makes his decision or takes more time to reflect upon it or asks the person who presented it to consider it further or asks other companions to reflect upon this evidence or even to make the decision. This supposes true spiritual liberty in the superior, an absence of pre-determined judgments, an ability truly to listen to others.

60 Ibid., II, 372.
61 For numerous references to letters illustrating Ignatius' practical attitude towards representation, see J. Lewis, op. cit., pp. 23-33.
62 *EppIgn,* IX, 89.

He is seeking to discern the will of God, and this requires the peaceful consideration of all the evidence available.

Ignatius adds that the decision given by the superior is not necessarily the end of the dialogue. Evidently, this would be untrue if it were a decision which must be carried out immediately. He says that the companion should not present further arguments immediately after the superior has stated his decision.[63] But Ignatius goes on to give very explicit instructions on how to re-represent matters to the superior, even after he has given a decision more than once. If the companion feels (*sentir*) that some other judgment would be better or that he has solid reasons to advance, he should make another representation after three or four hours or on another day. Even if the superior's decision is repeated, after a month or even a longer time the subject "may again represent what he feels" or describe the results of an order already given. Ignatius adds a very characteristic reason to explain the necessity of this reiterated representation in the discernment process: "because experience and the passage of time reveal many things," and also circumstances change greatly as time goes on.[64]

The great realism of Ignatius and his remarkable understanding of human nature are manifest in the following advice to the companion making representations to adapt his manner and moment of approaching the superior to the latter's temperament and natural capacities. Thus, the companion should speak very clearly, and he should choose the most opportune time possible to make his representation. Ignatius was perfectly aware that a superior can suffer from fatigue, from tension, from headache and indigestion which would leave him humanly indisposed to give an objective hearing to the representation — to be truly present during the dialogue. The companion is to observe the personal disposition of the superior not out of any

---

63 The phrase used is *"no aya réplica ni razones algunas por entonces"* (*EppIgn,* IX, 90). The word used in texts *a* and A of the Constitutions to forbid repetition of representations to the superior is also *replicar* (*Cons*MHSJ, II, 151, 574). In view of this document of 1555, concerning the manner of treating with superiors, it would seem legitimate and even necessary to interpret the Constitutions' passages as also meaning that one should not repeat the representation "immediately."

64 *EppIgn,* IX, 91.

self-seeking diplomacy, but because he is convinced after prayerful reflection that he has an obligation to help the superior to carry out his role of discernment of the will of God for the Company's service of Christ through the aid of souls here and now.

To summarize, during the second step of the discernment process, the gathering of evidence, the superior must retain great awareness of the complexity of the judgments he must make and of the need to understand the concrete circumstances of the actual situation. He must realize, too, his personal limitations, especially in matters demanding special competence. As the number of competent members of the Company increases, he should avail himself more and more of the means of consultation, asking for the opinions of those who may aid his judgment and creating structures to make this dialogue easier and more fruitful. Furthermore, he must establish personal relationships with all the companions under his immediate authority, based upon a profound and intimate knowledge of each one individually, and he must foster an atmosphere of confidence and freedom in the use of representation. It is clear that for Ignatius representation was an essentially important part of the process of discernment. His master was always living experience, and representation makes available to the superior the concrete experience of the members of the Company who are living and exercising the apostolate in the actual situations involved in his decision. Without this dialogue with the companions the superior could lose himself in abstract theories of the religious life and of apostolic activity and give orders based upon a priori or overly subjective judgments. Nevertheless, the superior can never simply cast upon others the weight of responsibility for making final decisions, which belongs to him as the principle of unity of the Company. But in order to discern the concrete will of God for the companions here and now, he must engage in the dialogue of mutual discernment of spirits which will enable him to find the Spirit of God.

Confirmation of Decisions   The final step in the discernment process is the effort to seek confirmation of the determination one has made of the actual will of God. This confirmation may be sought in prayer as it is at the end of the Election in the Spiritual Exercises and as it was by Ignatius in his deliberation on poverty as recorded in the

Spiritual Diary.[65] Confirmation may come from external authority as from the pope, as is exemplified in the constant effort of Ignatius to have papal approbation of the Company and its Constitutions through bulls and briefs.[66] The hierarchical structure of the Company gives to local superiors the means of confirmation of their decisions by the general.[67] The confirmation of the subjective discernment of a companion is found in his conformity and obedience, after representation, to the final judgment of the Company through the superior.[68] The principal means of confirmation of the decisions of the superior, however, are the mutual contentment of himself and his companions and the proof of living experience.

A very important word, therefore, in Ignatius' vocabulary of discernment is "contentment" (*contento*) or the almost equivalent "satisfaction" (*satisfecho*), "tranquillity" (*tranquilo*), "interior quiet" (*quieto*) and "peace" (*paz*). These terms refer to the psychological state which bears interior testimony that one has made a right decision. It issues from the *sentir* grounded in the radical attitude of soul of spiritual liberty and of the unique desire to serve Christ through the aid of souls in companionship. The dynamic thrust of human feelings reacting to the evidence appearing in the concrete situation and to the interior results of prayerful reflection upon this evidence finally comes to rest in the judgment which determines the decision how to fulfill the concrete will of God here and now. The result is satisfaction of desire resulting in an interior state of peace, tranquillity, contentment — the quieting of the fluctuation of feelings in the peaceful conviction that the will of God has been found in spiritual liberty.

The role of this psychological state of response or contentment is illustrated in Ignatius' mystical vocabulary in the

---

65 On the Spiritual Exercises, see above, p. 127.
66 Ignatius even used confirmation from the King of Portugal, stating that he would be of the same *pareçer* as the king concerning the use of the goods of one college to aid another, and that he was certain that all would agree "as appears to His Highness, and with spiritual joy in the Lord" (*Cons*MHSJ, I, 387). It is necessary to recall Ignatius' Castilian conception of kingship in judging this kind of confirmation.
67 *Cons*MHSJ, II, 164, 290, 464, 486, 488.
68 Ibid., II, 12, 594.

Spiritual Diary. The state of contentment continually serves as
a norm for judging the way for Ignatius to seek and find God in
his personal prayer.[69] *Contento* and *satisfecho* occur also in
passages specifically concerning the "election" of Ignatius concerning the relative or total poverty of the Company.[70] The
study of these terms in election contexts in the *Spiritual Diary*
shows the relativity of interior peace or contentment as a norm
of discernment in matters of practical policy for the Company.
At one time or another, one may be *contento* in the thought of
contrary decisions.[71] The state of interior peace may be so intense at times as to give the impression that final confirmation
of judgment has been given; but thereafter one can be impelled
to seek further confirmation.

From February 7, 1544, until he finally made his election of
total poverty for the Company ("having no fixed revenues")
on March 12, Ignatius repeatedly experienced moments of interior peace and contentment which led him to believe that his
election was finished.[72] This state fluctuated sufficiently, however, to make Ignatius feel again that the confirmation was not
yet certain. On February 18, he made an "ultimate" oblation
to elect total poverty; but immediately after this, he experienced
a need to pray for further confirmation.[73] This fluctuation of
feeling that he had sufficient or insufficient confirmation continued for several days. On February 23, he was granted the
"confirmation of Jesus" in the thought that since Jesus was
Head of the Company, this was the strongest motive for choosing total poverty. Ignatius felt certain that this reasoned conclusion was the right election, even though he received no consolation until afterwards.[74] It is striking that although Ignatius

69 *Cons*MHSJ, I, 97, 108, 110, 112, 116, 117, 121, 122, 131, 132, 133,
   137, 151.
70 Ibid., I, 89, 90, 95, 97, 98, 100, 102, 104, 107, 108, 113, 124, 126.
71 Although Ignatius' temperament and spiritual ideals predisposed
   him to choose the total poverty he finally elected, he found on February 7, that the thought of accepting some steady revenues came
   to him *"muy tranquillamente sin contradiçión alguna"* (*Cons*-
   MHSJ, I, 89). Codina proposes the odd interpretation here that
   Ignatius actually was still deciding to accept no fixed revenues (ibid.,
   I, 89, n. 12).
72 *Cons*MHSJ, I, 89-113.
73 Ibid., 99-100.
74 Ibid., I, 104.

found confirmation chiefly in feelings of peace and contentment, this powerful "confirmation of Jesus" was the result of thoughts (*pensamientos*) without consolation. During the following days, Ignatius stated that he no longer felt need of seeking confirmation; nevertheless, he continued to do so and when he finally brought the election to a close on March 12, he began in a state of darkness and aridity, "finding inner peace (*requiem*) in no way and desiring to finish in a time of great spiritual consolation and complete satisfaction." Since the decision itself seemed clear to Ignatius, he felt that he was asking for too many consoling signs "for my own satisfaction." Yet he feared that if he finished in dryness, "I would not be content afterwards." Having concluded that, nevertheless, he should immediately terminate the election in any case, he began to be consoled "with great interior satisfaction." [75] During the entire following day, Ignatius enjoyed "contentment and spiritual joy" as a result of his election.[76] Throughout the *Spiritual Diary* it is evident that confirmation of practical decisions through prayer and interior peace is relative. It may seem final on one occasion and afterwards be called into question.

The inner peace and contentment experienced in making a decision confirms that one is choosing in true spiritual liberty motivated by the unique desire to praise and serve God. The content of the decision is not given with this peace but is formulated by gathering all the evidence, including that derived from mutual discernment.

One is tempted to have the temerity, in spite of the magnificent mystical value of the *Spiritual Diary*, to feel that in this election Ignatius allowed himself to remain too exclusively on the level of subjective discernment of spirits, finding confirmation of what he most profoundly felt to be his personal vocation.[77] That Ignatius himself was somewhat aware of this is

75 Ibid., I, 124.
76 Ibid., I, 126.
77 Close study of the "motions" and "intelligences" and "visitations" described by Ignatius in the *Spiritual Diary,* especially the great graces of "reverence" and *"acatamiento,"* leads to the conclusion that Ignatius confused an aspect of his personal vocation in his approach to God (absolute interior poverty, total surrender to the way God would choose to give Himself to him) with the regime of total poverty for the Company in accepting no fixed revenues (*Cons-*

shown by his remark that he had received such intense interior confirmation never to change the election of absolute poverty, that he would not do so for all of heaven or earth, but that this was for his part, in so far as it depended on him, because of the decision the companions had already made to mitigate poverty for the greater apostolic service of Christ.[78] However, Ignatius' election on poverty was never specifically submitted to discussion and mutual discernment. The dispersal of the companions on apostolic missions made this practically impossible.[79] Perhaps, the results might have been different had Ignatius' determination been submitted to mutual discernment.[80] Divine confirmation of the spiritual way in which Ignatius should go in his own life of prayer and of seeking and finding God is one thing. Divine confirmation of the content of a particular decision of the superior affecting the life of the Company is quite another.

The study of the vocabulary of discernment of Ignatius forbids the assertion that he received a divine and definitive con-

---

MHSJ, I, 128). In view of his spiritual orientation, it was quite understandable that he chose material poverty as the visible sign of man's interior poverty before God.

78 *Cons*MHSJ, I, 36-37, 62-63, 70.

79 The profound reverence of the companions for Ignatius and their confidence in his wisdom and in the aid of the Holy Spirit granted to him also made them ready to leave judgments about the life of the Company to him. In 1548, when Ignatius submitted his rough drafts of Constitutions to Laynez, Salmerón, Broët, and Jay, they gave global approval to all that he had already written or would write in the future. They explained that they did this because of their confidence in Christ, that His divine goodness had guided Ignatius in the government of the Company thus far and would continue to do so in the future (*Cons*MHSJ, I, 245).

80 Ironically, precisely the Election recorded in the *Spiritual Diary* — the rejection of all fixed revenues for houses of the Company — has been the source of much practical difficulty and juridical ambivalence in the history of the Company. The fact that in terms of the economic and social structures of his own epoch this regime of poverty seemed to Ignatius the best way to signify interior poverty and to follow Christ, the Head of the Company, is quite understandable. At this time "living without any fixed revenues" and entirely upon alms was quite feasible, and Ignatius could not foresee the changes that history would work in the future and the consequent difficulties that this provision would cause the Company. Nevertheless, had the companions specifically submitted this decision to mutual discernment, the conclusion might have been different.

firmation of the content of this election of absolute poverty. Reverence for the sanctity of Ignatius and for the profound union with God manifested in the *Spiritual Diary,* together with the exaggerated notion of divine "revelation" of the Constitutions has caused the Company considerable difficulty over the centuries. Yet in this election as in all others concerning the life of the Company, the essential norm of discernment is the "scope of our vocation"; and all else, even the regime of poverty, must be judged in terms of concrete circumstances as means to the end of the service of Christ through the aid of souls in companionship here and now.

In carrying out his role of discernment a superior (even one endowed with the extraordinary mystical gifts of Ignatius) should not rely simply on the first step of the discernment process: prayer for light. He must at the same time use all the means possible for the gathering of evidence; and he should seek confirmation not merely in his subjective contentment and spiritual peace in prayer (which may follow upon a divine lesson for his personal manner of seeking and finding God, rather than as divine approval of the content of his decision for the companions), but also in the contentment of all the companions and, above all, in the signs of the will of God revealed through living experience.

The effect of this mutual contentment and interior peace on the life of the Company is reflected in the statement that the superior is responsible "to preserve the tranquillity (*quietud*) and well-being of the Company." [81] The tranquillity of order realized in the formation of an apostolic community of love is the very being of the Company and the essential end of the role of the superior. The mutual contentment of the superior and the companions is, therefore, indicated as a sign of confirmation of discernment.[82] This is particularly notable in the General Examen. Indeed, in text *a* the discernment of a candidate's vocation is always described in terms of this interpersonal dialogue terminating in the contentment of both parties.[83]

---

81 *ConsMHSJ,* I, 59; II, 92, 102, 106, 108, 114, 116, 146-147, 198, 272.
82 Ibid. See also *Cons,* [119, 121, 142, 514].
83 Cf. F. Roustang, *Constitutiones de la Compagnie de Jésus,* 2 vols. (Paris, 1967), II, 44. Roustang insists upon the "mutual conversation" structure of the Examen. He also develops this theme in his

True contentment on the part of both the superior and the companions supposes a clear knowledge of all the concrete factors that make up the "scope of our vocation." Ignatius knew that discontent is often the result of lack of understanding of all the issues. This is why he is so insistent upon communication and interpersonal dialogue.

The interior state of contentment, then, is of great importance in the confirmation of the result of discernment. It provides personal testimony to the spirit whose desires are directed uniquely to the divine service that the decision made does express the actual will of God here and now. Obviously, as a source of confirmation of judgment of the will of God, this contentment must issue from a *sentir* grounded in true spiritual liberty, rather than be the satisfaction of self-seeking. When this interior peace is shared by the two interlocutors in a dialogue of mutual discernment, it unifies them in the tranquil pursuit of the scope of our vocation through the unifying command of the superior confirmed by their mutual contentment. It supposes as clear a knowledge as possible of all the concrete circumstances of the situation of discernment, so that both superior and companions can share one *pareçer* and *sentir* and *juzgar* with interior peace. It brings about the union of wills — the mutual love — which must unite all the members with one another and with their head for the service of Christ through the aid of souls in companionship. It should always be sought as the psychological state of all the companions at the moment of perfect obedience which brings the Company to be.

Finally, in accord with the dynamic mental structure of Ignatius, decisions are always subject to reform, even after there has been unanimous agreement and mutual contentment concerning them, if experience shows that they are no longer ordered to the "scope of our vocation." This study has revealed repeatedly the central position of the teaching of living experience in the mental structure of Ignatius. It was in actual life situations and through natural and supernatural experiences

discussion of Part I of the Constitutions. He believes that in text B Polanco has destroyed the interpersonal dialogue between the Company and the candidate presented in text *a* and has substituted a structure wherein the candidate becomes an object presented to the knowledge of the Company.

that he sought to discern the actual will of God, rather than in some system of a priori principles from which he deduced practical conclusions. For this reason the proof of experience is the ultimate and only sure confirmation of the decisions of the superior for the life and action of the companions of Jesus.[84]

To make a decision that is a true determination of the actual will of God demands that the superior's opinion and felt-knowledge and judgment be formed by faithful attention to the real circumstances of each concrete situation. The effort to force these situations into a preconceived rigid mold would not only be unreal and totally alien to the mental structure of Ignatius; it would also be an act contrary to that spiritual liberty which alone would make it possible to find the will of God manifested in times and events and persons here and now.[85] The profound awareness of Ignatius of the need to pay attention to all concrete circumstances is often expressed in a phrase following upon a statement of general procedure that this must be adapted "according to the circumstances of persons, times and places," or the equivalent: "for special reasons or particular circumstances," "according to the capacity of each person," "according to the different customs of countries," "for any exigencies or events that might occur." [86]

In the Constitutions, for example, these qualifying phrases appear in passages giving norms for admission and dismissal,[87] discussing practical matters of the life and training of those in formation,[88] and the order of life and study in the colleges.[89] Some of these are especially interesting for understanding the mental structure of Ignatius and his idea of the role of the

84 *Cons*MHSJ, I, 19, 63, 323; II, 145, 154, 166, 237, 276, 640, 652, 666.
85 This attention to concrete circumstances is already evident in the Spiritual Exercises in admonitions to the director to adapt the Exercises to the age, the disposition, the temperament and the personal needs of each exercitant (*SpEx,* [9, 14, 17, 18, 72, 205]).
86 *Cons*MHSJ, I, 18, 37, 255, 258, 311, 320; II, 19, 50, 52, 124, 133, 145, 149, 151, 152, 153, 154, 166, 167, 168, 169, 176, 177, 178, 179, 181, 187, 189, 192, 196, 205, 219, 221, 222, 242, 277, 292, 360, 368, 412, 418, 424, 426, 434, 440, 468, 470, 472, 474, 478, 544, 546, 590, 592, 598, 612, 618, 622, 630, 680.
87 Ibid., II, 133, 145.
88 Ibid., II, 150-169.
89 Ibid., II, 169-196.

superior. Seven hours of sleep a night are recommended, but it is immediately added that each one should decide how much he needs and ask the superior's approval "because there is such great diversity of persons and their habits and temperament." [90] Norms are given for the clothing of scholastics, "and this in general, because in particular cases this may be done differently for various reasons." [91] The common rule is that scholastics make one hour of prayer, but the rector may lengthen or shorten the time "for an individual person for special causes." [92] Daily order and externals of life may be changed according to "the various customs of countries" where the colleges are located. [93] These qualifying phrases also occur in the Sixth Part concerning the poverty of incorporated members,[94] and in the Seventh Part on missions.[95] Text B in a Declaration in the Seventh Part adds that, "since in certain places it is possible that at a given time these [apostolic] means or some of them would not be effective, the constitution will not oblige except when the superior thinks that it should be followed." [96]

Adapting the Constitutions   In order to understand more fully this characteristic of the mental structure of Ignatius of complete freedom from a priorism and openness to the signs of the will of God manifested in the contingent circumstances of actual situations, it is useful to study his attitude toward the mutability of the Constitutions.[97]

Already in the Rules for Thinking Rightly within the Church in the Spiritual Exercises, Ignatius reveals an awareness of the

90 Ibid., II, 152.
91 Ibid., II, 177.
92 Ibid., II, 178.
93 Ibid., II, 179.
94 Ibid., II, 205.
95 Ibid., II, 219, 221, 222.
96 Ibid., II, 598. Text B states that the superior must have much communication by letters with those on missions and as much as possible be kept informed of the success of all initiatives, so that he may provide counsel and all other possible aid, "according to the exigencies of persons and affairs" (*Cons*MHSJ, II, 590); and the extent of this aid and counsel will depend on the importance and difficulty of the affair and the qualities of the persons sent on the mission (ibid., II, 592).
97 In the light of the evidence of Ignatius' constant, dynamic openness to the teaching of living experience, his long period of groping through rough drafts and his conscious adaptation of structures found in older religious orders during the gradual development of the final

development of doctrine and the evolution of theology. He says that we should praise both positive and scholastic theologians. It is the glory of the former to move our affections to the love and service of God in all things and of the latter "to define or explain for our times" the things necessary for salvation and to expose and do battle against errors. The scholastic doctors, since they are more modern (*más modernos*) not only can take advantage of the right understanding of the Holy Scriptures and of the achievements of the holy positive doctors, but

---

form of the Constitutions, the conviction of Jesuits of an older tradition that the end of the Company and the substantials of the Institute were the result of a revelation strictly so called at the Cardoner and/or at La Storta and that the Constitutions were divinely inspired cannot stand. See, e.g., A. Astráin, *Historia de la Compañía de Jesús en la asistencia de España,* 7 vols. (Madrid, 1902-1925), I, 102-122. Historians and theologians today are much more aware of the need to study such texts in the light of the social and cultural formation of their authors. The inspiration theory was based on certain passages in the writings of the early followers of Ignatius, especially Ribadeneyra, Polanco and Nadal, which, read independently of other texts, seemed to suggest inspiration (cf. *FN,* I, 506; II, 137, 362, 428, 474; IV, 474). It must be realized that the mental structure and the language of these men were the honest reflection of a world view wherein natural causes (often unknown) were frequently attributed to immediate action or direct inspiration by God, as well as of their veneration for Ignatius which resulted in a near apotheosis of him after his death. Ribadeneyra even presented *postulata* (proposals) to the Fifth General Congregation insisting that the substantials of the Institute were indubitably divinely revealed and arguing the case with "proofs" from the lives of Pachomius, Benedict, Bernard and Francis that their rules were also the gift of divine inspiration through the dictation of an angel or some other extraordinary means. The proposals are quoted by A. Jimenez Oñate, *El origen de la Compañía de Jesús* (Rome, 1966), pp. 176-177. Oñate justly remarks that every great spiritual movement at its beginnings runs the risk of excessively emphasizing the illuminist tendency and that the Company was not exempt from this danger (p. 43). A remarkable expression of this mentality (and a fascinating example of baroque rhetoric) is the *Imago primi saeculi societatis Jesu a provincia flandro-belgica eiusdem societatis repraesentata* (Antwerp, 1640). Essentially, this vast tome is 952 pages of self-congratulation. Concerning the Spiritual Exercises it states flatly: *Scripsit illa quidem Ignatius, sed dictante Maria* (p. 73). With respect to the divine revelation of the Company, it asserts that its foundation had been prophesied by David, Isaiah, St. John the Evangelist, St. Vincent and Joachim the Abbot, among others (pp. 57-64). In reading theories about the inspiration of the Constitutions, one must always put them into their cultural context.

also being themselves enlightened by divine help, can be aided in their theological reflection by the teachings of the Church.[98] Not only does Ignatius declare himself in favor of modern thought and growth in understanding of the Bible and of patristics, but he asserts his conviction that this evolution is guided by Divine Providence and given direction through the historical development of the grasp of and enunciation of the apostolic testimony by the Church. If this is the conception Ignatius had of the development of Catholic doctrine, it seems most unlikely that he would have been intransigent about the possibility of an evolution in new historical situations of the manner to accomplish the scope of our vocation, which was expressed in his own language and in terms of his own time and culture in the Constitutions.

A study of the passages in the Ignatian documents concerning both "guarding" the Constitutions and dispensing from them and discussing the possibility of making changes in them bears out this conclusion. The first text treating of the mutability or immutability of the Constitutions is in the third bull of Paul III, *Injunctum nobis,* of 1543. After reiterating the permission to frame Constitutions, the bull continues: "by special privilege of the apostolic authority we grant permission to change or alter or entirely do away with those constitutions already made or which will be made in the future according to the different circumstances of places and times and events, and to make and validate other new ones which, after having been changed or altered or newly created, are hereby granted prior confirmation by the apostolic authority." [99] This statement is completely in accord with the mental structure of Ignatius as it has been revealed in this study. For him the one absolutely fixed principle was the "scope of our vocation:" the service of Christ through the aid of souls in companionship. Living experience would reveal the concrete will of God as to how to accomplish this vocation here and now. The end of the Constitutions was to aid the whole body of the Company to fulfill this vocation

---

98 *SpEx,* [363]. Text B of the Constitutions reflects this reasoning in allowing, with the approval of the general, the use of some *"suma o libro de theologia scolástica que paresca más accomodada a estos tiempos"* (*Cons*MHSJ, II, 476).

99 *Cons*MHSJ, I, 84-85.

by giving a concrete description of the means to bring the Company to be in the union of all its members in corporate life and apostolic action and the conservation and increase of its well-being.[100]

In the texts of the Constitutions distinctions are made between particular and mutable regulations and those more universal and immutable.[101] The Constitutions with their Declarations present the immutable things, which should be universally observed, while rules given in other forms enunciate the more specific and mutable matters. As has been shown in the study of the qualifying phrases in the Constitutions, these are open to dispensation and adaptation according to concrete circumstances. It is significant that text *a,* the most "Ignatian" of the texts of the Constitutions, gives three reasons for calling a general congregation. The first is to elect a new general, while the third is to treat of matters of permanent import. The second reason is a need "to treat of the constitutions of the Company to make innovations or changes, to add to them or subtract from them for the future" (*a,* 230).[102]

---

100 This end of the Constitutions is often expressly stated: *Cons*MHSJ, I, 20-21, 27, 72, 83, 84, 298, 376; II, 129, 260, 262. Polanco, nevertheless, manifested considerable disquiet because of "this very general clause" in the bull granting permission to change the Constitutions, "because of the danger that they might be changed for the worse." He suggests that at least certain exceptions should be made from this general permission, so that certain parts could never be changed "at any time" (*Cons*MHSJ, I, 312; cf. 331). Polanco would seem to have had considerably less confidence in the commitment to the "scope of our vocation" of companions in the future than did Ignatius. Although Polanco wanted these changeless parts to be enumerated in another bull or brief, this was not done; and when he posed the question to curial theologians "whether the confirmed Constitutions are immutable," the response was that, on the contrary, "the superior may change them after they are made, according to the differences of the times" (ibid., I, 354).

101 Besides Constitutions, text *a* mentions rules of houses or colleges and Declarations and notes (*avisos*) (*Cons*MHSJ, II, 129-130). Text A enumerates five classes of legislative documents (ibid., II. 262), which are condensed into three classes in text B (ibid., II, 264).

102 This second reason is omitted from text A and text B which were composed after the arrival of Polanco. Out of reverence for the work of Ignatius (and the influence of Polanco?), the First General Congregation determined that the "substantials" of the Constitutions as written by Ignatius could not be modified even by a general

A number of texts insist upon guarding and observing the Constitutions.[103] A very interesting remark on helps to conserve and increase the body of the Company is that moderation in spiritual and bodily labors and "keeping the Constitutions well-balanced (*mediocridad en las Constitutiones*), not going to extremes either of rigor or of weakness, and, thus, they can be better kept", will help for the permanent conservation in being of this body (*a,* 256). A logical deduction from this statement would be that on the hypothesis that any provision of the Constitutions had become either too rigorous or too lax as a result of the evolution of historical circumstances, it would no longer fulfill its end of conserving the being of the Company and, in the truest loyalty to the intention of Ignatius, it should, therefore, be changed.

The texts also grant the faculty of dispensing from the Constitutions. Just as the general must see to the observance of the Constitutions, "similarly, he may dispense in particular cases, taking note of the persons, places, times, etc.," with the discretion God gives to him, "reflecting on their end which is the greater divine service and the good of those who live in this institute." The passage specifies that the general may make dispensations with regard to the experiments of those in proba-

congregation. See the *Institutum Societatis Jesu,* 7 vols. (Avenione, 1827-1838), IV, 29; VI, 2. The Third General Congregation made this prohibition even stronger (ibid., VI, 34), and the Fourth considered adding a simple vow to the vows of the professed not to consider anything publicly or privately against the "essentialia Instituti et Constitutionum Societatis." Though this vow was rejected, the rule was made that in provincial congregations change of these essentials could not be discussed (ibid., IV, 283-284). The Fifth General Congregation repeated these prohibitions and defined the "substantials" of the Institute (ibid., VI, 64; cf. 362). It would seem to be legitimate to inquire, in the light of the papal bulls and of the Constitutions themselves, whether these congregations had the right to bind future congregations not to discuss changes. The legislation of the various general congregations requires considerable study in the light of the historical and cultural situations in which they took place. At any rate, this prohibition to discuss "substantials" and to make changes in the Constitutions would seem to have been contrary to both the letter and the spirit of Ignatius' legislation, which always envisioned necessary changes according to contingent circumstances in everything except the "scope of our vocation."

103 *Cons*MHSJ, I, 14; II, 16, 194, 207, 208, 241, 248, 256, 257.

tion "as in the other matters where he judges this to be the intention of the Constitutions" (*a,* 241).[104]

The Constitutions are the instrument of the Company to assure its well-being and its effectiveness in accomplishing its end of the apostolic service of Christ here and now. They are not an end in themselves. They do not offer to the superior an a priori block of fixed decisions to solve every case wherein he must exercise his role of discernment. To be faithful to the conception of the role of the superior of Ignatius, a superior must always be willing to undertake the difficult task of discerning the will of God as it is discovered through his *pareçer* and *mirar* and *sentir* and *juzgar* in the actual situation, which he must approach with an attitude of spiritual liberty and openness to the workings of divine providence in the circumstances of persons, places and times.

From the beginning, this study has shown that in the conception of Ignatius the Company of Jesus exists as a whole: *todo el cuerpo.* An individual member is a "companion of Jesus" only to the extent of his actual union with the whole body acting under the unifying direction of its one head for the service of Christ through the aid of souls in companionship here and now. The role of every superior on his own level is constantly to renew this mutual union and love, this united life and action of the companions: to bring the Company to be by making an apostolic community of love at each new moment of its history. The Constitutions present Ignatius' description of this ever renewed process of unification and direction of the whole Company. This process is essentially that of discerning at each given moment the will of God for the life and action of the companions — the concrete way they must here and now achieve the end of the Company as a whole. Thus, the concrete prescriptions of the Constitutions concerning authority, hierarchy, obedience, etc. all pivot around the common objective of discernment of the actual will of God. It is for this reason that

104 The parallel passages in texts A and B change the last phrase to: "the intention of those who ordered the Constitutions" (*Cons*MHSJ, II, 672). These texts also state that the rector may dispense from the Constitutions "según las occurencias y necessidades" with the authority of his superiors (ibid., II, 458).

prayer is the primary means; that consultation of the best informed members is so insisted upon; that such ample provision is made for the representation of the opinion of individual members to the superior; that the manifestation of conscience and the intimate knowledge of each individual companion is considered so essential. The manifestation and the practice of representation are not, in the last analysis, directed towards primarily personalistic or psychological ends. They are directed towards the discovery of the actual will of God through mutual discernment, enabling the superior to see all the evidence in the concrete situation, independently of his own or others' subjective desires, so that he can direct the whole Company to its end.

All of this mutual exchange of *pareçeres* is the "circulation" of the body of the Company in the dynamic unity of all its members with one another and with their head. That which is revelatory and clarifying for true discernment is the grasping of the objective situation made possible through this circulation, this mutual exchange. It is here that Ignatius' dialectic of the personal good and the universal good plays its role. At the end of the process of mutual discernment, it is the ultimate *pareçer* of the superior, his final decision of the concrete will of God, which must unite all the members in life and apostolic work, a union which is made actual through the perfect obedience of all the companions. It is in this moment that the Company of Jesus comes to be. It exists as itself in the moment of perfect union of wills — mutual love — directing the whole body to the service of Christ through the aid of souls in companionship here and now.

OBEDIENCE FOR
APOSTOLIC LOVE

THROUGHOUT THIS STUDY it has been shown that according to Ignatius the essential role of the superior is to make an apostolic community of love by unifying all the members of the Company for the service of Christ through the aid of souls in companionship here and now. The exercise of the authority of the superior, therefore, is by its very nature always dynamic: the ever repeated renewal of the union of all the companions in mutual love — bringing the Company to be — to achieve the "scope of our vocation." This is the significance and the justification of authority in the Company in all of its functions: admitting new members and forming the desire of those in training to seek only the service and praise of God, ordering the lives of the companions in their communities, supervising their studies, caring for their health and temporal welfare, guiding their spiritual progress. The superior is the living principle of unity who binds together all the companions for accomplishing the apostolic end of the Company. Ignatius recognized, therefore, that the central function of the superior would be the discernment of the will of God at any moment for the lives and actions of the companions.

In the mind of Ignatius obedience is the correlative of the unifying role of the superior. The Company actually comes to be in the moment of perfect obedience of all the companions to the command of the superior. This act of obedience constitutes the mutual union of wills — mutual love — of all the members with one another and with their head, and it realizes the end of the Company of the apostolic service of Christ in companionship here and now. Consequently, Jesuit obedience is not an end in itself. It is, rather, the most important means to integrate all the companions into one living apostolic body.

For Ignatius the essential meaning of obedience was precisely this function of unifying all the members of the Company in an apostolic community of love. This is clear in texts concerning entrance into the Company or full incorporation in it through unifying obedience. Candidates are admitted into the Company "for entire obedience and corporate living in our Lord." [1] An obvious impediment to entrance into the Company would be a temperament which makes it impossible for a man "to dispose himself to live in the manner of the Company and to be obedient." [2] Members of the Company are identified in the fourth bull of Paul III as all those who are committed to obedience to the general of the Company.[3] Full incorporation in the Company is effected by commitment to obedience.[4] The essentially unifying end of Jesuit obedience is made explicit in passages treating obedience as the primary means to union.[5] That the mental structure of Ignatius identified "love and obedience and union" [6] is especially clear in the Eighth and Tenth Parts of the Constitutions. "Because this union is constituted in large part through the virtue of obedience, it should be maintained always in full vitality." [7] This union is effected by "the bond of wills which is charity and love of one another" (*a*, 225), while the primary means to it is "the bond of obedience which unites the companions with their superiors and with one another, local superiors with the provincials, and all with the general" (*a*, 256).[8] It is difficult to conceive of a clearer enunciation of the fact that Jesuit obedience is not an end in itself, but is, rather, the most important means to make a community of love for the service of Christ through the aid of souls in companionship. Through their perfect obedience to the unifying commands of their superior, the companions enable him to fulfill his role of making an apostolic community of love.

---

1 *Cons*MHSJ, II, 114. See ibid., I, 247, 249, 254; II, 40, 114.
2 Ibid., II, 145.
3 Ibid., I, 358, 359, 369.
4 Ibid., II, 145, 197, 204, 222, 230, 242, 638.
5 Ibid., I, 4, 5, 6, 7, 16; II, 226, 255-256, 312, 616. See above, ch. 2, p. 52.
6 Ibid., II, 616.
7 Ibid., II, 226.
8 See above, ch. 3, pp. 79-83; ch. 4, pp. 84-93.

The ascetical significance of obedience was important for the personal motivation of the individual companions to aid them to achieve the spiritual freedom required for the perfection of obedience and, therefore, of mutual union for corporate apostolic service.[9] True obedience requires true humility — the liberation of the person from all ego-centered desires —, so that he desires only the service and praise of God to be achieved in companionship. This is why obedience and humility were quasi-identified in the mental structure of Ignatius.[10] Another virtue he integrated with obedience and humility was reverence. *Reverencia* or *acatamiento* referred both to external acts of reverence and to the profound interior attitude which these expressed.[11] The praise and service of God is the embodiment of the profound reverence which the creature must have for his Creator.[12] This reverence should exist in the depths of the spirit,[13] and should overflow into a man's total human comportment.[14] For Ignatius, reverence and honor and the sensitive and delicate care always to please and never to offend the person who should be reverenced were all united in a basic existential attitude governing all external actions.[15] This humble reverence found its perfection in love: *"reverencia amorosa."* [16]

Ignatius applies the rich content of his notion of reverence to the delineation of the attitude that the companions should have towards their superiors. For example, he declares in the Constitutions that "all should have great reverence, especially interiorly, for their superiors, having consideration and reverence for Jesus Christ in them and loving them as fathers in Him." [17] Since Ignatius repeatedly gives the statement that the superior

---

9 See below, Appendix II.

10 See above, 98 and fn. 57.

11 See Covarrubias, p. 909; cf. p. 33. See also A. Nebreda, "El camino de Ignacio. Estudio del *acatamiento* en los Ejercicios Espirituales," *Manresa*, XXXII (1960), 45-66, 127-138.

12 *SpEx*, [23].

13 Ibid., [114].

14 Ibid., [3].

15 Ibid., [38]; *Cons*MHSJ, I, 127, 129, 131, 260. This *reverencia* and *acatamiento* became the content of a profound and repeated mystical experience for Ignatius as he recorded in his *Spiritual Diary*.

16 *Cons*MHSJ, I, 108, 131, 132, 133, 217, 387; II, 84, 96, 98, 106, 118, 120, 122, 610.

17 Ibid., II, 208; see I, 217.

commands the companions "in the place of Christ our Lord" as the motive of the humble, loving, reverent obedience that they must give him, it is necessary to analyze this formula.[18]

The notion that all legitimate authority, whether spiritual or temporal, comes from God and, therefore, vicariously represents the dominion of Christ to whom has been given all power in heaven and on earth had been a part of the cultural heritage of Ignatius from the beginning.[19] The Spanish ecclesiastical writers in developing a theory of kingship had started from the constant doctrine of the Church that organized society required authority to maintain its being and that all legitimate authority was derived from God. The *Siete Partidas* declared: "Kings in their kingdoms are vicars of God, placed over the people to maintain them in justice and truth in the temporal order";[20] "The king holds the place of God to establish justice and law in the kingdom of which he is lord";[21] "The people should recognize that the king occupies the place of God in the land to deal out justice and mercy and that his people are his subjects obliged to serve and obey him.[22]

An indication of the kind of imaginative development Ignatius gave to this notion of human authority as representing God occurs in the narration in the *Autobiography* of his difficulties during his first months in Paris. On arriving in the city on

---

18 Ibid., I, 18-19, 29, 217, 304, 379, 385, 389; II, 66-68, 68-70, 96, 98, 102, 106, 118, 120, 122, 161, 167, 168, 194, 207, 208, 214, 244, 410, 462, 516, 526, 560, 572, 574, 590; *equivalent expressions:* ibid., I, 68; II, 140, 168, 200, 201, 380, 522, 574, 654.

19 See the texts from Scripture and the early Fathers given in GG, II, 336-343; cf. 421.

20 *Siete Partidas,* II, 172.

21 Ibid., II, 174.

22 In the Visigothic coronation ritual, which was typical of such Christian rites, the archbishop asked the new king: "Vis regnum tuum, a Deo concessum, secundum justitiam patrum tuorum regere et defendere?" He prayed that the king might rule justly the "populumque a te sibi commissuam" (GG, II, 580-582). In his very useful study *Images of Authority: A Consideration of the Concepts of Regnum and Sacerdotium* (New Haven, 1966), J. M. Cameron remarks that in both Church and state during the Middle Ages "the view of power is that it is exercised by those who act in the name and with the authority of God; but they are vicars, delegates, substitutes, representatives" (p. 2). See also *Siete Partidas,* II, 211.

February 2, 1528, he enrolled in Latin classes at the college of Montaigu, and, in the beginning, he lived in the hostel for Spanish students. Lack of money soon forced him to move across the river to the hostel of St. James for the poor. This involved a long walk to and from classes and the necessity of early arrival at the hostel every evening before the doors were locked. Ignatius considered seeking work as a servant at the college in order to have lodging there, but his efforts were unsuccessful. In planning his manner of doing this work if he obtained this employment, he had decided to imagine that the Master of the college would be Christ and that one of the students would be St. Peter, another St. John, and so on for each of the apostles. When he received an order from the Master he would consider that it was Christ who commanded him. This idea reflected the Castilian tradition of authority as representing God.[23]

The conception of the superior as obeyed in the place of Christ was for Ignatius a spiritual motive for perfect obedience, as well as a reflection of his cultural formation. He appeals to this motivation in the first description of the manner of obedience the companions should give to superiors in the Company, which he wrote in the Formula of the Institute: all should obey the superior "and acknowledge and fittingly reverence in him *Christum, veluti presentem.*"[24] This motive is often

---

23 In his memoir, Laynez puts it that Ignatius determined to serve them with all diligence "como lugartinientes de nuestro Señor" (*FN,* I, 98). See also *FN,* I, 466.

24 The statement of the presence of Christ in the superior is modestly cast in the subjunctive: "as if present." It is notable in the succeeding formulae that Ignatius says to be ready at the voice of obedience "as if" (*como si*) it came from Christ. The reason he gives for the reverence and obedience shown to the superior in the place of Christ is that the subject obeys "for His love and reverence." There has been a tendency to read too much theological assertion of some kind of special, quasi-sacramental presence of Christ in the superior into the expressions of Ignatius, especially in the letters. Carlos Palmes, *La obediencia religiosa ignaciana* (Barcelona, 1963), pp. 153-156, develops this idea and goes so far as to state: "As Christ is the Incarnate Word of the Father, so the superior is the incarnation of Christ and manifests the divine will in his word" (p. 153). Cf. J. Lewis, *Le gouvernement spirituel* . . . (Montreal, 1961), pp. 54-56. In the letters, however, as in the Constitutions the "in the place of Christ" formulae occur in contexts of exhortation and motivation, rather than as the presentation of doctrine. It is true that a tradition

repeated in the subsequent documents. It looks above all to the personal, spiritual motivation of the individual members of the Company. Based upon a long Christian tradition made concrete for Ignatius in Castilian notions of vicarious authority, it is presented in the description of Jesuit obedience as the personal foundation upon which to build the perfect obedience which will enable each member to integrate himself into the whole body, thus bringing the Company to be at each historical moment of its existence.

The end of each individual man born into the world is to serve and glorify God through the closest possible union with Christ. Concretely, for a man who has the vocation to become a member of the Company of Jesus, this personal end is realized in his total commitment of himself to the end of the whole Company: the service of Christ through the aid of souls in companionship. To achieve this end he must be ready to go anywhere in the world at the command of the vicar of Christ on earth or of his superior who, as vicar of the pope, represents Christ to him. The conception of obedience to the superior as speaking in the place of Christ rejoins all the ascetical and spiritual motives and methods of the Company. They are intended to help the individual Jesuit to achieve the spiritual liberty of desiring only the glory of God realized in the ever greater extension of the Kingdom of Christ through uniting all these individual vocations into the one, dynamic, living body of the Company, which will be a more effective apostolic instrument than any of these individual persons could be alone. The spirituality of the Company as envisioned by Ignatius is always outer-directed. Personal perfection is for the sake of the apostolate in companionship.[25]

Ecclesial Obedience   The superior represents Christ to the companions because of the essentially vicarious structure of authority in the Church. The authority of the superior of the Company is based upon

developed in Jesuit spirituality which asserted much more of a "special presence" of Christ in the superior than appears in the vocabulary of Ignatius. It is possible that this idea, like so many others in Jesuit spirituality, originated with Jerónimo Nadal. One hopes that scholars will undertake both historical and theological studies in depth of this question.

25 See above, ch. 4, pp. 94-100.

the place of the Company within the Church of Christ.[26] The convictions of Ignatius concerning the authority of the Church are exposed in the Rules for Thinking Rightly Within the Church in the Spiritual Exercises. In the thirteenth rule Ignatius expresses in extremely straightforward terms his vision of the structure of reality — that which gave coherence to all his experience and explained to him the meaning of life: we must obey the hierarchical Church with perfect submission of individual judgment, because we believe that in Christ our Lord, the bridegroom, and in the Church which is His spouse, there is one and the same Spirit — the Holy Spirit — who, through the Church, governs and directs us to the salvation of our souls; for our holy mother the Church is ruled and guided by the same Spirit and Lord who gave us the ten commandments.[27] This profound faith, carried here to its logical consequence in the practical order by total obedience to the hierarchical Church, was the faith that Ignatius had received in the Basque castle; the faith that had informed the entire structure of kingship and of loyalty to legitimate authority in the Castile of his youth; the faith that had been deepened by the great light at the Cardoner and that had guided him through all the long and difficult years of his pilgrimage. The Company of Jesus which he founded has meaning only as an apostolic instrument of the Church.

A man who commits himself to the Company of Jesus freely makes himself a part of this body of companions, whose very being is precisely to serve Christ through serving His Church.[28] This service means going to teach all nations the great command of love given by Jesus and baptizing all men into His death and resurrection. Obedience, essentially ordered to this end from the very beginning,[29] unites all the companions with one another and with their head who gives the unifying com-

---

26 See L. Mendizabal, "El hecho ecclesiástico de la obediencia ignaciana", *Manresa*, XXXVI (1964), 403-420. Cf. K. Rahner, "A Basic Ignatian Concept Some Reflections on Obedience," *WL*, LXXXVII (1957), 291-310.
27 This principle of control of subjective judgment even in highly spiritual experiences by obedience to ecclesiastical authority is eloquently developed by Ignatius in his letter to Teresa Rejadella, June 18, 1536 (*EppIgn,* I, 105). See also *SpEx,* [365].
28 *Cons*MHSJ, I, 16.
29 Ibid., I, 2.

mands. In obeying the general or his vicars, the subordinate
superiors, the companions obey the man who for them is the
vicar of the vicar of Christ on earth. Christ Himself willed the
ecclesial structure so that all might be one in Him. Thus, to
obey the superior who represents Christ in this structure is to
obey Christ Himself. Love and reverence for Him is the motive
for obedience to His representative. Ignatian obedience has
meaning only because it is ecclesial obedience.

The Church is the human means willed by Christ for the
continued exercise of His divine salvific action in history until
the consummation of the world. The Church through which
He never ceases to act is the People of God, united with one
another and with their unifying head, the vicar of Christ on
earth, in an apostolic community of love. It is in and through
His Church — this human, weak and sometimes scandalous
community of redeemed but sinful men — that Christ acts to
enable all men to have a direct encounter with God and to
achieve the end for which they were created. In spite of human perversity and the obstacles thrown in the way of
Christ's action by the weight of evil, the omnipotent providence of God rules the Church through His Holy Spirit. Authority in the Church is an instrument of Divine Providence.[30]
In spite of the lack of wisdom or positively evil actions of
given hierarchical superiors — even of a pope — the Church of
Christ in its totality is guided by Divine Providence towards the
final achievement of the end for which Jesus established it: the
extension to all men of the saving grace of His cross and
resurrection, the transformation of the world into a "new crea-
tion." The Company of Jesus is an instrument of the Church
for the fulfillment of this end. The authority of the superior
and the obedience of the companions are entirely within the
Church and for the Church.

A man who is incorporated into the Company of Jesus enters
in a special way into the order of Divine Providence for the
whole Church. He is embraced by the providential ordering
of the scope of our vocation for the service of the Church.
Obedience in the Company, therefore, inserts a companion into
this order of providence. The companion who happens to be
superior becomes the "minister" of Divine Providence through

30 Ibid., II, 20-22.

whom all the companions are united and directed to the service of Christ in His Church. The superior gives commands to
his companions "in the place of Christ." In spite of his human
limitations he is the instrument of Divine Providence for the
final achievement of the end of the whole body of the Company which requires that it come to be here and now through
the union of all its members with one another and with their
head. It is in view of this insertion of the Company into the
providential ordering of the Church of Christ to its divinely
appointed end that in a crisis situation "blind" obedience becomes possible and finds its justification.[31]

For Ignatius the "mystical" aspect of obedience followed
from its essential meaning as the bond of union of the companions of Jesus as a corporate instrument of the Church of
Christ. The personal, spiritual motive of seeing Christ in the
superior and of loving his commands as the manifestation of
the will of God for this individual here and now, which could
lead a companion to great heights of mystical union with God
in the very practice of perfect obedience to the superior "in the
place of Christ," received its value and its meaning from the
providence of God exercised through the Holy Spirit in the
Church and, so, in the Company of Jesus.[32] The individual
vocation would find its fulfillment and its perfection in personal
sanctity within the vocation of the whole Company as an instrument of Christ in His Church.

In reading the texts in which Ignatius treats of the practice *The Practice*
of obedience of the companions of Jesus, it is necessary always *of Obedience*
to keep in mind the essential meaning of obedience in the Company as the primary means to union in mutual love and apostolic action. The passages in the Constitutions concerning the
manner to obey are based upon a text in the early document
"Constituta et Annotata," (1544-1549) which specifically
treats of obedience as a means (*medio*) to the end of fulfilling

31 See below, Appendix II.
32 Cf. F. Taymans, "Missions divines et obéissance humaine," *NRT*,
LXIX (1947), 486-496; M. Pontet, "Sur la terre comme au ciel.
Essai de critique religieuse," *NRT*, LXXV (1953), 1067-1075, especially 1073-1074; G. Gilleman, "L'obéissance dans notre vie divine,"
Christus, no. 8 (1955), 466-487; H. Holstein, "Le mystère de
l'obéissance," *Études*, CCLXXVIII (1953), 145-157.

the scope of our vocation.[33] This obedience is based upon the vocation of each individual companion who must look only to God and must find in perfect obedience an expression of love (*con spiritu de amor*). This dynamic love will lead to perfection in realizing the end of the Company; but to achieve this perfection, it is most necessary to apply all effort to the strength and virtue of obedience. Having placed obedience in the Company very clearly as a means to its apostolic end, Ignatius goes on to declare in what manner it should be practiced. Of course, it should not be given if we can "judge or swear that this would be in any way sinful." Otherwise, the execution of the command should be prompt and total. Here Ignatius introduces the example of promptness from the monastic scriptorium: immediate obedience, even leaving the letter unfinished. He also appeals to the personal spiritual motive of responding to the voice of obedience as if it were spoken by Christ, "since we obey (the superior) in His place and for His love and reverence." Obedience of the will and understanding is presented as necessary for this prompt and perfect execution — a kind of "blind" obedience.

The earliest appearance of the expression "blind" obedience in the Ignatian documents occurs in a letter written around August, 1542, to John Baptist Viola, a scholastic studying at Paris, who had requested a change in courses rather than "wasting my time," unless obedience commanded him to do so. Ignatius wrote: "It seems to me that obedience ought to be blind. I call it blind in two ways: (1) where there is no sin the subject conforms his judgment and does what is commanded; (2) granted that the superior commands him or has commanded something, the subject feeling (*sentir*) reasons and difficulties concerning what is commanded, with humility represents these reasons and difficulties to the superior, not putting pressure on him one way or the other, in order that afterwards he may in interior peace follow the way which will be shown to him and commanded him." [34]

It is notable that in the passage in the *Constituta et Annotata,* the adjective blind refers to both the will and the obedient understanding.[35] Ignatius explains that as regards the will this

---

33 *Cons*MHSJ, I, 216-217.
34 *EppIgn,* 228. See also below, pp. 168.
35 *Cons*MHSJ, I, 217.

means that we obey the command promptly and with spiritual joy, while as regards the understanding it means that we deny our own opinion and judgment in all matters where we cannot swear that the command of the superior is sinful. It is here, therefore, that Ignatius emphasizes the necessity of total interior "self-abnegation." Prompt and joyful obedience is impossible without this complete liberation from all ego-centered desires in order to desire only the service of Christ. Without this perfect obedience the Company cannot come to be.

The passages in the Constitutions on the manner of obeying develop and explain the earlier text to a certain extent, but their fundamental structure is the same. The first passage occurs in the Third Chapter of the Third Part in a context discussing the means to dispose those in probation to virtue. After appealing to the personal spiritual motive of obeying the superior in the place of Christ, Ignatius explains the three-fold perfect obedience — of execution, of will, and of understanding or judgment.

Obedience of execution means the prompt performance of what is commanded, "with the necessary courage and humility," with no excuses or rancor, even when the order given is difficult and repugnant. As regards the interior, the companion must have "true resignation and abnegation of his own will and judgment." Such spiritual freedom is, once more, the essential condition for perfect interior obedience: "entirely conforming his desire and feelings to what the superior desires and feels" (*querer y sentir*), in all cases where sin is not evident.[36] Ignatius here introduces a new motive for obedience of will and of judgment: the subject conforms himself to the rule of the superior "in order to conform himself more truly to the first and highest rule of all good will and judgment which is the eternal Goodness and Wisdom."[37]

---

36 Ibid., II, 167.

37 The statement here that through obedience a member of the Company achieves greater conformity with the will of God rejoins the other expressions in the Constitutions about the rule of Divine Providence governing the companions through their superiors. It is presented as a personal, spiritual motive; but it does not have the same significance as did the ascetical practice of the monks of the desert seeking perfection through complete renunciation of their own wills to follow the decisions of their spiritual father. See below, pp. 168-173; also *Cons*MHSJ, II, 168.

In the Third Chapter of the Sixth Part of the Constitutions, Ignatius repeats the passage from the *Constituta et Annotata* with some further development. The perfection of obedience means that one should be outstanding in it (*señalarse*), obeying not only in matters of obligation such as those contained in the bull or commanded under obedience, but also in all other matters where sin is not evident, even though there is only a sign given of the will of the superior without an express order. The description of the three-fold obedience is more precise. All must strive "that holy obedience in execution and in will and in understanding be always perfect in everything." To the qualities of promptness and spiritual joy in carrying out the command that of perseverance is now added. The notion of "blind" obedience is expressed somewhat differently: "persuading themselves with blind obedience that what is commanded is good" (*justo*).[38] Once more, the "abnegation" of one's own opinion and judgment is made explicit as the means to achieve this perfect obedience.

Texts A and B of the Constitutions repeat this passage adding the personal, spiritual motive to let oneself be ruled "by Divine Providence through the mediation of the superior" and giving some of the examples of obedience Polanco was already collecting from the Fathers and from older religious rules: the dead body which allows itself to be taken anywhere and treated in any manner and the stick in the old man's hand which is entirely at his service.[39] These examples, of course, are more harmful than helpful in contemporary language and culture. For Ignatius, a man of his own epoch and language, they would not have been shocking, particularly since he immediately added the idea of obedience which he wished to express through them: "because in this way the obedient companion should joyfully labor in whatever work in which the superior wishes to employ him for the aid of the whole body of the religious institute," being certain that, thus, he conforms himself to the divine will better than he could by performing some other action according to his own will and judgment.[40]

---

38 *Cons*MHSJ, II, 207.
39 Ibid., II, 522; see also Appendix II.
40 *Cons*MHSJ, II, 522.

Text B adds a Declaration explaining exactly in what consists the three-fold obedience. Obedience of execution means that "the thing commanded is done"; of the will, that the one obeying "wills the same thing as the one giving the command"; and of the understanding, that he "feels (*sentir*) the same, having a good opinion (*pareçer*) of what is commanded." Obedience is imperfect if obedience of execution is not accompanied by this "conformity of will and *sentir* between the one who commands and the one who obeys".[41] The purpose of this practice of interior and exterior obedience is precisely the aid of souls in companionship, the joyful fulfillment of the scope of our corporate vocation made actual through the unifying command of the superior and the obedience of all the companions.

In the light of this constant presentation of obedience as a means to the end of union and mutual love for the apostolic end of the Company, it is possible to see what Ignatius meant by obedience of the understanding and the role of "blind" obedience. Perfect obedience means the prompt and joyful execution of the superior's command, possible only if the will and the judgment of the companion conform to the will and the judgment of the superior. Obedience of understanding means that the one obeying judges that the command is *justo,* and so removes all psychological obstacles to prompt and joyful execution.

"Blind" obedience is presented as the means to achieve obedience of the understanding in cases where the companion has an opinion or judgment contrary to the order of the superior. It would not be operative, therefore, when one sees clearly that the command of the superior is wise, because in such cases obedience of the understanding is immediately possible.[42] "Blind" obedience consists in persuading oneself that the superior's order is good, even though it contradicts one's own judgment and requires denial of one's own opinion. The justification of "blind" obedience is not found in the mind of Ignatius through some tortured theologizing resulting in a "proof" that God wills the content of the specific command as

41 *Cons*MHSJ, II, 524.
42 See below, Appendix II.

such.[43] Rather, it is grounded in the "scope of our vocation." Since it is the will of God that a member of the Company serve Christ through the aid of souls in companionship, it follows of necessity that each individual companion must be ready to deny his own will and judgment when this is required in order to integrate himself into the dynamic unity of the Company. Otherwise, the aid of souls in companionship would become strictly impossible. This consciousness of the value of the "scope of our vocation" gives to each one the interior force needed to deny further consideration of his own opinion, since the command given must be executed and there is no more time for further discussion and mutual discernment. "Blind" obedience means, then, not the shutting of one's eyes as such, but rather fixing one's attention uniquely upon the *quid agendum:* the fact that within the "scope of our vocation" the will of God is being indicated by the superior, although one does not know, anymore than did Ignatius at Jerusalem, whither it is leading.[44]

For a man who has the vocation to be a member of the Company of Jesus, the will of God is expressed once and for all in the "scope of our vocation": the service of Christ through the aid of souls in companionship. This will of God, therefore, includes all the necessary consequences of this vocation. Now, this vocation can be fulfilled only through the constantly renewed act of bringing the Company to be in the actual union of all the members with one another and with their head for corporate apostolic activity here and now. This union consists in the

43 C. Palmes, *La Obediencia Religiosa Ignaciana* (Barcelona, 1963), attempts to justify the notion that the specific command in its content represents the particular will of God for a subject. He begins with the general notion that God has an antecedent will for the sanctification of all men which includes all of the means to achieve this end (pp. 21-22). Specifically, God has this detailed and precise will for each individual religious in the perfection of his own vocation which extends to "each one of the circumstances of his life" (p. 62). To explain how the obedient subject attains in the least details of his life this specific, a priori will of God for each circumstance of his existence, even though the superior may depart from this divine will in his decision, Palmes is forced to introduce distinctions between the consequent will of God and two different antecedent wills (pp. 125-134). God has a *voluntad de signo* for the superior antecedent to his command (p. 130). It is the superior's fault if he does not find this will. But God has another antecedent will *de signo* for the subject (p. 131). If the superior transmits the first will faith-

mutual union of wills — mutual love — of all the companions. Obedience is the primary means to this union, its sine qua non condition. Perfect obedience at every moment to the actual command of the superior, consequently, is the will of God for each member of the whole body of the Company. The individual companion can be certain that in conforming his will and judgment to that of the superior he achieves greater conformity with the will of God than he could in following his own contrary opinion. The being of the Company consists in this constantly renewed companionship which is brought to be through perfect obedience to the actual command of the superior here and now. Therefore, the will of God is expressed to each companion at any given moment in the actual unifying command. Prompt and joyful execution of a command contrary to one's own will and judgment is possible through "blind" obedience, denying one's own position to prevent destroying this union and therefore the being of the Company, and finding good the command of the superior because it, even if unwise in itself, unifies the companions and brings the Company to be here and now. This command, consequently, is the actual will of God for each companion here and now according to the "scope of our vocation."

The conviction of the first companions that it was the will of God for them — their vocation — not to dissolve the union that he had led them to form, but rather to confirm it and make it more solid each day through mutual care and comprehension

---

fully, these two wills are identical. But if the superior is not faithful, God has yet another antecedent will for the subject (not just His consequent will), which is the original antecedent will plus the interpretation of the superior (p. 131). Thus, in obeying the order of the superior (who has not faithfully transmitted the antecedent will of God for him), the subject still fulfills the antecedent will of God for him, thanks to this "double antecedent will" posited by Palmes. This sort of reasoning suggests that God is a kind of pincushion! The theological basis, however traditional in scholastic theology of a certain type, is not very solid. God would seem to have a much more generic will for the salvation of men, leaving specifications of details to human liberty. It is not surprising to find Palmes complacently using the very unhappy image of the obedient subject who recognizes the voice of the Master in that of the superior and reflects "that it is Providence which moves from above the strings of the puppets" (p. 216).

44 See above, ch. 1, pp. 29-30.

was the result of their recognition that through united effort they could better serve Christ apostolically.[45] In the Deliberation obedience to "one of us" was chosen precisely as the way to fulfill "the good pleasure and the perfect will of God according to the scope of our vocation." [46] Because of this conviction, which is the foundation of the vocation to aid souls in companionship, it is psychologically possible for a member of the Company to deny his own will and judgment and to find good the unifying command of the superior even when it goes contrary to his own opinion as long as it is not clearly sinful.[47] The companion is aware that a corporate apostolic effort in the long run will result in greater service of Christ and more effective aid of souls than he could accomplish alone, even though in a given instance he may find that the command which must be executed is against his own considered judgment of the best way to serve Christ apostolically in the present situation. Thus, denying further consideration of his own opinion, he can find it possible to carry out the command promptly and joyfully. In an extreme or "crisis" case, this may mean to "blind" oneself to the content of a specific command, because he recognizes that this is the only way to bring the Company to be as an apostolic instrument of Christ. [48]

The individual companion knows that to be part of a community, to make it come to be as a community, supposes self-

---

45 *Cons*MHSJ, I, 3.

46 Ibid., I, 2.

47 Today, much more than during earlier, simpler times when the possibility that a superior might command something sinful was considered very theoretical, since sin tended to be identified with a list of clear negative commandments, superiors must be aware of the exigencies of conscience of their companions in view of sins of omission. Much more dialogue and consultation of experts is required nowadays than it was in former times to set the individual conscience at rest.

48 The possibility of a "crisis" case of obedience, wherein the companions clearly see that the evidence is contrary to the decision of the superior is much greater in contemporary situations where they often have a special competence which the superior lacks. If the superior has failed to use all the Ignatian means of discernment, the subject may be placed in a truly agonizing position. This "crisis" case, although somewhat over-optimistically considered to be extremely rare, has been discussed by the commentators in the context of what might be called the "casuistry of obedience." Most interpretations are based upon a distinction introduced by Suarez, *De*

sacrifice for the universal good of the whole community. He will see a "crisis" case of obedience as simply a particularly dramatic instance of the fundamental requirement of his vocation to be part of a community: with all his companions to fulfill the "scope of our vocation." Obedience of judgment is grounded in the overall judgment that the service of Christ in His Church through the aid of souls can best be achieved in its totality by an apostolate undertaken in companionship. This overall judgment allows for the objective fact that in an individual case personal apostolic action can be hindered rather than helped by a command of the superior. Here, the dialectic of the universal good and the individual good comes into play from the side of obedience. The superior general — or his vicar at the provincial or local level — is an emanation of the Company and must be regarded by the obedient member as the companion who incarnates the whole body of the Company in view of its corporate apostolic end, rather than as an individual who frustrates personal judgments and desires or a particular apostolate.

The motive which makes possible the self-persuasion that the superior's command, although contrary to one's own judgment, is *justo* is that persons living under obedience should allow themselves to be ruled by Divine Providence through the mediation of the superior. Thus, a companion can allow himself to be employed by the superior in the aid of souls with certitude that he conforms himself better to the divine will through this obedience than he could in following his own different will and judgment. According to Ignatius, denial of one's own judgment

---

Religione Societatis, IV, 15-16, between the particular end intended by the superior in the command and the general end which he intends in all things and which the subject must pursue in all things: obtaining the kingdom of God. Through blind obedience the subject closes his eyes to the first end and considers only the generic one which he can affirm. More recent commentators have emphasized the mysterious workings of Divine Providence, ultimately turning all things — even human malice and error — to the good for which God created mankind and stressing that, in itself, no natural means can be adequate to achieve a supernatural end. See, for example, A. Valensin, "Notes sur divers points concernant l'obéissance", *RAM,* II (1926), 173 ff.; M. Giuliani, "Nuit et lumière de l'obéissance," *Christus,* no. 7. (1955), 349-368; K. Rahner, "A Basic Ignatian Concept . . ." , *WL,* LXXXVII (1957), 291-310, and *The Christian Commitment* (New York, 1963), pp. 14-37, 60-61.

should make it psychologically possible for the companion to persuade himself that the command of the superior is itself *justo*. The reason for this is evident from a consideration of the structure of discernment according to Ignatius. Ignatius nowhere states that the superior is necessarily correct in his final judgment. He insists upon prayer for light and expresses hope in the grace of state, but he does not assert that the superior infallibly arrives at the best possible decision. Indeed, the judgment of the superior is never beyond possibility of error, and so it must always be open to reform should experience show it to have been wrong. But what is true of the judgment of the superior is, in principle, even more true of the judgment of the individual companion who normally does not have at his disposal all the means of discernment available to the superior. The decisions to be made are in the practical order for the conservation and growth of a community of love and for the choice of apostolic missions and methods. As judgments of the practical order they rarely will be grounded in evidence so overwhelming as to exclude the possibility of a different and possibly wiser choice.[49] Furthermore, Ignatius was very aware of the difficulty of being liberated from hidden prejudices and subtle self-seeking. The whole long process of the Spiritual Exercises bears witness to the effort needed to achieve spiritual liberty and to make choices based on the desire only to serve and praise God. A companion who is aware of the relativity of human judgments in the practical order (his own as well as those of the superior) and who is conscious of the risk he runs of deceiving himself through self-centered desires often will find it possible through no longer considering his own judgment to persuade himself that the command of the superior is *justo*, especially if he sees that the superior really makes use of all the means of discernment available to him.

If a superior truly follows the Ignatian way of discernment: through authentic dialogue, through personal knowledge of the various human beings who are his companions, through fully

---

49 Ignatius gave as the motive for the special vow of obedience to the pope that the companions could not be certain where they could best serve God (*Cons*MHSJ, I, 160). In principle, the pope should be in the best position to decide what missions should be undertaken to best serve Christ anywhere in the world.

adequate communication, and through constant openness to the teaching of experience in the concrete circumstances of time and place and persons, he rarely will be forced to give a command which will require a companion to practice an extreme form of "blind" obedience. A truly Ignatian superior must make his own the essentially dynamic mental structure of Ignatius himself — always "on the way," always ready to recognize the signs of the actual will of God manifested in each new concrete situation, never bound within a closed system of government and of a priori decisions simply imposed upon subjects who are expected to "grit their teeth," blind their minds and woodenly obey. It must always be remembered that for Ignatius an important sign of confirmation of the discernment of the will of God was the mutual contentment of the superior and the companions.

Through the study of Ignatius' conception of the meaning and practice of obedience in the Company of Jesus, it is possible to disengage the essential structure of Jesuit obedience. First, Jesuit obedience must be total, perfect, loving, joyful. Second, this obedience is essentially a means to the apostolic end of the Company, the "scope of our vocation" which supposes the total commitment of each companion to the corporate vocation, and as a result is a means to the bond of love uniting all the members with one another and with their head — a union realized in perfect obedience. Third, a personal spiritual motivation of seeing Christ giving commands through the superior because of the role of the Company as an apostolic instrument of the Church helps the companions to love and reverence the superior and, so, to obey him perfectly. Fourth, perfect obedience is threefold: prompt and joyful execution of the command by the companion based on conformity of his will and of his judgment to that of the superior. Fifth, for one to obey promptly and joyfully and to persevere in obedience, "blind" obedience may be necessary. The expression refers to the perfect obedience of understanding achieved when that which is commanded, being contrary to one's own will and judgment, is found good because of the "scope of our vocation." Sixth, in conforming himself perfectly to the judgment of the superior in perfect obedience, the companion achieves greater conformity with the will of God according to the "scope of our vocation."

The Structure of Jesuit Obedience

Seventh, external and interior obedience is possible only if one has attained true spiritual liberty, centering his desires not upon himself, but uniquely upon the service and praise of God.

The Role of the Superior The essential role of the superior according to Ignatius is to make the apostolic community of love which constitutes the Company of Jesus here and now for the service of Christ through the aid of souls in companionship. Only through a misinterpretation of the fundamental meaning of authority and obedience in the Company can one conclude that the primary role of the superior is to be the spiritual director of each one of the companions in order to lead them to personal perfection.[50] It has been shown that the personal perfection of the members is always ordered to the apostolic end of the whole body of the Company.[51] It is quite true that the superior must exercise an ascetical and pedagogical role in the formation of young members of the Company to lead them to spiritual liberty and the desire only to serve Christ which is necessary if they are to unite themselves fully to the Company. This role of the superior is directed towards the progressive incorporation of members into the body of the Company. Full incorporation supposes total freedom from self-love for the sake of the mutual union of wills — mutual love — which constitutes the being of the Company. This is the reason for the long duration of formation and experiments before full incorporation in the Company. The superior also has the role of aiding even fully formed members to advance in personal sanctification. But these roles are simply parts of his essential role of being the living principle of unity for all the companions of Jesus in their union of life and apostolic action.

50 C. Palmes, op. cit. p. 60, states that the *"primer officio"* of the superior is to interpret the divine will for his subjects. He explains that if the role of the superior as the head of the community is important, much more important is his role as "director of each one of the souls of his subjects" (p. 61). Further on, he declares that for Ignatius the superior was not only responsible for ordering the community to the common good, but also and "above all" (*sobre todo*) to be the "spiritual father who must rule the subject for his personal perfection" (p. 274). This, indeed, is to misunderstand the dialectic of the individual good and the universal good in the role of the superior according to Ignatius.

51 See above, ch. 4, pp. 94-100.

His role requires all the dynamism of the mental structure of Ignatius himself, an openness to all the indications of the actual will of God revealed by experience in each new concrete situation. The superior can never take refuge in a priori categories woodenly imposed upon his obedient subjects. He must seek their help to discern the will of God for the Company at each new moment of history. He must avoid all escapism into a voluntaristic security based upon the notion that whether he commands well or ill, God must manifest His will to the companions through the orders of the superior.[52] The superior must make it possible for his companions to form a true community united by mutual love, rather than by mere external forms. True community supposes the conscious and free commitment of each individual member to the scope of our vocation, the total engagement of complete and mature persons in the great cause of the apostolic service of Christ in companionship. A superior who through fear or mistaken loyalty attempts to impose and defend orders against the evidence of concrete circumstances of place and time and persons not only imposes an unjustifiable burden upon his subjects but also acts in direct opposition to the notion of Ignatius of the role of the superior.

A truly Ignatian superior in his ordering of the spiritual and the temporal lives of his companions and in his commands to them to undertake apostolic missions in the service of the Church will bring the Company to be by making the practice of perfect, loving, joyful obedience the normally spontaneous response of all the companions to his government of them "in the place of Christ." [53] Through intimate, personal knowledge

---

52 Cf. L. Mendizabal, *El modo de mandar selon San Ignacio* (Bérriz, Viscaya, 1966), pp. 28-29. He is careful to limit his affirmation of the serene, moral security of the superior to one who has really done his best to discover the concrete will of God. There is a psychological risk, however, for superiors to run too quickly to this providential security.

53 This ideal of the attitude and the actions of the superior in relation to his subjects is eloquently expressed in *Perfectae Caritatis,* the decree of Vatican Council II on the religious life: "Governing his subjects as God's own sons, and with regard for their human personality, the superior will make it easier for them to obey gladly. . . . Let him give the kind of leadership which will encourage religious to bring an active and responsible obedience to the offices they shoulder and the activities they undertake." *The Documents of Vatican II,* ed. Walter Abbott (New York, 1966), p. 477.

of each one of his companions (at least through the hierarchical structure of subordination), he will be enabled to care and provide for the spiritual and the temporal needs of all. Using all means for ever more effective interpersonal communication, he will usually find it possible to resolve the dialectic of the individual good and the universal good in an harmonious synthesis of united life and action which will issue in an ever more effective apostolate. Endowed with a dynamic mental structure like that of Ignatius himself — the spiritual liberty to be always "on the way," always open to every new indication of the actual will of God — he will seek the divine will with great fidelity to the structure of discernment outlined by Ignatius. With the help of his companions he will make decisions according to the circumstances of time, place and persons which most often will give mutual contentment to all. His companions, aware of their superior's knowledge and love of them and of his capacity to govern them, will obey him with love and joy. If, on occasion, they must practice "blind" obedience, they will find it possible to do so with interior peace, because they will be profoundly and concretely aware of the transcendent value of the "scope of our vocation." The truly Ignatian superior, in short, will carry out the role of the superior as Ignatius conceived of it. He will constantly bring the Company to be anew by making an apostolic community of love for the service of Christ through the aid of souls in companionship here and now.

MAKING AN APOSTOLIC
COMMUNITY OF LOVE

IN THE INTRODUCTION TO THIS STUDY the writer admitted to astonishment at some of the questions he was led to pose by the method of vocabulary analysis and at the answers to which this analysis led. Having been formed within a certain tradition of authority and obedience in the Company of Jesus, one is surprised to find that the fundamental idea of St. Ignatius of the end of the Company and of the role of the superior differs from this tradition in many important ways. In this final, brief chapter an effort will be made to sum up the conclusions of this study of the language of St. Ignatius expressing the role of the superior.

The mental structure of a man consists of his awareness of his personal identity and of the psychological characteristics of his own manner of grasping reality — of structuring the natural and supernatural experiences which he shares with others, but which are distilled within his self-consciousness into a coherent whole which is his own answer to the search for the meaning of his life. Personal identity is shaped and finally discovered through the interplay of many forces within self-awareness. Self-awareness is incarnated from the beginning in a certain human body, a family, a culture, a history. All of these factors enter as "material" into a man's consciousness of his irreducible selfhood, material which he must form into a certain personal manner of living. The constant accumulation of new experiences joined with the evolution of one's own personal history in time constitute his "past," carried into the moment of his present self-awareness and giving meaning and value in his free choice of his future.

The Mental Structure of Ignatius

On the psychological level the "election" of a vocation is a kind of definitive discovery of personal identity. All of the factors of one's past and of his present self-awareness are seen to find their coherence in the commitment of oneself to a certain permanent life-form. At this privileged moment a man can say: "This is myself. Here I find my own true identity. All that is to follow in my life, my personal history, will find its significance and its value within this identity." Such a commitment is, consequently, an engagement for life to this vocation and all its known and unforeseen consequences, because to deny it is to deny one's own painfully acquired personal identity. The understanding of the vocation will constantly grow through living it, and the realization of the depth of commitment will become ever clearer as its consequences are faced; but it is grounded in this moment of free election of self-identity.

In following the spiritual evolution of Ignatius Loyola which culminated in the foundation of the Company of Jesus, it has been possible to trace his gradual formation and discovery of personal identity. In discovering his vocation he was led successively from the ideal of personal service of God to the realization of this service through the aid of souls and, finally, to the accomplishment of this apostolic action in companionship. Ignatius then spent the rest of his life concretely realizing this vocation in the Company of Jesus and striving for the preservation and growth of the Company by framing Constitutions and by delineating the role of the superior. The vocation of Ignatius Loyola wherein he found his personal identity became the vocation of all those men who would incorporate themselves into the body of the Company: the service of Christ in His Church through going anywhere in the world at the command of His vicar to aid souls in companionship.

The basic psychological characteristic of the manner of grasping reality of Ignatius has been shown to have been concreteness. He saw reality in all its existential richness and density, the complex intertwining of the many circumstances that form every actual situation. Thus, his mental orientation was markedly visual, expressed in his constant search for light and clarity; and it was essentially dynamic, because the concrete real is always moving forward towards the fulfillment or the frustration of its being. He saw the praise and reverence and service of God as identified with the ever greater aid of souls through the vocation of the Company. He saw the being of the Company as the ever renewed mutual love of the companions realized constantly through the role of the superior, the living principle of their union. He saw the exercise of authority as fundamentally the exercise of love, and obedience as the response of love to love. Ignatius expressed the process of discernment, an essential for the superior, in terms of his concrete experience of the dynamic intermingling of psychological states: forming opinions based upon actual evidence, refining these opinions through prayerful reflection and mutual discernment, noting the orientation of concomitant feelings, gradually forming and reforming judgments in order finally to arrive at decisions.

The dynamism of the mental structure of Ignatius caused him always to look to living experience as the clearest indication of the concrete will of God being expressed through His providence — His active love in history. His spiritual liberty, won through the Spiritual Exercises, freed him from theoretical "straitjackets." This mental structure of Ignatius Loyola is expressed in his language and underlies his conception of the role of the superior.

The role of the superior according to Ignatius is completely dynamic. One of the astonishing results of the analysis of his language describing this role has been the basic unity and simplicity of the superior's function. All of the concrete specifications of the various ways to carry out this role — giving commands to undertake apostolic missions, ordering the spiritual and the temporal lives of the companions and providing for their needs, forming new companions into members fully incorporated into the body of the Company — all these roles were seen to be the realization of the essential role of the superior: making an apostolic community of love. The superior is the living principle of unity in the Company as he brings the Company to be anew by uniting all the actual companions with one another and with himself in true mutual love, the profound interior union which incarnates the love of God of each individual member and which makes possible the service of Christ through the aid of souls in companionship. Through the process of discernment the superior must endeavor to synthesize the individual good and the universal good in the ever more effective accomplishment of the "scope of our vocation." Despite the necessity of analyzing the various functions of authority, one is always led back to the amazing simplicity and richness of Ignatius' concrete idea of the role of the superior.

One must distinguish carefully those specific prescriptions concerning the use of authority which are expressions of Ignatius' own culture and language from his basic dynamic notion of the role of the superior as such, which must be carried out in different ways in other times and places if one is to be truly loyal to Ignatius. For instance, the ascetical and pedagogical role of the superior essentially is ordered to the formation of the desire of new companions: to lead them to true spiritual liberty, freedom from self-seeking and self-love, so that they will desire only the apostolic service of Christ in companionship. The concrete manner to form this spiritual liberty and desire will differ from one time and place to another. It is possible that specific ascetical methods proposed by Ignatius as a result of his own temperament and of the concrete circumstances he confronted would not only not be helpful, but would be positively harmful for different companions in different historical and cultural circumstances. The Company at any given moment of its history must discern how to preserve spiritual continuity across cultural discontinuity. With his dynamic mental structure, Ignatius would have been the first to follow the teaching of living experience in order to discern the way to achieve the end of the formation-role of the superior here and now.

Ignatius enunciated just such a principle to Francis Borgia in a letter written on September 20, 1548: "Nevertheless, I feel in the same Lord (*sentiendo en el mismo Señor nuestro*) that if we have need of certain exercises for a time, whether these be spiritual or bodily, at other times we have need of others; and those which are good at one time are not constantly so at another time" (*EppIgn,* II, 233-234). This principle should be applied, *mutatis mutandis,* to all the specifications of the role of the superior made by Ignatius and even to necessary adaptations of the Constitutions. One thing is required: to remain absolutely faithful to Ignatius' conception of the essential role of the superior — to make an apostolic community of love here and now.

The study also revealed that for Ignatius Jesuit obedience is not an end in itself. Correlative to the role of the superior, it is the absolutely necessary means to bring the Company to be. Because of his faith in Christ and in His Church and because of his personal commitment to the "scope of our vocation" which can be realized only in mutual union and love, the companion of Jesus finds it possible to obey perfectly, even when forced to practice "blind" obedience. The individual Jesuit knows that through obedience to the unifying commands of the head, he finds God. The way to perfection of the individual companion of Jesus is the way of obedience. By his total gift of himself to the Company through obedience, he lives love: the self-communication which culminates in communion with God, with all his companions, and with all mankind whom he serves.

On the other hand, the superior is not God, nor does he receive revelations from the Holy Spirit of the content of the decisions he must make for the life and action of the Company. The structure of discernment as it is presented by Ignatius emphasizes the difficulty of finding the actual will of God and the necessity that the superior avail himself of the help of mutual discernment in dialogue with his companions. The superior as an emanation of the Company is responsible not only to God, but also to the whole Company who must care for him and watch over him and, if necessary, correct him and depose him. In the conception of Ignatius the superior is not a father governing paternally, but a companion who must make the final decisions that will enable all the companions to fulfill the "scope of our vocation" here and now through their perfect, loving, joyful obedience to his unifying commands.

The role of the superior according to Ignatius of Loyola is not easy. The duties of any state of life impose certain risks upon a human being. God gives to each man the graces necessary for serving Him in a particular state of life and, if this is an "outer-directed" role for the service of others, those special charismatic graces needed to carry out the role. This "grace of state" does not operate magically. It requires the cooperation of the person receiving it, as does any grace given to any man. A superior can vitiate his grace of state if he gives way to the particular temptations involved in his state of life.

Many of the "temptations" of a superior can be the result of false notions concerning this role, rather than temptations in the classical sense. In a man of good will who is a superior, these "temptations" probably rarely operate on a fully conscious level. If anything, this increases the danger that they will keep him from carrying out his role as Ignatius intended. The superior, therefore, has the duty of daring to delve into the hidden depths of his subjective motives in order to discover what could impede him from making an apostolic community of love.

It seems to the present writer that nearly all the "temptations" of a superior, apart from childish ones such as ambition or favoritism, are reducible to some form of fear. Confronted with the responsibilities and risks involved in carrying out his role, he is in danger of giving way to a subtle kind of fear which can be hidden by unadmitted self-deception, but which will result in the destruction rather than in the realization of the mutual union which constitutes the being of the Company.

There is the fear of the risks involved in entering into true personal relationships with his companions. To escape the insecurity of such relationships, the superior may be tempted to isolate himself from real contact with his companions — to hide behind the office of superior and to become a "personage" rather than a person. True knowledge of the individual companions may make painful demands upon the superior and complicate his life; so, he may be tempted to escape into the security of turning the manifestation of conscience into a mere formality, rather than seeking to create conditions which invite the companions to use it as Ignatius intended. The superior may seek the security of losing himself in the administration of the house or of its apostolic works to avoid personal contact with the companions. Instead of confronting those individuals who have committed errors or caused difficulties, he may take refuge in generalized rules posted on the bulletin board and thus he affects all the members of the community in a negative way.

There is the fear of the risk to the superior's security in his own judgment if he enters into a dialogue of mutual discernment with his companions. To avoid taking this risk the superior may be tempted to impose a wooden a priori organization on the community. He may circumvent the companions' use of representation by condemning those who do so as lacking in perfect obedience of judgment. He may opt for ruling "paternalistically" in a way that reduces his subjects to children who are to be seen but not heard.

There is the fear of making mistakes and being found out in them, the fear of admitting to having been wrong. This can lead to the temptation to refuse to reform decisions that experience shows to have been ill-advised. It can also tempt the superior to do nothing when true leadership is called for, not to have the courage to give a unifying command when the time available for mutual discernment is exhausted and action should be taken here and now.

There is the related fear of being honest about evidently bad situations due to circumstances beyond the superior's own control: the refusal to take the risk of having confidence in the personal commitment of the companions to their vocation and in their mature recognition of the complexities and difficulties inherent in all human enterprises — the weight of time and matter. Rather than admitting the present impossibility of solving a problem or of changing an almost intolerable situation, the superior may be tempted to escape into the security of demanding heroic virtue of his companions by needlessly multiplying occasions demanding "blind" obedience. He may be tempted to try to cover up problems under the rhetorical generalities of pious exhortations, appealing to the "Holy Institute" while neither explaining it to the companions nor understanding it himself.

Finally, the superior may be tempted to blame all difficulties upon the bad will and immaturity of his companions rather than upon the weight of circumstances or his own personal limitations.

Much of the battle of conquering these temptations can be won simply by bringing them to consciousness. Then, a superior who truly has grasped his role according to Ignatius will find the way, with the help of his companions, to make an apostolic community of love. True dialogue, true personal relationships require the courage to make oneself present to the other. There are many subtle ways to refuse this presence. Openness to the reality of the other precludes the fabrication in one's own consciousness of a falsifying image of the other or the projection of a falsifying image of oneself. It is a presence that must always be renewed, a risk that must be repeatedly taken. Perhaps more than most men, the superior needs the courage to make himself present to those other men who are the companions of Jesus committed to his care. If through the Ignatian formation of Jesuits all the companions have a profound sense of the "scope of our vocation" constantly fostered by the superior, he need not fear to show his human limitations and to share the problems of his role with them. The superior, too, is a companion and he, perhaps more than the others, needs to be supported by the mutual love and comprehension and aid which is the reason for being the Company of Jesus.

On the other hand, superiors must be formed in such a way as to be capable of carrying out their role as Ignatius conceived it. If the only preparation for understanding this role has been exercising the role of subject in a primarily administrative structure, the man newly appointed to this responsibility cannot be expected to exercise it differently than his predecessors. The superior must be trained in techniques of interpersonal relations and of creating structures of communal dialogue, mutual aid and mutual love. Mere exhortation will not achieve these ends. The superior, helped by this formation, must have the personal quality of creative imagination: to know how to make a community of the particular individuals committed to his care, with all the complexity of their individual temperaments and backgrounds and strengths and limitations and their varying degrees of spontaneous comprehension or lack of mutual understanding. He must know how to create a community of companions on the human level through the imaginative use of recreation and of other means to establish interpersonal relations. Through the practice of mutual discernment, he must give his companions the consciousness of being treated as persons constituting together an apostolic community of love, rather than as "cogs-in-the-wheel" who feel that they are treated as so many numbers in an administrative process seeking external results through "togetherness."

Above all, the superior must have the dynamic mental structure of Ignatius himself, the spiritual liberty to be open to all the indications of the actual will of God in the concrete situation here and now.

The role of the superior is to bring the Company to be. The being of the Company of Jesus is love. Through making an apostolic community of love of all the companions here and now, the superior will carry out the role of the superior according to St. Ignatius of Loyola.

THE DELIBERATION OF THE
FIRST FATHERS

THE DELIBERATION OF THE FIRST FATHERS bears a Spanish notation in the hand of Ignatius: "1539. During three months. The manner to interiorly structure (*ordenarse*) the Company". The document is written in Latin. It is not certain who actually wrote the manuscript, although arguments have been given that it was either Codure or Favre.[1] The Deliberation has been discussed and analyzed at length in this study and has been shown to be the key document in interpreting the role of the superior according to Ignatius. It is also a clear model of the Ignatian method of mutual discernment.

An invaluable technique to facilitate the dynamics of mutual discernment is demonstrated in the decision of the companions to discuss the arguments against obedience and those in favor of it on separate occasions. This is a technique which can be most useful to religious congregations in this time of community discussions, general chapters, committees, commissions, and so forth. Those who have tried this technique testify to its efficacy.

The argument is sometimes given that thus to divide the discussion of negative and affirmative arguments will result in the waste of time. Experience shows the contrary to be true and a little reflection explains why this is so. Confrontation of opposing arguments during the same meeting almost inevitably leads to debate rather than to dialogue — especially within the American culture. One does not truly listen to the point of view of the other, but is concerned with forming counter-arguments. The result often is a lack of harmony and the need of more meetings to continue the debate.

On the other hand, following the Ignatian dynamics of the Deliberation should result in at least the possibility of resolving a

---

1 *Cons*MHSJ, I, xxxv-xl.

question in mutual contentment after two meetings. Having prayed in order to achieve true spiritual liberty and openness to the Spirit and to form the desire only to seek the will of God in the concrete situation, all the interlocutors first state honestly and sincerely the negative reasons that they have seen through prayerful reflection on the evidence. At the end of this session, conducted with none of the blinding heat of a debate, the total weight of the disadvantages of the decision should be clear to everyone. At the end of the following session, after the affirmative arguments have been heard, it should not be difficult to determine which way the balance scales of judgment are tipped by the weight of the arguments and thus, to choose with mutual contentment that which appears through this mutual discernment to be the will of God in the concrete situation.

THE TEXT

[1]. Near the end of Lent the time was drawing near when we would have to be dispersed and separated from one another. We were very eager for this, recognizing it as necessary in order to reach the goal we had already fixed upon and thought about with intense desire.

We decided to come together for some days before separating to discuss with one another our vocation and manner of life. After doing this for several days, we were divided by different ideas and opinions concerning our state of life, some of us being French, others Spanish, others Savoyards or Portuguese. There was unity of mind and purpose: to seek the gracious and perfect will of God according to the scope of our vocation; but there were various opinions concerning the more effective and more successful means both for ourselves and for our fellowmen.

It should surprise no one that this difference of opinion occurred among us weak and frail men, since even the Apostles, princes and pillars of the most holy Church, as well as many most perfect men with whom we are unworthy to be even remotely compared, had points of view which were different and at times in direct contradiction, and they have left these contrary opinions in writing. Since we judged matters differently, we therefore were anxious to seek and find some truly open way that we could follow in offering ourselves as a holocaust to our God, to whose praise and honor our all might be surrendered.

Finally, we decided and determined unanimously to give ourselves to prayers and sacrifices and meditations with greater than usual fervor and, after using all our own resources, to cast all our concerns upon the Lord, hoping in Him who is so good and generous that He denies His good spirit to no one who asks with a humble and single heart. Indeed, He gives with largesse to all men disappointing no one. Certainly, He would not fail us; but so great is His goodness, He would help us beyond our desires and understanding.

[2]. We began, therefore, to use all our human efforts and to bring forward our common problems deserving of careful and mature consideration and planning. Our custom was to reflect and meditate and pray over the questions throughout the day. In the evening each man proposed to the rest what he judged to be more correct and more expedient, in order that all might unanimously embrace the opinion that was truer and that had been examined and proved by stronger reasons and by the votes of the majority.

[3]. The first evening we came together, this question was proposed: after we had offered and dedicated ourselves and our lives to Christ our Lord and to His true and legitimate vicar on earth, so that he might dispose of us and send us wherever he might judge we could be most effective — whether to the Indies, the heretics, or among any of the faithful or among non-Christians — would it be better for us to be so joined and bound together in one body that no physical dispersal, however great, could separate us? Or perhaps would this be inexpedient?

A clear example of the problem was the Pope's sending two of us to Siena. Should we have concern and mutual comprehension for those going there, and they for us? Or should we perhaps have no greater concern for them than for persons outside our Company. Finally, we decided affirmatively, namely, that since the most kind and loving Lord had deigned to unite us to one another and to bring us together — weak men and from such different places and cultures — we should not sever God's union and bringing together, but rather everyday we should strengthen and more solidly ground it, forming ourselves into one body. Everyone should have concern for and comprehension of the others for greater apostolic efficacy, since united strength would have more power and courage in confronting whatever challenging goals were to be sought than if this strength were divided into many parts.

Now, in all that has been recounted and yet will be, we wish it to be understood that we adopted nothing at all from our own "spirit" and subjective notions, but only (whatever it might be) what the Lord inspired and the Apostolic See confirmed and approved.

[4]. Having decided and solved the first problem, we faced another more difficult one worthy of no less reflection and foresight. Having already pronounced perpetual vows of chastity and poverty before the most reverend legate of His Holiness when we were working in Venice, we now asked whether we should pronounce a third vow, namely to obey one of us in order that we might carry out the will of our Lord God more sincerely and with greater praise and merit and, at the same time, carry out the will and command of His Holiness to whom we had most willingly offered our all: will, understanding, strength, and the rest.

[5]. After many days of reflection and prayer, nothing had transpired to fill our souls with peace in solving this problem. Hoping in the Lord, we began to discuss mutually some means to solve the problem. First of all, we asked whether it might be good for all of us to withdraw to some hermitage and to remain there for thirty or forty days, spending all our time in meditations, fasting, and penances to the end that God might respond to our desires and deign to impress upon our minds the solution of the problem. Then, we asked whether three or four in the name of all should retire in this way for the same purpose. Or whether — although no one would go to a hermitage, all remaining in the city — we should devote ourselves to this one affair, so that we might give a larger and more ample place to meditation, reflection, and prayer, spending the rest of the day in our usual works of preaching and hearing confessions.

[6]. Finally, after discussing and examining these proposals,

we decided that all would remain in Rome for two reasons especially: first, so as not to cause rumors and scandals in the city and among the people who, since men are so inclined to rash judgment, might conclude and suppose that we had taken flight or begun to work at something new or had little stability and perseverance in carrying out what we had begun; secondly, so that through being absent we would not in the meantime lose the great results we were seeing in hearing confessions, preaching, and other spiritual exercises, the demands for which were so great that if we were four times our number we could not satisfy all, as we cannot do at present.

Concerning the problem we have been discussing, in order to find the way to solve it the three following preparations of soul were proposed to one and all. The first was that each one should so prepare himself, should so devote himself to prayers, sacrifices, and meditations, that he make every effort to find joy and peace in the Holy Spirit concerning obedience, working with all his powers to have a will more disposed to obeying than to commanding when the effect would be the equal glory of God and praise of His Majesty.

The second preparation of soul was that none of the companions should talk to another companion about this matter or should inquire about his arguments, so that no one would persuade another or incline him more in favor of obeying or of not obeying or the contrary, but that each one would desire as more expedient only that which he derived from prayer and meditation.

The third: that each man should think of himself as not being one of our Company, into which he never expected to be received, so that from this consideration he would not be pushed toward his opinion and judgment by any emotions, but as an outsider he might freely propose his idea to us concerning the resolution of obeying or not obeying, and finally he would confirm and approve by his judgment that alternative which he believes to be for the greater future service of God and the more secure permanent preservation of the Company.

[7]. With these antecedent spiritual dispositions, we ordained that the following day all would come together prepared. Each one would state all the possible disadvantages of obedience, all the arguments which arose and which each one of us had thought of individually in reflecting, praying, and medi-

tating; and he should propose in his turn what he had drawn from this.

For example, one said: "It seems that this name of a religious institute or obedience does not have the good reputation it should among Christian people, on account of our failings and sins."

Another said: "If we wish to live under obedience, perhaps we will be obliged by the supreme pontiff to live under some already established and constituted rule. If this happens, since it might not give us the opportunity and scope to work for the salvation of souls, which is our unique purpose after concern for our own souls, all of our desires, which in our judgment we have received from the Lord our God, would be frustrated."

Still another said: "If we vow obedience to someone, not so many men will enter our company to work loyally in the vineyard of the Lord where the harvest is so great but so few true laborers are found. The weakness and inconstancy of men is such that many seek selfish ends and their own will, rather than the desires of Jesus Christ and their own total self-abnegation."

In the same way another man gave other reasons and thus a fourth man and a fifth, and so on, stating the apparent arguments against obedience.

The following day we discussed the opposite, bringing before the group all the advantages and benefits of this obedience which each one had drawn from his prayer and meditation. Each one in turn proposed the results of his prayerful reflection, sometimes by deducing impossible conclusions, sometimes simply by direct affirmation.

For example, one reduced the case to the absurd and impossible: "If our Company attempted to take care of practical matters without the sweet yoke of obedience, no one would have a specific responsibility, since one would leave the burden of such responsibilities to another, as we have often experienced."

Similarly: "If this Company exists without obedience, it cannot long remain in being and continue. Yet, this is in conflict with our primary intention of perpetually preserving our Company in being. Consequently, since nothing preserves a company more than obedience, it seems necessary — especially for us who have vowed perpetual poverty and who live our lives in arduous and continual labors both spiritual and temporal, in which a company is less likely to continue in being."

Another spoke affirmatively thus: "Obedience brings about constant actions of heroic virtue. For a man who lives under obedience is most prompt to carry out whatever is demanded of him, even if this be extremely hard or even if it leads to his being embarrassed and laughed at and to being a spectacle to the world — for example, if it were commanded me that I should go through the public streets naked or dressed in eccentric clothes (granted that this might never be commanded). When a man is perfectly ready to do this, denying his own will and judgment, he is constantly practising heroic virtue and increasing his merit."

Similarly: "Nothing so lays low all pride and arrogance as does obedience. For pride puffs up and follows one's own judgment and will, giving way to no one, striving for grandiose and spectacular projects beyond one's powers. Now, obedience directly counters this, for it always follows the judgment and will of another, gives way to everyone, and is identified as much as possible with humility, which is the enemy of pride."

And: "Although we have given ourselves over to all obedience both universal and particular to the supreme pontiff and pastor, nevertheless, he would not be able to take care of our particular and occasional needs, which are innumerable — nor would it be fitting for him to do so if he could."

[8]. And so after many days of thinking through the many pros and cons of our problem and examining the more serious and weighty arguments, while carrying out our usual exercises of prayer, meditation, and reflection, at last, with the help of the Lord, we arrived at our conclusion, not just by a majority but without even one dissenting: that it would be more expedient and even necessary to vow obedience to one of our companions in order that we might better and more exactly fulfill our principal desires of accomplishing the divine will in all things, and in order that the Company might be more surely preserved in being, and finally, that all individual matters that might occur, both spiritual and temporal, might be provided for properly.

[9]. Retaining the same method of discussion and procedure in all remaining questions, always proposing both sides, we continued in these and other deliberations for nearly three months,

Appendix I: The Deliberation of the First Fathers

from the middle of Lent through the feast of John the Baptist. On this day everything was terminated and concluded joyfully and in complete concord of spirit — not without having previously engaged in many vigils and prayers and labors of mind and body before we had deliberated and made our decisions.

THE LETTERS ON OBEDIENCE

THE ANALYSIS OF THE IGNATIAN LANGUAGE of obedience and of the important texts describing the manner to practice obedience in the Company has shown that for Ignatius this obedience is a correlative of the role of the superior. Obedience is not an end in itself; rather, it is the essential means to bring the Company to be here and now through the response of perfect obedience of all the companions to the unifying command of the superior. The command and the obedience together bring about the actual mutual union of wills and of corporate action which constitutes the apostolic community of love for the service of Christ through the aid of souls here and now.

The essential meaning of Jesuit obedience must never be forgotten in interpreting the occasional letters on obedience written by Polanco under the direction of Ignatius. Over the generations a great deal of misunderstanding has arisen concerning the fundamental meaning of Ignatian obedience because the commentators traditionally have based their interpretations of it upon these letters, especially "the" letter on obedience written to the companions in Portugal dated March 26, 1553. Even the most modern commentators on Jesuit obedience have tended to consider this letter as the final step in a process of evolution in Ignatius' conception of obedience and, therefore, to interpret the Constitutions in the light of this letter. Actually, the letters and also the biographical anecdotes concerning Ignatius' manner of government during his own generalate must be interpreted in the light of the presentation of obedience in the Constitutions in order truly to understand them. The Constitutions are intended precisely to describe the essential role of the superior and of the companions in conserving and increasing the being of the Company, its union of mutual love and of apostolic action in companionship. The Constitutions themselves simply develop the implications of the "scope of our vocation" expressed in the election of obedience in the Deliberation and in the delineation of this vocation in the Formula of the Institute.

Most of the commentators on Ignatian obedience have greatly overstressed the aspect of personal, spiritual motivation — an asceticism directed towards personal perfection according to the ends of early monasticism —, because they have grounded their interpretation on the letter of 1553.[1] This letter indeed emphasizes personal spiritual motivation. The reason that it does so is clear from a study of the historical events which led to its composition. There is a danger when discussing the writings of a great saint to proceed as if he were not a man situated in a definite historical and cultural milieu and as subject to the laws of human expression and communication as any other man. His sayings are presented as more or less inspired oracles all having the same weight, or nearly so.[2] This has been particularly true

1 C. Palmes de Genover, *La obediencia religiosa ignaciana* (Barcelona, 1963), for instance, states that he wishes to discover the one basic idea which gives unity and life to Ignatius' notion of obedience and that he wishes to avoid all a priorism in doing so (p. 5). But he then takes as his point of departure "the" letter on obedience, without placing it in its historical context, and proceeds to interpret the Constitutions in function of this letter. This leads him to the strange affirmation that the motive for the choice of obedience by the first companions in the Deliberation was that the vows of poverty and chastity had not satisfied their anxiety for personal perfection. They sought "a greater dependence, which would reach to the smallest details of their daily life." By obedience to one of their own, their lives would become "a total consecration to God under His immediate representative who would continually manifest the divine will to them" (pp. 99-100). He concludes that for Ignatius obedience was "the supreme concretization of all his spiritual thrusts and aspirations and constitutes the *very essence of the vocation of the Company*" (p. 100. My emphasis). Nevertheless, in discussing the apostolic vocation of the Company, he does concede that in Ignatian obedience "this apostolic aspect constitutes an element of the same importance as personal sanctification" (p. 147).

2 During the last generation there has been a tendency to use isolated passages or sentences of the letters of Ignatius as "proof texts," that is to say, to begin with a "thesis" about Ignatian spirituality and then to search for corroborative texts in the various letters with little attention given to contexts, occasions for writing these letters and all circumstances of time, place and persons. This is particularly true of the otherwise extremely valuable articles by I. Iparraguirre, but examples could be multiplied.

of commentaries on this letter on obedience.[3] But this letter is an exercise in rhetoric.[4] It is an effort to persuade a particular group of individuals having very definite difficulties and susceptible to a specific kind of motivation. Anyone who has taught a class, engaged in spiritual direction, or written letters to particular groups or persons with the aim to persuade them of the truth of a certain position or the desirability of certain conduct knows that he adapts his presentation of motives and his emphasis of certain details to the particular persons he wishes to convince. No one wishes to have these modes of presentation torn from their specific context and presented as his complete and definitive thought on the subject. When he wants to present this, he will choose other far more objective modes of expression. Similarly, to understand the true meaning of Ignatian obedience, it is necessary to go to the Constitutions rather than to the letter of 1553.

The difficulties of the Company in Portugal during the early years arising from the character and manner of government of Simao Rodrigues and from the too rapid increase of members are well known and have been thoroughly discussed by historians.[5] What is significant for understanding the background of this letter on obedience is the fact that Simão's spiritual

Historical Background

---

3 A classical commentary on Ignatian obedience is that of M. Espinosa Pólit, *La Obediencia Perfecta,* 2nd ed. (Mexico, 1961). A translation of the 1st edition is *Perfect Obedience,* trans. W. J. Young (Westminster, Md., 1947). It is an interpretation of "the" letter of 1553 according to the scholastic method of terms, classification of parts, etc. Pólit presents the letter as a "finished monument of universal character." He asserts, therefore, that it may be "considered independently of every external circumstance." Granting that it was inspired by a specific occasion, he states that in reality this had no noticeable influence on the composition of the text. It gives a doctrine which is absolutely general "without limitation of time or persons" (p. 11).

4 For Polanco's ideas on the use of rhetoric see his *Industriae: Quinta Industria de los Medios y Modos que se han de usar par el Fin dicho de Aiudar el Proximo* (*PolCompl,* II, 790-805). Cf. I. Iparraguirre, "La conversación como táctica apostólica de San Ignacio de Loyola," *Razon y fe,* CLX (1959), 11-24.

5 Cf. *PolChron,* II, 694-717; A. Astráin, *Historia de la Compañía de Jesús en la Asistencia de España,* I (Madrid, 1902), 585-638; F. Rodrigues, *História da Companhia de Jesus na Asistência de Portugal,* I/II (Pôrto, 1931), 9-281. Astráin places very heavy blame on Simão

direction had tended to lead the Portuguese companions to impetuous and indiscreet acts of fervor and excessive penances going as far as public flagellations in the streets and half-naked preachers giving extravagant sermons. Simão's own taste for the life of a hermit and long hours of contemplation had widespread influence. At the same time his manner of government was so mild and lacking in firmness that a general relaxation of obedience was the result.

The appointment of Diego Miró as provincial to correct the situation turned out to be most unfortunate. Having begun with overseverity and a mania for regulating everything himself, down to the manner of ringing bells, he soon became ridiculous and rendered himself insupportable to his subjects. Then he simply gave up in despair and fled from the responsibilities of superior to the work of giving parish missions. The province was left without a true head until Torres and Gonçalves da Câmara were given the task of trying to improve matters. Meanwhile, the conduct of Miró had strengthened the disposition of the companions to have contempt for their superiors.[6]

The problem which called forth the letter on obedience, then, was that of needing to restore in the members of the Company in Portugal the true spirit of obedience which requires perfect, loving, joyful execution of the commands of the actual superior, whoever he be. Now, the dispositions of the companions in Portugal were such that the most effective motivation for this obedience would be an appeal to their fervent desire for mortification, sacrifice, penances and personal perfection. One can almost see Ignatius instructing the diligent Polanco to search out in his classified notes all possible examples and expressions and images from the Bible and the saints which would bring out this ascetical side of obedience and, so, would be truly persuasive for the group to whom the letter was to be written.[7]

Rodrigues for the events in Portugal. F. Rodrigues, on the other hand, writes an apology for Simão and tends to make Da Câmara the villain of the piece. The historical facts are well documented by both authors, in spite of their very different interpretations. In his discussion of "the" letter (228-232), Rodrigues tries to insist upon its general import for the whole Company in order to remove some of the stigma from Portugal.

6 Astráin, *op. cit.*, pp. 598-603.

The precise occasion of the letter of 1553 was a request Da Câmara sent to Ignatius from Portugal on January 6, 1553. Da Câmara reported that things were so troubled "that there is no order to be found in anything." [8] He implored Ignatius to write to the province a letter especially on obedience, because the subjects had been treated in such a condescending manner that they were turning out to be the superiors and the superiors, subjects. Da Câmara then touched upon the problem which would be at the heart of the letter on obedience. He assured Ignatius that a letter from him would result in much improvement, and he advised him that he should treat especially of the great harm and loss of respect for obedience "because of discredit for the person" of the superior. The source of much of the difficulty in Portugal was precisely the failure of the companions to reverence and obey the superior whatever his personal temperament or limitations might be. Da Câmara continued that the most important thing to explain to the Portuguese Jesuits would be the mind of Ignatius "concerning abnegation, mortification and obedience" and the rigor with which superiors should demand improvement of these.[9]

What Da Câmara requested, therefore, was a letter weighted with the personal authority and prestige of Ignatius that would insist upon the necessity of obeying any superior, whoever he might be, and that would give a clear exposition of the interrelation of abnegation, mortification and obedience. Thus, the letter of 1553 was called forth by a very specific situation and was deliberately expressed in rhetorical language intended to persuade the Portuguese companions of the ascetical value of perfect obedience to any superior, whatever might be his personal qualities or limitations. The presentation of obedience in the letter of 1553 was developed over a period of years and its evolution can be followed in two letters to Gandía in Spain and two to Coimbra in Portugal.

---

7 This imaginative projection is, of course, conjecture, although it would seem to be solidly founded in the character of Polanco and in the nature of things. An efficient secretary does build up a classified file of useful material.

8 *EppMixt,* III, 31.

9 Ibid., III, 41.

The first letter in the series was sent to the companions at Coimbra, May 7, 1547.[10] It presents the general means to personal perfection with the intention to instill in these men the discretion to avoid excessive fervor. It reminds the companions that all Christian states of life are ordered to the glory of God, personal salvation and the aid of the neighbor. Those called to the Company have a special vocation to make themselves "a continual sacrifice for the glory of God and the salvation of men." Thus, companions of Jesus must aid souls not only by good example, but also by the use of all apostolic means.[11] The entire letter, then, is placed in the context of the "scope of our vocation" which orders the pursuit of personal perfection (the vocation of all mankind) to the aid of souls in companionship.

The letter then proposes various motives for seeking personal perfection,[12] followed immediately by a warning against extremes of indiscreet fervor, listing its dangers and especially that of not persevering in the way begun.[13] Obedience is proposed as the source of discretion as well as the best form of mortification. Certainly, the penances of the saints are praiseworthy but for those who have "control over self-love," the means of discretion is better, "not departing from obedience." [14]

Obedience is then joined directly to the mutual love to which it is always ordered: "joined with that virtue and compendium of all other virtues" which Christ called His great commandment: to love one another. In the Company this mutual love is specifically ordered to the apostolic end: "not only to conserve this continual union and love among yourselves, but also to extend it to all men, instilling within your souls ardent desires for the salvation of men." [15] The remainder of the letter explains how the life of obedience during the period of studies is entirely ordered to apostolic effectiveness.[16]

The structure of this letter reveals the essential meaning of Ignatian obedience. All is ordered to the "scope of our vocation" — the service of Christ through the aid of souls in com-

10 *EppIgn*, I, 495-510; English in *LettersIgn,* pp. 120-130.
11 Ibid., I, 498.
12 Ibid., I, 499-502.
13 Ibid., I, 504-506.
14 Ibid., I, 507.
15 Ibid., I, 507.
16 Ibid., I, 508-509.

panionship. The pursuit of personal perfection is for this end and is achieved above all through obedience, which is itself a means to mutual union and love, the being of the Company which enables it to achieve its apostolic end. The special stress in this letter upon personal spiritual motives is the result of the concrete occasion that inspired it, but these motives are not presented as ends in themselves. On the contrary, they are specifically directed to the achievement of the end of the Company as a whole.

On July 29, 1547, a letter explaining the role of the superior *The Letter* and the meaning of obedience was sent to the companions at *to Gandía* Gandía to prepare them to elect one of their number as superior.[17] The letter insists upon the necessity of having one superior for the well-being of the Company, since he is the principle of unity.[18] Personal spiritual motives for obedience are then suggested. Obedience will help individual companions to avoid many errors of their own judgment and faults of their own will, not only in particular situations but "in their whole state of life." This is true because the more fully a man resigns himself to God through obedience to his "minister" (who is any superior to whom he subjects himself for the love of God), the more he "obliges (according to our manner of speaking) Divine Providence to rule and guide him." [19]

The language in this passage is important. Divine Providence rules those under obedience *en todo el estado de vida,* that is to say, in the achievement of the "scope of our vocation." The realization of this vocation in particular situations depends upon the unifying role of the superior whose commands make the apostolic community of love and direct the companions in the aid of souls here and now. A companion is freed from the limited and possibly erroneous or sinful thrust of his subjective will and judgment and is inserted into the providential ordering of the "scope of our vocation" within the Church through his perfect obedience to the command of the superior who speaks in the name of the whole Company. The more perfect the

17 Ibid., I, 551-562; *LettersIgn,* pp. 140-146.
18 Ibid., I, 522-554.
19 Ibid., I, 555-556.

companion's obedience, the more completely will he be united to all the members and their head and, consequently, the more will he share in this providential ordering of the whole body of the Company to its apostolic end. It is in this sense that we must interpret the notion of "obliging" Divine Providence to rule and guide us in proportion to the totality of our commitment to the "scope of our vocation" through obedience. The letter is very careful to point out, moreover, that this is a human manner of speaking. Later commentators have greatly exaggerated this notion of "obliging" Divine Providence, treating the vow of obedience as a kind of contract binding upon God.[20]

After continuing to suggest personal spiritual motives for obedience, the letter observes that these "concern more the individual members"; they are considerations intended to move each companion to give himself fully to the "scope of our vocation." [21] The remainder of the letter is concerned with the essential meaning of authority and obedience in the Company: the preservation of its being through the mutual union realized through obedience to the superior. For this, it is essential to give perfect obedience to any superior, whoever he be, not acting differently according to who the "minister" himself is, "but recognizing Christ in each one of them, faithfully obeying Him in His vicar." [22]

Now, the local superior is the vicar of the general and should be obeyed as the companions would obey Ignatius himself if he were present.[23] All the authority which Ignatius himself would have were he at Gandía to help the companions to the greater glory of God, he desires their rector to have "for the same end." They should respect the rector as they would Ignatius and, in reality, not the rector nor Ignatius "but Jesus Christ our Lord, whom you obey in both of us and for His sake His ministers." [24] The presentation of the superior as the minis-

---

20 Cf. J. M. Aicardo, *Commentario a las Constituciones de la Compañía de Jesús, I,* (Madrid, 1919, 746-747; Pólit, *op. cit.,* pp. 162-164; Palmes, *op. cit.,* pp. 115-116; I. Iparraguirre, "Perspectivas ignacianas de la obediencia," *Revista de Espiritualidad,* XXI (1962), 75, 84.

21 *EppIgn,* I, 556-558.

22 Ibid., I, 559.

23 Ibid., I, 561.

24 Ibid., I, 561.

ter of Christ clearly rejoins the entire structure of vicarious authority explained in treating the phrase "in the place of Christ." [25]

This letter again manifests the essential meaning of Ignatian obedience as ordered to the apostolic end of the Company by bringing it to be in the union of all the members with one another and with their head and the fact that personal spiritual motivation is a means to this end.

The Letter to Coimbra

The earliest letter to Coimbra did not succeed in convincing the companions there that they should moderate their extremes of mortification and contemplation and seek their personal perfection through obedience. A second letter entirely concerned with motivating perfect obedience was sent to Coimbra on January 14, 1548.[26] The argument of this new letter once more is based upon the necessity of obedience for the union of all the companions which constitutes the being of the Company: "all having one feeling and one desire . . . all being one thing in our Lord Jesus Christ" (*un mesmo sentir de todos y un mesmo querer . . . siendo todos una mesma cosa*). Since union of many persons cannot be maintained without order "nor order without the required bond of obedience of subjects to superiors," perfect obedience must be given to all superiors in the hierarchical structure of the Company "with no distinction of persons, recognizing Jesus Christ our Lord, since all obedience given to anyone should be given to Him and for Him." [27] The growing disquiet caused by the tendency of the Portuguese Jesuits to distinguish between superiors worthy or not of obedience, which was to reach its climax in Da Câmara's letter to Ignatius in 1553, is already clear here.

The threefold obedience of execution, will and understanding is presented precisely as a necessary means to union: "This obedience, since union is constituted and conserved by it, must be not only external but also interior, for it is not possible to conserve union of wills if different points of view are retained." [28] If perfect obedience of will and understanding is

---

25 See above, ch. 7, pp. 160-162.
26 *EppIgn*, I, 687-693; *LettersIgn,* pp. 159-162.
27 Ibid., 688-689.
28 Ibid., I, 689.

achieved, "then union will be solid and enduring," and peace and interior tranquillity will be imperturbable.[29] All — the superior and the companions — will be *contentos*.

To convince the enthusiastically fervent companions at Coimbra that obedience is the most noble of personal sacrifices to God, Polanco brings up a battery of examples from the Bible and the saints.[30] The companions are warned against practices good in themselves "like mortifications and contemplations and other things" done contrary to the will of the superior because a companion prefers to follow his own will.[31] It is recalled that the superiors are "ministers" of the Divine Majesty standing "in the place of Jesus Christ our Lord," [32] and that Divine Providence rules and guides the companions through their superiors to help them arrive at greater personal perfection "and the aid of your neighbors." [33]

In spite of the rhetorical stress on ascetical motives for obedience required by the occasion and the recipients of this letter, all is ordered once again to the apostolic end of the Company. Personal perfection is directed to the "scope of our vocation," the aid of souls in companionship.

The Letter to Oviedo at Gandía   On March 27, 1548, Polanco composed a letter under his own name, *ex commissione* from Ignatius, to Andrés de Oviedo, rector at Gandía.[34] A remarkable thing about the letter, which shows how complete and well-documented Polanco's note file of arguments and examples to use in letters of obedience had become, is the fact that it contains sixteen paragraphs which are repeated in essence and sometimes word for word in the letter of 1553.[35]

Oviedo had a temperament similar to that of the companions in Portugal. He had written to Ignatius asking permission to spend seven years in the contemplative life of a hermit.[36] Thus, the exigencies of rhetorical persuasion in this letter and that of

---

29 Ibid., I, 690.
30 Ibid., I, 690-692.
31 Ibid., I, 690.
32 Ibid., I, 691.
33 Ibid., I, 696.
34 Ibid., II, 54-65; *LettersIgn,* pp. 164-172.
35 Ibid., II, 57-63, nos. 12-28.
36 *EppMixt,* I, 467.

1553 were very similar. Polanco tells Oviedo that Ignatius had found his representations of his desires for a solitary life too insistent;[37] and, therefore, the threefold obedience is developed at greater length than in previous letters and an examination of conscience on obedience of understanding is proposed in the final paragraph.[38] Although ascetical motives are given much emphasis, the ordination of obedience in the Company to mutual union for the aid of souls is clearly expressed.

Antonio de Araoz had been named provincial of Spain on September 1, 1547. Polanco reminds Oviedo that he should discuss all his affairs with Araoz and obey him as he would obey Christ "since you have him in His place." [39] To prepare for this admonition, Polanco composed several paragraphs on the need for hierarchical subordination in the Company especially in view of the rapid increase in the number of companions. In every large group of men it is necessary to have order for the avoidance of confusion. When there is a multiplication of subordinate superiors, it is necessary to have an order of authority and subordination among them, in order to "conserve unity among them and through it the being and good government of the Company." [40] The essential meaning of Jesuit obedience is once more given as the foundation and end of the presentation of personal spiritual motives for obedience.

The reason for maintaining the being of the Company is that it may achieve its apostolic end. This is made clear by Polanco's remark to Oviedo that his desire for seven years of prayer and solitude would be a dangerous example "for the manner of action of the Company" and that, because of this, Ignatius feels that it requires more consideration. This consideration consists of the rhetorical presentation of obedience which follows.

The first of the personal spiritual motives for obedience recalled by Polanco is that of peace of soul. Obedience is "a firm anchor to stabilize and assure the soul." [41] Obedience supposes interior liberty, and Polanco here introduces a little examen on the quality of indifference necessary for true obedience. He then

---

37 *EppIgn,* II, 56-57.
38 Ibid., II, 64-65.
39 Ibid., II, 56.
40 Ibid., II, 55.
41 Ibid., II, 57.

begins the long presentation of the threefold obedience, especially that of the understanding, which will be repeated in the letter of 1553. For the fervent Oviedo he stresses that obedience is "an holocaust" in which the whole man, withholding nothing of himself, offers all that he is "in the fire of the love of God" to his Creator and Lord. It is a perfect resignation of himself by which the man dispossesses himself of everything, putting himself into the hands of God through his minister.[42]

The language here is eloquent and is intended to persuade Oviedo of the spiritual perfection of obedience as a personal sacrifice to God. It will be repeated to the ardent Portuguese in 1553. It is the language of Polanco, nevertheless, and it is employed for a highly rhetorical purpose. It should not be erected into the foundation of Ignatian obedience as commentators have done with the terms holocaust and the fire of the love of God.[43]

Polanco proceeds to a consideration of the practice of perfect obedience, presenting as its motive the commitment of oneself to the rule of Divine Providence through God's ministers, the superiors whom one has in the place of Christ. Obedience of the understanding is explained more fully than heretofore. The important fact is recognized that the understanding cannot be influenced by the will to deny what it is forced to see as evidential. In most instances, however, this is not the case, and there is the possibility of assenting to one position or another. It

---

42 Ibid., I, 57.

43 Palmes, *op. cit.*, analyzes Ignatian obedience into three essential elements: (1) a total holocaust in the fire of charity; (2) in order to be possessed and governed by God through His providence (3) through the mediation of the superior (p. 57). Cf. L. Mendizabal, "Naturaleza del orden de subordinación primariamente pretendido por San Ignacio," *Manresa*, XXXVII (1965), 113-140. His position is more nuanced than that of Palmes and is based upon an interpretation of religious obedience in general. Thus, he finds that holocaust to Christ is the generic element in all true religious obedience (p. 118). Cf the same writer's "Riqueza eclesial y teológica de la obediencia religiosa," *Manresa*, XXXVI (1964), 283-302. However, obedience was chosen by the first companions in the Deliberation not as a means to embrace the religious life for its own sake, but rather as the means to conserve their union of companions already offered as a holocaust to Christ through His vicar on earth for the aid of souls. In a sense, the fact of becoming a religious order properly so called was a by-product of the "scope of our vocation."

is in these non-evidential situations that the will should incline the understanding "to feel (*sentir*) what the superior feels," seeking reasons in favor of his decision and not against it. Polanco then presents "blind" obedience as "an easier and more secure" way to obedience of the understanding, which was used by the holy Fathers. Making an analogy with the assent of the mind in matters of faith, which are believed as truths revealed by God, although not comprehended by human understanding, he says that one should presuppose "that everything which the superior orders is ordered by God and His most holy will." In this way, "blind" obedience will consist in the prompt execution of the command "without any questioning" (*sin inquisición ninguna*) by the force of the will, presupposing that "what is commanded is holy and conforms to the divine will without further inquiry" (*sin más inquirir*).[44]

What has sometimes been overlooked by commentators is that the entire discussion of blind obedience is in function of a situation where a personal judgment contrary to that of the superior is in play.[45] This was quite clear in the passages on "blind" obedience in the Constitutions.[46] Even in this letter "blind" obedience is discussed in the context of a situation where the companion needs to seek reasons in favor of the superior's command. The question of "blind" obedience would not arise when a companion saw immediately the wisdom of the superior's decision and, so, spontaneously assented to it. It arises

---

44 *EppIgn,* II, 59-60.
45 See M. Olphe-Galliard, "La lettre de saint Ignace de Loyola sur la vertu d'obéissance," *RAM,* XXX (1954), 7-28, especially p. 21. H. Parenteau, "La notion d'obéissance aveugle, d'après saint Ignace de Loyola," *RAM,* XXXVIII (1962), 31-51, 170-194, presents a critique of the positions of major modern commentators (pp. 177-185). His own interpretation is that blind obedience is simply one of the means to arrive at obedience of judgment (p. 42). However, he presents this blind obedience as a more perfect means than that of seeking reasons in favor of the command of the superior. This would contradict the entire structure of discernment according to Ignatius. It is quite clear from the analysis of the Ignatian vocabulary of authority and obedience that he considered intelligent sharing of the motives for a command of the superior as the normal situation for the practice of the perfect, loving, joyful obedience based upon mutual union of wills which would find all the companions and the superior *contentos.*
46 See above, ch. 7, pp. 169-175.

only when the companion's judgment (evidently after consideration which has shown him that the command is not sinful as well as after all necessary reflection and representation demanded by the Ignatian process of discernment), remains contrary to that of the superior at the moment when execution is required immediately. No more time is available for further consideration or representation. The action of the Company unified by the command of the superior is necessary here and now for ordering the life of the Company to the service of Christ through the aid of souls in companionship. It is at this moment that "blind" obedience is the "easier and more secure" way to achieve the obedience of the understanding which is necessary for the prompt and joyful execution of the superior's command. It is at this moment that without further inquiry into the reasons for the command (which are, perhaps, humanly deplorable), the companion obeys with confidence that Divine Providence rules him and all the companions in the fulfillment of the "scope of our vocation" through the unifying role of the superior.

Continuing the letter to Oviedo, Polanco draws upon his card file for examples of blind obedience from the Bible and the saints, also giving arguments from the divine ordering of the material universe.[47] To counter the extreme fervor of Oviedo, Polanco develops the argument that he should conform to the superior's judgment, since our own will and judgment can easily err, especially in spiritual matters, if we proceed without discretion. This is true even in human affairs if we confide only in our own prudence, especially in personal matters "where men usually are not good judges because of passion." [48] This argument reflects Ignatius' awareness of the difficulty of achieving spiritual liberty and of escaping from blindness to the will of God resulting from ego-centered desires.

A most important reason for insisting upon obedience of the understanding is that without it obedience of the will and of execution will be impossible — that perfect obedience which is

---

47 *EppIgn,* II, 60-61. For an interesting discussion of the "astronomical" image of the orderly movement of the heavens in the letters, see J. Bussolini, "A propósito de un simil astronomico usado por San Ignacio en la carta de la obediencia," *Ciencia y Fe,* XII (1956), 57-59.

48 *EppIgn,* II, 61.

given "with love and joy." Perseverance is lost as are simplicity and humility and courage: all the qualities required for the perfect obedience necessary for the union of members with one another and with their head which constitutes the being of the Company. If a companion's own judgment is contrary to the command he must obey, he will experience feelings of repugnance and rebellion which will cause interior disunion and disturbance. Once more, the obedience of the Company is explicitly ordered to the conservation of its union and existence: "the union which sustains the being of every community, which is constituted by ordered subordination and made firm by the bond of obedience, will certainly be destroyed if this bond is not complete — of will and understanding."[49]

Finally, Polanco again recalls the personal spiritual motive that obedience is the most noble sacrifice man can make to God, "the whole man a living and pleasing victim offered to His Divine Majesty, keeping back nothing for himself." Polanco stresses for the fervent Oviedo the aspects of mortification and difficulty in going against natural inclination to follow the will of another.[50] The material to be repeated in the letter of 1553 ends here, and the letter closes with the examination of conscience on obedience of understanding presented to Oviedo.[51]

In this rhetorical presentation of personal spiritual motives for obedience, Polanco stresses seeing the superior in the place of Christ,[52] and as the "minister" through whom Divine Providence rules the companions.[53] He develops the Lucan text, "He who hears you, hears me; and he who rejects you rejects me," and the pertinent texts from St. Paul.[54] He also appeals to the "grace of state," saying that when a companion doubts whether or not the superior's command is sinful, he should trust that God, whom he obeys in His minister, will give the superior

---

49 Ibid., II, 62.
50 Ibid., II, 63.
51 Ibid., II, 64-65.
52 Ibid., II, 56, 58, 64.
53 Ibid., II, 57, 59, 61, 64.
54 Luke, 10:16; Col., 3:23-24; Eph., 6:5-7; Heb., 13:17; cf. I Peter, 3:13. That neither Polanco nor Ignatius were aware that in the Lucan text, as the modern exegesis has shown, the sense of Christ's words referred to all His disciples — all the People of God — rather than to the Apostles and hierarchical superiors is of no real importance. The use of the text is an application of Scripture to the notion

"more light and rectitude to know and conform to His divine will." [55] This would refer, of course, to a real positive doubt where the fear of sinfulness would be vague and undefined and not based upon what seems evidently binding upon the conscience.

The Letter of 1553 to Portugal By 1553 the situation in Portugal had gone from bad to worse and Da Câmara made his appeal to Ignatius for a letter exhorting the companions to perfect obedience. This letter — "the" letter on obedience — puts even more rhetorical stress on personal spiritual motives for obedience, especially ascetical ones of sacrifice and mortification, than had the previous letters.[56]

At the very beginning with a citation from St. Gregory, Polanco stresses that obedience brings all other virtues to the soul and maintains them there. While other religious orders are renowned for external practices of mortification and for prayer, the Company should be outstanding for interior abnegation of will and judgment through perfect obedience, "not looking at the person whom they obey, but in him at Christ our Lord for whose sake they obey." [57] The rhetorical device employed by Polanco is obvious. He immediately appeals to the thirst of the Portuguese companions for impressive acts of self-sacrifice by directing it towards perfect obedience to any superior whomsoever — a direct response to the special difficulty of contempt for certain superiors reported by Da Câmara.

Repeating the reference to the Lucan and Pauline texts used in the letter to Oviedo, Polanco insists even more that the superior is to be obeyed not because he is prudent or very good or endowed with many divine gifts, but because he represents the authority of God.[58] He then develops the meaning of the three-fold obedience, especially of the understanding, at greater length than in the Oviedo letter, though with much repetition of its content.[59] Laying great stress upon motives of personal

of vicarious authority and the working of Divine Providence through the "scope of our vocation." Cf. J. McKenzie, *Authority in the Church* (Milwaukee, 1966), p. 112; also *EppIgn,* II, 58.

55 *EppIgn,* II, 64.
56 Ibid., IV, 669-681; *LettersIgn,* pp. 287-295.
57 Ibid., IV, 671.
58 Ibid., IV, 671-672.
59 Ibid., IV, 672-677.

sacrifice in practicing perfect obedience, Polanco gives many examples from the lives of the saints.[60] He also warns against extremes of "fasts, prayers and any other pious actions" contrary to the will of the superior." [61]

Polanco recalls that obedience is ordered to the conservation of the mutual union and being of the Company.[62] This introduces a discussion of the means to achieve the obedience of the understanding necessary for union. Polanco enumerates three means to this end: (1) not to consider the superior as a man subject to mistakes and miseries, but to see Christ in him; (2) to seek reasons to justify the wisdom of the superior's command rather than to criticize it; (3) "blind" obedience.[63] The presentation of "blind" obedience is repeated almost word for word from the letter to Oviedo,[64] although the letter of 1553 adds a paragraph on the practice of representation and the need of interior indifference in proposing one's point of view to the superior.[65]

In a passage recalling the hierarchical structure of subordination, Polanco shows that obedience is directly ordered to the mutual union and love which constitutes the being of the Company: subjects should obey their superior; rectors and local superiors, the provincials; provincials, the general; and the general, the vicar of Christ on earth; "because in this way subordination will be completely maintained and, consequently, union and love without which the well-being and government of the Company cannot be preserved, as can that of no other congregation." [66]

The letter closes on the rhetorical note of ascetical motivation in the "glorious victory over yourselves," conquering the highest and most difficult level of self, the will and judgment, thus allowing God to lead them to the last blessed end of eternal beatitude.[67] The document is in many ways a masterpiece of rhetorical persuasion directed to persons susceptible to particular

60 Ibid., IV, 673-676.
61 Ibid., IV, 677.
62 Ibid., IV, 677.
63 Ibid., IV, 678-680.
64 Ibid., II, 59-60.
65 Ibid., IV, 680.
66 Ibid., IV, 680.
67 Ibid., IV, 681.

motives of personal perfection. For instance, even more frequently than in the letter to Oviedo, Polanco appeals to consideration of the superior as being "in the place of Christ," the "minister of Divine Providence" and the "interpreter of the divine will." [68] Nevertheless, the ordination of personal perfection to the apostolic end of the Company is always implicit in the explicit ordering of obedience to the conservation of the mutual union and being of the Company which exists for the "scope of our vocation" — the service of Christ through the aid of souls in companionship here and now.

This lengthy analysis of the evolution of the rhetorical presentation of personal spiritual motives for obedience has been necessary to show that, in fact, this letter on obedience simply repeats the essential meaning of obedience exposed in the Constitutions and does not constitute a shift in Ignatius' conception of obedience in the Company. Even in this letter obedience is presented not as an end in itself, but as the essential means to bring the Company to be in the union of all its members with their head for apostolic service of Christ in companionship.

There is no doubt that there was an evolution in Ignatius' choice of concrete structures through which the authority of the superior and the obedience of the companions would accomplish their purpose of forming an apostolic community of love here and now, an evolution that must always continue in the Company "according to the circumstances of persons, times and places." This evolution was brought about by the practical exigencies of uniting the rapidly growing numbers of companions and of forming new members in the spirit of the "scope of our vocation." It would certainly be false, however, to posit an evolution in the basic conception of Ignatius of the essential role of obedience in the Company: namely, to assert that the rhetorical presentation of ascetical motives in "the" letter on obedience represents a shift from the notion of obedience in the Company as the correlative of the superior's role of constantly unifying all the members for the apostolic service of Christ, to a notion of Jesuit obedience as being essentially and above all an holocaust ordered to personal perfection.

Careful study of the letter of 1553 in its historical context and in the series of letters on obedience makes clear the reasons

68 Ibid., IV, 671, 672, 673, 674, 675, 676, 678, 680.

for its rhetorical structure and ascetical presentation. In order to understand the essential meaning of obedience in the Company, it is necessary to study it in the Constitutions which were specifically intended to give a concrete description of what concerns "the whole body of the Company" for its "union and good government and conservation in well-being to the greater divine glory." [69] It should be noted, too, that text B of the Constitutions was completed in 1556, three years after the letter was sent to the companions in Portugal. Any true evolution in the fundamental conception of Ignatian obedience should have found clear expression in this text; but, as was shown in Chapter VII, Ignatius remained true to the end of the conception of obedience first expressed in the Deliberation.

The austere and virile obedience of the companions of Jesus is ordered to the ever renewed union of mutual love which brings the Company to be for the service of Christ through the aid of souls here and now.

69 *Cons*MHSJ, II, 269.

ABBREVIATIONS

used in the footnotes[1]

AHSJ—*Archivum historicum Societatis Iesu*

Cons—The *Constitutions of the Society of Jesus*

*Cons*MHSJ—Constitutiones et Regulae Societatis Iesu (Rome, 4 vols. [1934-1948]). The critically edited texts of the Constitutions and Rules, in their original languages.

*Cons*MHSJ, I—Vol. I. *Monumenta Constitutionum praevia.*

*Cons*MHSJ, II—Vol. II. Textus hispanus. Texts *a*, A, B, and D.

*Cons*MHSJ, III—Vol. III. Textus latinus.

*Cons*MHSJ, IV—Vol. IV. Regulae Societatis Jesu.

Covarrubias—*Tesoro de la Lengua Castellana o Española* (Madrid, 1611 and Barcelona, 1943)

DirSpEx—*Directoria Exercitiorum Spiritualium, 1540-1599* (Rome, 1955)

EppIgn—*Sti. Ignatii Epistolae et Instructiones.* 12 vols.

EppXav—*Epistolae Sti. Francisci Xaverii.*

FN—*Fontes narrativi de Sancto Ignatio.* 4 vols. (Rome, 1943-1960)

GG—A. García-Gallo, *Manual de historia del derecho español.* 2 vols. (Madrid, 1964)

LettersIgn—*Letters of St. Ignatius,* translated by W. J. Young

MonNad—*Epistolae P. Hieronymi Nadal.* 6 vols. (Rome, 1898-1962)

PolChron—*Chronicon Societatis Iesu, auctore J. A. de Polanco, S.J.* 6 vols. (Rome, 1894-1898)

RAM—*Revue d'ascétique et de mystique*

SpEx—The *Spiritual Exercises of St. Ignatius* or his *Exercitia Spiritualia*

WL—*Woodstock Letters*

---

1 For fuller descriptions of the above books and a more extensive list of abbreviations, see pages 358-362 of St. Ignatius of Loyola, *The Constitutions of the Society of Jesus, Translated with an Introduction and a Commentary* by G. E. Ganss, S.J. (St. Louis, 1970).

BIBLIOGRAPHY

For an EXTENSIVE BIBLIOGRAPHY on St. Ignatius, the reader is referred to St. Ignatius of Loyola, *The Constitutions of the Society of Jesus, Translated with an Introduction and a Commentary* by G. E. Ganss, S.J. (St. Louis: The Institute of Jesuit Sources, 1970). Here below are listed additional references which supplement that bibliography or are especially important for the present book. References to works cited in the footnotes can be located under the authors' names in **Index II** below, pages 230-231.

Bataillon, M. *Érasme et l'Espagne: Recherches sur l'histoire spirituelle du XVIᵉ siècle*. Paris, 1937.

Bernard-Maître, H., S.J. "Les fondateurs de la Compagnie de Jésus et l'humanisme parisien de la renaissance (1525-1536)." *Nouvelle Revue Théologique*, LXXII (1950), 811-833.

————"La préréforme humaniste de l'université de Paris aux origines de la Compagnie de Jésus (1525-1536)," in *L'homme devant Dieu: mélanges offert au Père Henri de Lubac*. 3 vols. Paris, 1964. In II, 223-233.

Blet, P., S.J. "Note sur les origines de l'obéissance ignatienne." *Gregorianum*, XXXV (1954), 99-111.

Calveras, J., S.J. "La ilustración del Cardoner y el instituto de la Compañía de Jesús según el P. Nadal." *Archivum Historicum Societatis Iesu*, XXV (1956), 27-54.

————"Notas exegeticas sobre el texto de los Ejercicios." *Manresa*, XXIV (1952), 373-383.

Cameron, J. M. *Images of Authority: A Consideration of the Concepts of Regnum and Sacerdotium*. New Haven, 1966.

Cantin, R., S.J. "L'illumination du Cardoner." *Sciences Ecclésiastiques,* VII (1925), 23-56.

Capelle, C. *Le voeu d'obéissance des origines au XIIe siècle: étude juridique.* Paris, 1959.

Carrougas, M. "Saint Ignace maître des images." *La Vie Spirituelle,* XCV (1956), 58-67.

Casanovas, I., S.J. *San Ignacio de Loyola, fundador de la Compañía de Jesús.* Trans. M. Quera, S.J., Barcelona, 1944.

Certeau, Michel de, S.J. "L'éprouve du temps." *Christus,* no. 51 (1966), 311-331.

———Trans. and ed. *Mémorial du Bienheureux Pierre Favre.* Paris, 1960.

Codina, A., S.J. "Los Ejercicios Espirituales de San Ignacio de Loyola y las constituciones de la Compañía de Jesús." *Manresa,* VIII (1932), 133-147, 245-262.

———*Los origenes de los Ejercicios Espirituales de S. Ignacio de Loyola.* Barcelona, 1926.

———"Regulae antiquorum ordinum et praeparatio constitutionum S.I." *Archivum Historicum Societatis Iesu,* I (1932), 41-72.

Collección de documentos ineditos para la historia de Guipúzcoa. San Sebastián, 1958.

Courel, François, S.J. "La fin unique de la Compagnie de Jesús." *Archivum Historicum Societatis Iesu,* XXXV (1966), 186-209.

Covarrubias, Sebastián de. *Tesoro de la Lengua Castellana o Española, según la impresión de 1611, con las adiciones de . . . 1674.* Ed. Martín de Riquer. Barcelona, 1943.

Dalmases, C. de, S. J. "El ideal apostólico de San Ignacio." *Estudios Eclesiásticos,* XXX (1956), 305-324.

———"Las meditaciones del reino y de dos banderas y la vocación a la Compañía de Jesús, según el P. Nadal." *Manresa,* XX (1948), 311-320.

Diaz, J.S. *Manual de bibliografía de la literatura española.* Barcelona, 1963.

Favre-Dorsaz, A. *Calvin et Loyola: deux réformes.* Paris, 1951.

Fessard, G., S.J. *Autorité et Bien Commun.* Paris, 1944.

Filograssi, G., S.J. "Familiarità e unione con Dio nell'orazione secondo S. Ignazio." *Gregorianum,* XXXVII (1956), 391-416.

Francis, E.J., "Toward a Typology of Religious Orders." *The American Journal of Sociology,* LV (1950), 437-449.

Futrell, John Carroll, S.J. "Ignatian Discernment." *Studies in the Spirituality of Jesuits,* II, no. 2 (April, 1970), 47-88. St. Louis: The American Assistancy Seminar on Jesuit Spirituality, 1970.

———*Making an Apostolic Community of Love: The Role of the Superior according to St. Ignatius Loyola.* Unpublished dissertation, Institut Catholique de Paris, 1967.

Gagliardi, A., S.J. *Ad patres ac fratres Societatis Jesu de plena cognitione instituti.* 3rd ed. Bruges, 1841.

Galeotti, N., S.J. and A. van Westherhout, S.J. *Imagines praepositorum generalium Societatis Jesu.* Rome, 1748.

García-Gallo, A. *Manual de historia del derecho español.* 2 vols. Madrid, 1964.

García-Villoslada, R., S.J. *Ignacio de Loyola: un español al servicio del pontificado.* 2nd ed. Zaragoza, 1956.

———*La universidad de Paris durante los estudios de Francisco de Vitoria, O.P.* Rome, 1938.

Gilleman, G., S.J. "L'obéissance dans notre vie divine." *Christus,* no. 8 (1955), 466-487.

Giuliani, M., S.J. "Compagnons de Jesús." *Christus,* no. 22 (1959), 221-239.

Godet, M. *La congrégation de Montaigu.* Paris, 1912.

Granero, J.M., S.J. *La acción misionera y los metodos misionales de San Ignacio de Loyola.* Bilbao, 1931.

———"La espiritualidad de San Ignacio: estudio de sintesis." *Manresa,* XXVIII (1956), 489-514.

———"Libertad en la obediencia." *Manresa,* XXXIV (1962), 15-28.

———"Loyola y Erasmo." *Manresa,* XXXVIII (1966), 155-164.

Holstein, H. "Le mystère de l'obéissance." *Études,* CCXCI (1953), 145-157.

Imbart de la Tour, P. *Les origines de la réforme.* 4 vols. Paris, 1905-1914.

Iparraguirre, Ignacio, S.J. "Armonia sobrenatural de la acción de Dios y del hombre en san Ignacio de Loyola." *Estudios Eclesiásticos,* XXX (1965), 343-361.

———"Fuentes y estudios de la espiritualidad ignaciana." *Manresa,* XXVIII (1956), 7-28.

Bibliography

Leturia, Pedro de, S.J. "Perchè la Compagnia di Gesù divenne un ordine insegnante." *Gregorianum,* XXI (1940), 350-382. English translation in *Jesuit Educational Quarterly,* IV (1941), 30-54.

Liuima, A., S.J. " 'Devoción como rúbea' in sancti Ignatii ephemeride spirituali." *Gregorianum,* XXXVII (1956), 530-541.

Llamera, O.P. "La crisis actual de la obediencia y las razones tradicionales e ignacianas de su necesidad." *Teología Espiritual,* I (1957), 417-452; II (1958), 11-42.

Menendez de Pelayo. *Historia de los heterodoxos españoles.* 2 vols. Madrid, 1966.

Nebreda, A.J., S.J. "El camino de Ignacio: estudio del acatamiento en los Ejercicios Espirituales." *Manresa,* XXXII (1960), 45-66, 127-138.

Neyron, G., S.J. Saint Ignace de Loyola en présence des idées de son temps." *Revue d'Apologétique,* LIII (1931), 129-153.

Nicolau, M., S.J. *Jerónimo Nadal, S.I. Sus obras y doctrinas espirituales.* Madrid, 1959.

———*Pláticas espirituales del P. Jerónimo Nadal, S.I., en Coimbra (1561).* Granada, 1945.

Nouvel, E. *Le collège Sainte Barbe.* Paris, 1948.

Olmedo, F.G., S.J. *Introducción a la vida de S. Ignacio de Loyola.* Madrid, 1944.

Olphe-Galliard, M., S.J. "Érasme et Ignace de Loyola." *Revue d'Ascétique et de Mystique,* XXXV (1959), 337-352.

Pfandl, L. *Introducción al siglo de oro: cultura y costumbres del pueblo español de los siglos XVI y XVII.* Barcelona, 1929.

Pinard de la Boullaye, H., S.J. *La spiritualité ignatienne.* Paris, 1943.

Pontet, M. S.J. " 'Sur la terre comme au ciel.' Essai de critique religieuse. *Nouvelle Revue Théologique,* LXXV (1953), 1067-1075.

Quera, M., S.J. *Los Ejercicios Espirituales y el origen de la Compañía de Jesús.* Barcelona, 1941.

———"San Ignacio legislador de la Compañía de Jesús. *Estudios Eclesiásticos,* XXX (1956), 363-390.

Quicherat, J. *Histoire de Sainte-Barbe.* 3 vols. Paris, 1860.

Renaudet, L. *Humanisme et renaissance.* Genève, 1958.

Rodriguez-Grahit, I. *Ignace de Loyola et le collège Montaigu:*

l'influence de Standonck sur Ignace. Genève, 1958.

Roques, R. *L'univers dionysien: structure hiérarchique du monde selon le Pseudo-Denys.* Paris, 1954.

Rouquette, R., S.J. "Ignace de Loyola dans le Paris intellectuel du XVIᵉ siècle." *Études,* CXC (1956), 18-40.

Salaverri, J., S.J. "Motivación histórica y significación teológica del ignaciano 'sentir con la Iglesia.' " *Estudios Eclesiásticos,* XXXI, (1957), 139-172.

Silos, L. "Cardoner in the Life of Saint Ignatius of Loyola." *Archivum Historicum Societatis Iesu,* XXXIII (1964), 3-43.

Solano, J., S.J. "Fundamentos neotestamentarios y dogmáticos de la espiritualidad ignaciana." *Manresa,* XXVIII (1956), 123-134.

———"Jesucristo bajo las denominaciones divinas en San Ignacio." *Estudios Eclesiásticos,* XXX (1956), 325-342.

Solignac, A., S.J. "Le réalisme apostolique de saint Ignace de Loyola." *Revue d'Ascétique et de Mystique,* XXVII (1951), 205-236.

Taymans, F., S.J. "Missions divines et obéissance humaine." *Nouvelle Revue Théologique,* LXIX (1947), 486-496.

Tenneson, A., S.J. "L'obéissance à l'église d'après saint Ignace." *Revue d'Apologétique,* XLVII (1928), 522-562.

Tillard, J.M., O.P. "L'obéissance religieuse, mystère de communion." *Nouvelle Revue Théologique,* LXXXVII (1965), 377-394.

Truhlar, K., S.J. "La découverte de Dieu chez S. Ignace de Loyola pendant les dernières années de sa vie." *Revue d'Ascétique et de Mystique,* XXIV (1948), 313-337.

Vasse, D., S.J. "L'autorité du maître." *Études,* CCCV (1967), pp. 274-288.

INDEX I, the General Index

The numbers refer to pages

A

Abnegation, meaning to Ignatius, 97-98
  and obedience, 167-168
Alfonso VIII, 58
Alfonso XI, 58
Approval, Ignatius' use of the term, 90-91
Aquinas, St. Thomas, O.P., 4
Araoz, Antonio de, S.J., 205
Authority of the superior
  cultural context of Ignatius' conception of, 56-61, 160-162, 181
  descends from Christ, 83-86, 160-162
  exercise of, 86-93
  images of, 93-94
  See also Hierarchical structure; Obedience; Superior

B

Beda, Noel, 30
Bobadilla, N., S.J., 23, 77
Borgia, St. Francis, S.J., 78, 182
Broët, Paschase, S.J., 25, 108

C

Câmara, Gonçalves da, S.J., 27, 198, 199, 203
Carafa, Cardinal, 137, 138
Cardoner, Ignatius' illumination at, 20-22, 109, 163
Care, Ignatius' use of the term, 92-93
Certeau, Michael de, S.J., 10, 11
Charles V, 29, 62
Circumstances, concrete, attention to, for discernment, 149-150
Codure, Jean, S.J., 25, 34, 187
Cognet, Father Louis, Oratorian, 12
Collateral, the, 76-79
  office disappeared, 78-79
Command, Ignatius' use of the term, 86-87
Community, living in
  and the genesis of interior union, 41, 48-51
  profound mutual love is the basis of, 92-93
Company of Jesus, meaning of the title, 25, 25 n. 29, 26 n. 31
  use in this book, 3 n. 2
  bringing it to be, 9, 39, 40, 45-47, 52, 55, 56, 81-82, 84, 89, 90, 104-105, 106, 118, 121, 124, 136, 155, 156, 157, 162, 170-171, 177, 178, 181, 182, 186, 195, 212-213
Companionship, to serve Christ through the aid of souls in, 22-28
Confirmation. *See* Discernment
Constantine, 4

223

Index I, the General Index

224

motive for choosing in the Deliberation of 1539, 27, 34, 40
correlative of authority, 10, 52, 109, 121, 157, 182, 195, 212
means to achieve the apostolic end of the Company, 17, 81, 157-158, 175, 182, 195, 212-213
the most important means to love and union, 52, 81-83, 100, 157, 165, 169, 171
quasi-identified with love and union, 45, 158
an expression of love, 166, 181
its ascetical significance, 159
ecclesial, 162-165
mystical aspect of, 165
and humility, 100, 159
structure of, 175-176
—"the" Letter on Obedience
misunderstood, 195-199, 210-213
an exercise in rhetoric, 195-197
historical background, 197-200
and the letter to Gandía, 201-203
and the letter to Coimbra, 203-204
and the letter to Oviedo at Gandía, 204-210
See also Polanco
Olave, Martín de, S.J., 102
Order, Ignatius' use of the term, 87-90
quasi-identity with Union, 89
Oviedo, Andrés de, S.J., 204, 205, 206, 208, 209, 210, 211, 212

P

Pactista theory of authority, 62-64, 74, 85, 90 n. 26
Paternal government, not Ignatius' notion, 69 n, 100-104, 183
Paul III, Pope, 34
Paul, St., 112
Pelayo, Alvaro, 62
Perfection, personal
its relation to the apostolic end of the Company, 35-37, 69, 95, 162, 176

the means to, 95-100
Permission, Ignatius' use of the term, 90-91
Polanco, Juan de, secretary and procurator general of the Company, 64-65
his logical, scholastic mentality, 5, 65
wished public documents to be edifying, 36-37, 117 n. 30
his images of obedience, 168, 198
and the letter on obedience, 195, 204-212
Poverty, Ignatius' election of, in the *Spiritual Diary*, 144-146
Profound intention underlying cultural expressions, 4, 10, 11, 55, 97
of the companions founding the Company, 17
of Ignatius in describing the superior's role, 56-61, 82-83, 89, 91-93, 132-133, 155, 168, 182
See also Cultural structures; Ecclesial end; Scope of our vocation
Provide, Ignatius' use of the term, 92-93
Putten, Theodore van der, S.J., 12

R

Rector, qualities and duties of the, 74-76
essential role of the, 75
Representation as dialogue for discernment, 137-142
Reverence and obedience, 159-160
Rodrigues, Simão, S.J., 23, 24, 77, 197, 198
Rules for Thinking Rightly Within the Church,
riposte to Erasmus, 30
commented on, 150-152, 163

S

Salmerón, Alonzo, S.J., 23, 108

INDEX II, to Authors Referred to in the Footnotes

230